WHO DO YOU SAY I AM?

WHO DO YOU SAY I AM?

*Daily Reflections on the Bible,
the Saints, and the Answer
That Is Christ*

CARDINAL
TIMOTHY M. DOLAN

I

IMAGE
NEW YORK

Some of the essays in this work were originally published on Catholic New York
(www.cny.org) and subsequently on Zenit (www.zenit.org).

Grateful acknowledgement is made to Our Sunday Visitor Publishing
for permission to reprint an excerpt from *Priests for the Third Millennium*
© Cardinal Timothy M. Dolan. Published by Our Sunday Visitor Publishing.
1-800-348-2440. www.osv.com. Used by permission.
No other use of this material is authorized.

All Scripture quotations are taken from the
New American Bible Revised Edition.

LIBRARY OF CONGRESS CATALOGING-IN-PUBLICATION DATA
NAMES: Dolan, Timothy Michael, author.
TITLE: Who do you say I am? : daily reflections on the Bible, the saints,
and the answer that is Christ / Cardinal Timothy M. Dolan.
DESCRIPTION: New York : Penguin Random House, 2019.
IDENTIFIERS: LCCN 2019016893 (print) | LCCN 2019980718 (ebook) |
ISBN 9781984826725 (hardcover) | ISBN 9781984826732 (ebook)
SUBJECTS: LCSH: Devotional calendars—Catholic Church.
CLASSIFICATION: LCC BX2170.C56 D65 2019 (print) |
LCC BX2170.C56 (ebook) | DDC 242/.2—dc23
LC record available at https://lccn.loc.gov/2019016893

Printed in Canada

2 4 6 8 10 9 7 5 3

FIRST EDITION

Book design by Carole Lowenstein

To my new grandnephew, Timothy Michael Elfman,
whose name I love, and who gives me
great joy and trust in the future.

INTRODUCTION

What do you think is the most important question in life?

If you're very sick and contemplating surgery, I guess it's "Doctor, am I going to live?"

If you're a young man head over heels in love, I suppose it's "Will you marry me?"

If you're a student who just completed a pivotal exam, it's "Did I pass?"

If you're on the Atkins diet, it's "How many carbs are in that?"

What is the most important question in life? I propose to you that we need look no further than one asked by Jesus: *"Who do you say I am?"* Upon the answer to that most important question, everything else depends.

Actually, Jesus asks two questions. The first is, "Who do the crowds say I am?" So He asks us out of curiosity today, "Who does the world—the public opinion polls, the culture, society, the experts, other people—who do they all say I am?" That's easy to answer: "Well, Lord, they think you're a nice guy, a loving leader, a marvelous teacher, a good model for us, a great religious figure who ranks up there with Abraham, Moses, Muhammad, Confucius, Buddha; some think you're a revolutionary, a healer, a reformer, a positive thinker, a giver."

Jesus smiles . . . and then comes that most important question of all. "Fine: That's who *they* think I am. But who do *you* say I am?" Upon the answer to that question hangs everything—the direction of our life, our attitude to life, how we act, what we say, what we hope for, the salvation of our souls—*"Who do you say I am?"*

We can reply, "Lord, I've never really thought about it." Sad, tragic, hypocritical really, since we check the box marked

"Christian" or "Catholic" when asked to designate our religion, and we are at His supper on the first day of the week. . . .

We can answer, "Lord, I have different opinions about you and haven't made up my mind yet. I don't want to be closed-minded about this." Sad, tragic, an insult, since He has, as a matter of fact, already revealed to us the answer to that pivotal question and since we belong to a Church that has cherished the reply for two millennia as a supreme act of faith.

Or we can give the correct answer, the one given by Saint Peter: "You are the Christ, the Son of the living God; you are my Lord and Savior; you are my beginning and my end; you are the way, the truth, and the life; you are God from God, light from light, true God from true God, begotten not made, con-substantial with the Father, from whom all good things come. You are the most important person in my life; Jesus, who lives in me, who accompanies me always, who knows me better than I know myself, who loves me so much that you died for me, who rose from the dead and wants me to spend eternity with you. You are the answer to the questions posed by every human life. That's who you are, Jesus, my Lord, my God, my all."

There's the right answer! There's the act of faith! There's the reply of Peter and of the Church founded on the rock of his faith.

Now get ready, because the answer to that question has towering implications in our lives—how we live, what we say, what we choose, how we treat ourselves, how we treat others.

Every day we must ask ourselves this question anew: "Who do you say I am?"

I hope this book helps you journey every day toward answering—and living out—that question.

JANUARY 1

Feast of the Solemnity of Mary, Mother of God

Last week, billions of people celebrated a mother and the birth of her baby. Children around the world pointed at the newborn child in the Nativity scene and asked, "Who's that?" and parents and grandparents whispered, "That's Jesus, Our Lord and Savior." Then the same children pointed to Mary and inquired, "And who's that?" and the answer was: "That's His mother. Without her, Christmas could not have happened."

We Catholics passionately love our Church. As in our families, we are "born into" the Church at Baptism. Like a mother, she feeds us in the Eucharist, forgives us in Reconciliation, strengthens us in Confirmation, consoles us with the Anointing of the Sick, and gives us away in Matrimony or Holy Orders.

In this family of faith, we look to Mary as our own spiritual mother—a mother who guides and protects us. Mary never went to college, yet we call her *Sede Sapientiae*—"the Seat of Wisdom"—as she gave flesh to Wisdom, to the Word, to the eternal Son of God. Her virtues? Listening, reflecting, pondering, wondering, serving, and trusting. Her *fiat,* her proclamation: "Be it done unto me according to thy word." Mary is wise because she accepts God's will. She gives us Jesus, who shows us the way, teaches us the truth, and shares with us His life.

That's why the Blessed Mother is the greatest of all the saints, because she is the closest to her divine Son and wants nothing more than to draw us close to Him.

JANUARY 2

He will never fail you or forsake you.
—DEUTERONOMY 31:6

One of the central messages of Christianity is this: We have a God who simply will not take "no" for an answer!

Think about it: It started in the Garden of Eden. Adam and Eve had everything, every gift, all happiness, intimacy with God, eternal life, no woe, war, or sickness—and they told God *no* as they disobeyed His only request. God could have legitimately responded, "Go to hell!" But not our God!

He saw a world destroying itself by sin and selfishness and sent a flood to cleanse it . . . but the world once again said *no*!

He made a covenant with Abraham and bound Himself by a covenant with His people . . . but we once again were unfaithful and told Him *no*!

He saw His people enslaved, so He sent Moses, Aaron, and Joshua to lead them miraculously to freedom . . . but they all replied *no*!

He gave us commandments, and we worshipped molten images; He sent David, Jeremiah, Isaiah, and Ezekiel to teach us and call us back to Him, and we said *no*!

He offered us mercy, salvation, happiness, and eternal life—and we said *no*!

And then He sent us His Son. . . .

The good news, my friends, is that we have a good God who simply will not take "no" for an answer! So what will bring us happiness? Saying *yes* to Him.

JANUARY 3

Give thanks to the Lord, who is good,
whose love endures forever.
—CHRONICLES 16:34

A new year brings renewed thanks for the blessings of the past year and the hope of many blessings in the year to come. The Irish sisters who taught me at Holy Infant School in Ballwin, Missouri, invited us to say every morning as we awoke, "Thank you, Lord, for the gift of a new day," and as we went to sleep at night to whisper, "Thank you, Lord, for the gift of the past day."

We remember those words as we enter a new year, for gratitude keeps us from arrogance, self-satisfaction, smugness, and selfishness. When we view everything as a gift, we treat everything and everyone with awe and respect. That unfortunate sense of entitlement—the feeling that people owe us things or that we have certain privileges coming to us—is never ours, since we are so thankful for all that we have received.

When we acknowledge that everything we are and everything we have comes to us undeserved from a lavishly generous God, we desire to live a life of praise to that good and loving Father and we shudder at wounding Him with our sin. Because we view everything we are and have as unmerited, we must be charitable and share what we have with others. Since God has been so good to us in the past, we are confident that He will take care of us in the future. In this coming year, let us place all of our concerns in His providential hands.

JANUARY 4

Where is the newborn king of the Jews?
We saw his star at its rising and have come to do him homage.
—MATTHEW 2:2

Today is the tenth of the twelve days of Christmas, as we build toward the revelation (that's what the Greek word *epiphany* means) of Jesus as Savior to all the world, represented by those mysterious wise travelers from a faraway country.

What do you think those three kings felt when they found Jesus in Bethlehem? Awe? Faith? Gratitude?

But—bear with me here—I wonder if what those wise men initially felt was disappointment! You heard me. Disappointment! The star, their research, their travels, their inquiries in Jerusalem, their consultation with Herod, their anticipation of finding the long-awaited king . . . all for this? A little baby in the arms of a young mother in a stable! Where are the trumpets? Where is the palace? He was not the kind of king they expected to find. Yep, I think those Magi were disappointed. At first, anyway. Then their faith, awe, and gratitude kicked in, and they adored the Messiah and presented Him with their gifts.

Now the lesson for us: The Lord's epiphanies, His revelations, in our world, in our lives, are usually without trumpets, palaces, drama, and glitz. He usually comes to us in gentle, unassuming, simple ways. Our God manifests Himself in ordinary, "disappointing" ways that make it easy to miss Him.

No one should seek his own advantage,
but that of his neighbor.
—I CORINTHIANS 10:24

So many of us, of every and no faith, loved and admired Mother Teresa. You always had the sense that she was leading someone to God. She was telling the truth about the dignity of our lives by serving. And she was never stingy about giving advice, either. And so, in her characteristic simplicity, she wanted us to know what it means to have our priorities in life straight. For the Christian, it means:

J—Jesus
O—Others
Y—You

Her advice, of course, is a bit countercultural. Don't we typically start with "me"? She knew from experience that the key to joy is humility. Humility puts things in perspective.

For the Christian, it means the words of Saint Paul: "Whoever boasts, should boast in the Lord." For all of us, it keeps us from a self-centered sense of entitlement that can become quite the dangerous spiritual and emotional malady. You can see the caution here, can't you, about constantly feeling sorry for oneself?

If we're walking around licking our wounds, thinking about the ways we have been overlooked, taken for granted, or under-appreciated . . . look out! We're setting ourselves up for a fall, friends. Can you see how this attitude would lead to cynicism, negativism, and behavior that can get us into all kinds of trouble and poison not just our souls and our health but our relationships?

Mother Teresa was, not surprisingly, onto something. When we focus on Jesus first and then on others, we live a selfless life. Not a selfish life. And that is a life of joy.

JANUARY 6

Epiphany

Happy Feast of the Epiphany!

Epiphany means "revelation." Those Magi from the east represent every nation, every age, every race, every language, every culture, adoring the newborn Savior of the world, *revealed* to them as God's Son. On Christmas we acclaim Him the newborn King of Israel; on Epiphany we confess Him as the *Savior of everyone*.

So, you see, Epiphany is the day when we profess that Jesus is the Light of the World, revealed as the Savior of all. Thus the charge: We must bring His saving Person and His transforming Word to the nations. That's called evangelization. That's the *missionary* identity of the Church.

I figure that most of you have taken down the tree and the lights and put the crib away. Just make sure that Jesus is not put in the attic. Just make sure that you've once again seen the light. Just make sure that, like the three kings, you have adored Him as Savior. And just make sure that Jesus has been reborn in you—and then, it's missionary time! There's a dark world out there waiting for His *Epiphany*, His star, His light.

JANUARY 7

*Now this is eternal life, that they should know you,
the only true God, and the one whom you sent, Jesus Christ.*
—JOHN 17:3

Right after I was ordained a priest, I received a telephone call from a grade-school classmate who wanted to visit me. I had not seen "Eddie" in years but had heard that life had not been very good to him, that his years of service in Vietnam had scarred him, and that he had become a drug addict. How surprised I was when he showed up at the rectory looking happy, healthy, and confident.

He sensed my amazement and began to explain: "Tim, you know that I've been through tough times. I had lost everything—family, friends, faith, future. One day I almost lost my life. Another addict and I were in the basement of an abandoned warehouse shooting up heroin. I watched as he loaded up our two syringes with a triple, lethal dose. 'Let's cut to the chase,' he whispered. 'Neither of us can find any purpose to life. Unless one of us can come up with a reason to live in the next thirty seconds, let's go out on a high with this triple dose of gold.'"

"I was desperate, sure," Eddie recalled, "but not ready to end it all, so my scrambled brain went into overdrive to discover some meaning to life. What came to mind was something you and I learned in second grade from our catechism: 'Why did God make you? God made me to know him, love him, and serve him in this world, and to be happy with him forever in the next.'"

Eddie continued: "That's what I blurted out just as the other guy said, 'Time's up,' and began to look for his vein. 'Say that again,' he asked. And I did." Eddie had tears in his eyes as he finished the story. "The other guy shrugged and said, 'Sounds good to me,' and we both dropped our syringes. That 'wisdom' I remembered from second grade saved—and changed—my life."

It's precisely that wisdom we claim today. It is the wisdom that saved Eddie's life.

This is my beloved Son, with whom I am well pleased.
—MATTHEW 3:17

When Christ was baptized by John the Baptist, the Spirit of God descended like a dove, and God expressed the joy He had for His Son.

Our baptism day was just as joyous. On that day, wonderful things happened!

We became a child of God.

The waters of the sacrament washed away Original Sin.

Our souls were flooded with the radiance of grace—God's very own life.

Jesus Christ claimed us as His own, a beneficiary of the salvation He won for us by His cross and Resurrection!

We became a member of a supernatural family, the Church.

God invited us to spend eternity with Him in heaven.

Jesus told Satan—who wanted us so very badly—to get lost, since we now belonged to Christ.

The gifts of faith, hope, and charity were instilled in our hearts!

Every other blessing in life flows from that glorious event.

When we stand before God at the end of our lives, He won't ask to see our passports, our stock portfolios, a résumé, or our academic degrees. But a baptismal certificate will be of immense interest!

Because of baptism, we're in God's hands. He's known us since before we were in our mother's womb. He washed us clean and claimed us as His own on the day of our baptism, and He wants us on His lap for all eternity.

*And he put all things beneath his feet and gave him as head
over all things to the church, which is his body.*
—EPHESIANS 1:22-23

"Christ, yes! Church, no!"

That seems to be a popular sentiment these days. Many want a king without a kingdom, a shepherd but not the fold, a general with no army, a spiritual family in which I am the only child, faith but no faithful.

Whenever I read surveys on religion in America, I'm struck that many, we are told, want Christ without His Church. A quarter of our people raised Catholic no longer consider themselves such. The faith of our fathers apparently has no claim on them. Some seem more loyal to the baseball team they cheered as a kid than to the Church in which they were baptized and raised. Believe, yes; belong, no.

These people want the Lord, my Lord, not *Our* Lord. It cuts to the core of Catholicism, for of course we believe that Christ and His Church are *one*. As we pray every Sunday at the Creed and have been praying for seventeen centuries:

"We believe in God, the Father Almighty. . . . We Believe in Jesus Christ, His only Son, Our Lord. . . . We believe in the Holy Spirit, the Lord and giver of life. . . . We believe in one, holy, catholic, and apostolic Church. . . ."

It's a package deal for a Catholic: Jesus Christ and His Church.

And this moves us to rejoice in the Church as a golden bond keeping us tethered to Christ, not as handcuffs that we try to unlock.

*Yes, you are my flock: you people are the flock of my pasture,
and I am your God.*
—EZEKIEL 34:31

In the catacombs in Rome you will see ancient Christian art, and one of the more common scenes is of a shepherd—a depiction of a strong man holding a lamb. From the earliest days of the Church, the image of Jesus we have found most consoling, most compelling, and most revealing is that of the Good Shepherd. Jesus is the Good Shepherd.

Although He is indeed the Good Shepherd, He often works through others. Throughout our lives He sends people to assist us. Many years ago, I was at a children's hospital to visit a sick baby, and I was touched by the personal care and attention of the nurses on duty. They were helping Jesus shepherd a sick little lamb. When I entered the hospital room, a good friend of the mother's sat with her. That friend was certainly an agent of Christ. Then I watched the tender love and care that the mother had for her child. The Good Shepherd was visible in her, too.

We see this in the Church as well, with those who shepherd in a sacramental way. Deacons, priests, and bishops nurture as proxies for Jesus. They shepherd us, their flock, through good times and bad. That's why we call our priests that beautiful title *pastor.*

However, there is only one eternal, ever-reliable, unfailingly Good Shepherd, and that is Jesus Christ.

Hail, favored one! The Lord is with you.
—LUKE 1:28

Christmas seems to come and go more quickly each year, doesn't it? We usually notice this sometime around the first week of January and complain that we want it to last just a bit longer. We can rejoice in the fact, however, that the Church has ways of extending the message and meaning of Christmas throughout the year. One way would be through the Angelus. This simple prayer relives the conversation between the Archangel Gabriel and Our Lady in the first chapter of Luke. It is a prayer wonderfully appropriate during Advent and at Christmas and one that allows us to keep Christmas going all year. I encourage you to pray it at least once a day.

V. The Angel of the Lord declared unto Mary.
R. And she conceived of the Holy Spirit.

Hail Mary . . .

V. Behold the handmaid of the Lord.
R. Be it done unto me according to thy word.

Hail Mary . . .

V. And the Word was made Flesh.
R. And dwelt among us.

Hail Mary . . .

V. Pray for us, O holy Mother of God.
R. That we may be made worthy of the promises of Christ.

Let us pray:

Pour forth, we beseech Thee, O Lord, Thy grace into our hearts, that we to whom the Incarnation of Christ Thy Son was made known by the message of an angel, may by His Passion and Cross be brought to the glory of His Resurrection. Through the same Christ Our Lord. Amen.

*Those who conceal their sins do not prosper, but those who confess
and forsake them obtain mercy.*
—PROVERBS 28:13

Going to confession is like a trip to the dentist: We know it's
good for us, and we sure feel better afterward, but we're anxious about doing it.

The simple truth is that we are sinners. We acknowledge
that our sins not only offend our loving God and harm ourselves but hurt everybody else.

We claim to be people of love, but sometimes we are hate-
ful. We pretend to be selfless yet often are the opposite. We say
we're honest and on occasion lie and cheat.

We have disregarded the commandments, the Beatitudes,
the Bible, and the teaching of Jesus and His Church. We admit
it. We've hurt God, ourselves, and our neighbors. We're sorry.

We know God forgives us when we ask Him to, because He
told us so. We experience that in confession. We sometimes
find it hard to forgive ourselves. And we ask those we have offended to pardon us for our failure to practice what we preach.

I guess that's why we describe ourselves as "practicing
Catholics," because we keep trying to get it right.

On the way to His cross, Jesus fell three times, which means,
in the Bible, "a lot." We slip and fall a lot, too!

So even though we may feel jittery as we prepare for confession, let us remember that it is the only way to pick ourselves
back up and continue our ongoing attempt to follow Christ
more faithfully and generously.

*Let us not grow tired of doing good, for in due time
we shall reap our harvest, if we do not give up.*
—GALATIANS 6:9

I spent many happy years as archbishop of Milwaukee, Wisconsin. And I did my best to always offer the 8 A.M. Mass at the Cathedral of St. John the Evangelist.

One morning somebody said to me, "Archbishop, I want to let you know something that you do that has influenced me and has had a good effect on me." Well, I was expecting her to speak about visiting someone in the hospital or working in the soup kitchen, or one of my sermons, or a project. To my complete surprise, she told me that what most affected her was that half hour before my Sunday morning Mass when she saw me praying my Divine Office in the Blessed Sacrament Chapel of the cathedral. Now, I didn't think that this would have an influence on anyone. But it did. For her to see me as a bishop taking my prayer seriously, for her to know that I recognize that I am no good unless I am completely reliant on the grace and mercy of the Lord, that spoke volumes to her.

We are all sort of Cal Ripkens—the great ballplayer on the Baltimore Orioles who simply showed up for every game and broke records because of his consistency. He was just there.

Most of life is just showing up. And as Christians, we need to show up. We are at times witnesses to Jesus Christ in our words. And at other times, simply in our presence. So let this be our noble goal: that we never give up trying.

Do not damage the land or the sea or the trees until we put the seal
on the foreheads of the servants of our God.
—REVELATION 7:3

The Sign of the Cross is perhaps the most compelling and enduring symbol in our spiritual lives. When our parents and godparents presented us for baptism, the priest claimed us for Christ and traced the Sign of the Cross on our foreheads. When our bodies are carried to church for our funeral Mass, once again the Sign of the Cross will be traced over us. Every day since childhood, I hope, we have made the Sign of the Cross at least once. Many of us wear the cross as a sacramental, and in our homes we find the crucifix as a powerful expression of faith.

We concentrate on the cross in our prayers and in our penance as we unite our own acts of mortification with the ultimate sacrifice of Jesus on the cross. And we center on the cross in our charity, in solidarity with those who, because of sickness, hunger, struggles, violence, disaster, or poverty, bear a heavier share in Our Lord's Passion.

I have a friend who received a cross to wear as a bishop from Saint John Paul II. When the Holy Father gave it to him, he said, "This cross will hang upon your heart. Make sure it sinks down into it. For you are to wear the Sign of the Cross on your heart."

Think of his words when you make the Sign of the Cross. Let that cross sink into your mind, your soul, and your very being.

There is neither Jew nor Greek, there is neither slave nor free person, there is not male and female; for you are all one in Christ Jesus.
—GALATIANS 3:28

Some years ago I preached at a retreat for seminarians. At breakfast almost every morning, the men would comment on how they were dreaming so much at night. I told them that one of the directors on a retreat I once had observed that whenever we were in a reflective mood, whenever we were praying well, whenever we were "getting back to basics" in our lives, we usually slept well and dreamed well. Since reflection, prayer, and a return to basics were precisely what a retreat was all about, I remarked to the seminarians that I was hardly surprised that they were sleeping well and dreaming a lot.

Today we celebrate the birthday of Reverend Martin Luther King, Jr., a prophet who shook us to the core by preaching a return to the foundational, normative values of the Bible, of human nature, and of our nation's principles. Can I propose to you that it's a good day to be in a mood of reflection, praying, and getting back to basics?

We are made in the very image and likeness of God, given the sacred gift of life by our creator; thus, we are all brothers and sisters, owing ourselves and one another dignity and respect, endowed—not by government but by the Creator—with certain inalienable rights, the first of which is life itself. I learn those basics from my faith, you bet, but also from my own nature and from the guiding principles of a nation founded on divine and natural law. Can you "dream" a bit about what would happen if we really believed those basics?

JANUARY 16

Remain in me, as I remain in you.
—JOHN 15:4

Our vocation in life is to know Jesus so well that when He whispers to us in silence, we will hear His voice and follow His call.

Think for a moment about the wording of the call, the invitation, that Jesus gives us. Does He summon us to work with Him, to plan with Him, to organize with Him, to build with Him, to act with Him, or to do something with Him?

Not at all! What words does He use in His summons to us?

Abide in Me.

Stay with Me.

Watch with Me.

Come with Me.

Live in Me.

These are all "being" words, not "having" or "doing" words. This reminds me of the plea of Augustine: "What I now longed for was not greater certainty about you, but a more steadfast abiding in you."

Here is our identity in Christ. And to deepen that identity, to enhance it, and to strengthen it in all its supernatural and natural dimensions is the task of every one of our valuable programs and missions within the Church.

Ultimately, all we have is Jesus Christ. To rekindle our love for, faith in, and knowledge of Him has to be the ultimate goal of everything we do.

We must fall in love with Him again. "Because," as Saint Thomas More wrote to his daughter from the Tower of London, "when all is said and done . . . it's not about reason at all. It's all about love."

JANUARY 17

Feast of Saint Anthony of the Desert

Jesus teaches us important lessons not just by what He says but by what He does. We learn some of these lessons in the Gospel of Mark, where we see Him teaching, visiting, and healing during the day but going off alone in quiet prayer at night.

Jesus teaches us that life must have those two components. There has to be hard work, but we have to balance it with hard prayer. And we're doomed if we don't have both of them.

Most of us err on the side of hard work. We're pretty good at working hard. We're diligent, we're responsible, and we know what we have to do. But we tend to be slackers when it comes to the prayer part, the quiet part, the being by ourselves with Christ part.

Saint Anthony of the Desert is a good example to follow in learning to improve our prayer life. He believed that he needed to follow Christ in solitude and in quiet, and so he went into the desert to spend his life in prayer, penance, and contemplation. He did a lot of writing, teaching, and service to the poor, but basically his life was lived in solitude and communication with God.

Christ calls us to always grow closer to Him, but we cannot do that if we lead unbalanced lives and if our lives are missing that one integral component—prayer.

I write these things to you so that you may know
that you have eternal life, you who believe
in the name of the Son of God.

—1 JOHN 5:13

Saint Augustine wrote, "We come from You, O Lord, and our hearts are restless until they return to You for all eternity." It is this wisdom that was preached dramatically by Jesus and His Church but is treasured as well by Judaism, Islam, Eastern religions, Native Americans, and philosophers of no particular creed, namely, that we have within us the spark of the divine, that we are destined for eternity, that life is so beautiful, so noble, and so sacred that it will never end.

It is this wisdom that is our priceless legacy as Catholics. The self-help author Stephen Covey claims that a habit of a successful person is to have a clear, constant goal and focus in life. Our highest goal is eternal union with God.

I don't know of anyone who has expressed it more eloquently than the founder of the Jesuits, Saint Ignatius of Loyola, who called it "The First Principle and Foundation." It goes like this: We are created to praise and serve Our Lord, and by this means to save our soul. Everyone and everything on earth is created to help us reach the end for which we are created. Hence, we make use of all things insofar as they help us reach our eternal destiny, and get rid of whatever hinders us from attaining our ultimate goal.

Today I invite you to think of the end—our eternal destiny—and to thank our God who passionately desires us to spend that eternity with Him.

Why are you terrified, O you of little faith?
—MATTHEW 8:26

We always need hope, but I think you will agree that on some days more than others we need a booster shot of it.

One of my favorite episodes in the life of Jesus is the storm at sea, when the Apostles were in a boat on the Sea of Galilee, caught in the middle of a storm so severe that even the seasoned fishermen were scared that they were about to capsize and drown. And where was Jesus? Asleep! He was napping in the back of the boat. In desperation, the Apostles finally woke Him and clamored, "Lord, are you not concerned? We are going to sink!" Whereupon He got up, quieted the winds, calmed the waves, and all was at peace. The boat was safe.

This is what Christ does in our lives. He settles the waves and calms the storms. One of the best definitions of hope I've ever heard is that hope is the virtue that keeps us steady even when it seems the Lord is asleep.

Let's face it, many of us are tempted to think that Jesus is asleep during those days when winds and waves threaten to overwhelm the boat we call our lives. We suffer pains, crises, difficulties, loss of trust, or problems with faith. These storm winds and waves can scare us, but they will never sink us. We have His word on that.

Jesus might seem to be sleeping, but He is still in charge.

Most blessed are you among women,
and blessed is the fruit of your womb.
—LUKE 1:42

Early on in my life, it dawned on me that people I loved and respected very much were attached to the rosary. I remember seeing the beads on the nightstand at both of my grandmas' homes; as Dad would empty his pockets when he came home from work, there it was again; the priests I looked up to would often be reciting the rosary outside of church. As a kid, I learned that loyalty to the rosary helped the faith in Ireland survive when Mass and the sacraments were outlawed.

When I concelebrated Mass in the Holy Father's chapel, there it was in his kneeler. On almost every Communion call as a parish priest, I knew the sick person would have one close by.

So you see, not just as a child but also as a priest and a bishop, I got the message that the rosary is a beloved, effective prayer. I would never let a day pass without saying it.

Saint John Paul II called for a revival of devotion to this great prayer. In fact, he even added five new "luminous mysteries"—the baptism of Jesus, the wedding feast of Cana, the call to conversion, the transfiguration, and the institution of the Eucharist—to the more historical joyful, sorrowful, and glorious mysteries.

Think of the value of this prayer: It is simple, it is biblical, it is Jesus-centered, it can be prayed anywhere, it is communal in that at any given time thousands of others somewhere in the world are praying it, and, best of all, it is prayed in union with the Mother of Jesus.

Do yourself a favor: Look in your drawers, your jewelry boxes, your storage closets, and find your old rosary. Teach it to your kids; start saying it again yourself. It never fails to bring us closer to Jesus and His mother. It is indeed a source of "life, sweetness, and hope."

JANUARY 21

*So let us confidently approach the throne of grace
to receive mercy and to find grace for timely help.*
—HEBREWS 4:16

One of the many joys I have as a bishop is administering the Sacrament of Confirmation to our young people. Most of them, as part of their preparation for the sacrament, write me a letter requesting that I confirm them.

They usually give a number of reasons why they should be confirmed: They have worked hard to prepare; they have completed service projects; they want to acknowledge publicly that they are mature Catholics; they come from a Catholic family and it is part of their tradition—all decent enough reasons, I suppose. But I always smile with satisfaction and appreciation when one of them mentions the best reason of all: "I want the Sacrament of Confirmation *because I need it!*"

Do we ever! And not just the grace of that sacrament but the grace that comes from all the other ones, too: Baptism, Eucharist, Reconciliation, Anointing of the Sick, and those called to Marriage and Holy Orders. Simply put, we need God's help. The sacraments bring that help in a uniquely powerful way.

To live a faithful, generous, virtuous life, the kind of life that Jesus and His Church challenge us to live, is downright tough. It takes prayer, grit, commitment... and, most of all, God's grace. That grace comes to us, powerfully and uniquely, in the seven sacraments.

The truth will set you free.
—JOHN 8:32

Veritas: Latin for "truth." *Veritas* calmly, rationally, tirelessly, creatively, and effectively presents the basic, inescapable truth about human life: that from the moment of conception, a unique, unrepeatable human life is present—a life that merits respect and that deserves equal protection under the law.

Abortion is not a theological issue but a biological one; it is not a Catholic, evangelical, or orthodox Jewish issue but a civil rights issue. I am not opposed to abortion because I am a baptized Catholic but because I am a thinking human being and a citizen of a country founded on the protection of inviolable human rights.

We must confront certain popular untruths that continue to challenge us. One is that our personal right to choose trumps all other rights.

We know that the rightness or wrongness of the choice depends on what is chosen. To choose Chablis over Burgundy is certainly a right; to choose your sixth glass of it before driving home is not.

Likewise, we must acknowledge the truth that the choice to destroy an innocent human life is the most indefensible choice of all.

JANUARY 23

The seventh day is a sabbath of the Lord your God. You shall not do any work,
either you, your son or your daughter.
—DEUTERONOMY 5:14

His Christmas card from 2008 had brought good news: He had landed a very prestigious and high-paying job as a geologist—the profession he cherished—at a mining exploration company in Montana. I was so happy for him, a friend since high school. He had explained in his card that the job was three weeks at a time in a very isolated area of the mountains, then a week back home in Illinois with his wife and three children. He regretted being away, but he and his wife had agreed that this career opportunity was well worth it.

Then came the Christmas card for 2009. He had quit that job. Was it the money? Hardly, the card explained, since the salary was exceptional. Lack of challenge? Just the opposite, the news went on, as he really enjoyed the work. Why, then, had he quit?

Listen to this: "I missed my wife and kids, and I missed Sunday Mass. Up in the mountains, at the site, we were over a hundred miles from the nearest Catholic church, so I could only go to Mass one Sunday a month, when I was home. The job—as much as I loved it—was ruining my marriage, my family, and my faith. It had to go!"

Talk about an inspirational Christmas card!

The power, the meaning, the beauty, the necessity of Sunday Mass . . . Just ask my friend. What role does it play in your life?

The one enthroned in heaven laughs.

—PSALM 2:4

By nature, we are impatient. Any confessor would report if he could that impatience is the most common sin he hears in the Sacrament of Reconciliation.

We hate to wait in the checkout line, at the stoplight, in the doctor's office, at the license renewal agency. We no longer wait for marriage to express sexual love, and some people even advocate not waiting for natural death before ending a life. We do not even like to wait for the Lord to answer our prayers.

As the psalmist sings, "The one enthroned in heaven laughs." He smiles at the impatience of His children. For God, of course, as it says in 2 Peter 3:8, "one day is like a thousand years and a thousand years like one day."

The Lord knows that all good things come to those who wait. He realizes that life's best events cannot be hurried. God teaches that waiting, hoping, and longing are tonic for the soul. His prophets constantly encouraged His people of Israel never to lose heart, to "be stouthearted, wait for the Lord!"

Our patient expectation expands the soul and creates a space that only the Lord can fill. This anticipation only enhances the joy—the pleasure of the gift—once it arrives. Our longing exercises the muscle of trust, as we have to admit humbly that God knows what He is doing, that our schedule is not His, and that He has no deadlines or calendars as we do.

JANUARY 25

Conversion of Saint Paul

Many people spend a lot of time asking, "What is the Church?" Before long, they discover that the answer can be found only if they reword the question: "*Who* is the Church?"

Simply put, as Saint Paul teaches, the Church is Christ. He learned this lesson on the road to Damascus, when the Lord told him that in persecuting the Church, Paul was persecuting Jesus Himself.

What does Jesus bellow to Saul? "Saul, Saul, why do you persecute . . ." My people? No. My Church? No. My followers? No.

"Saul, Saul, why do you persecute me?"

"But who are you, sir?" Saul asked.

"I am Jesus, and you are persecuting me!"

Paul's conversion was one of the watershed moments in Christian history. After three days of blindness, the scales fell from his eyes and he could see. Yet it wasn't just his surroundings that he could see. It was so much more than that.

He could see himself as a sinner, and he was immediately changed.

Our own experiences may not be so dramatic, but what about conversion in our own hearts and lives? Saint Teresa of Calcutta, that shining symbol of holiness and self-sacrifice, said it best when she was asked, "If you could change one thing in the world, what would it be?" She replied, simply, "Me."

All of us need to ask: Am I living up to what I profess? Where do I fall short, and what about my life needs changing?

He said to them, "Why are you sleeping?
Get up and pray that you may not undergo the test."
—LUKE 22:46

On the night before He died, at His Last Supper, as one of His last gifts to those He loved, Jesus gave us the Holy Eucharist.

We Catholics hold three beliefs about the Eucharist:

First, we profess that it is a sacred meal in which we unite as a family of faith to hear God's Word, to be fed with Christ's body and blood, to strengthen the spiritual bonds of community, and to be fortified to bring the fruits of our sacred meal to those beyond us.

Second, we believe that the Mass is a sacrifice. Every Eucharist is a re-presentation of the eternal, unending sacrifice offered by God the Son to God the Father on the cross of Calvary. Thus, the Holy Sacrifice of the Mass is the supreme act of adoration, sorrow, thanksgiving, and satisfaction because, first and foremost, it is the action of Jesus for and with us.

Third, the Eucharist is presence. We believe that Christ is really and truly present—body, blood, soul, and divinity—in the Most Blessed Sacrament.

A simple, sincere, childlike reverence for the awesome presence of Jesus in the Holy Eucharist is the hallmark of genuine Catholic life.

One of the saddest questions Jesus ever posed came only a couple of hours after the Last Supper. He had asked His Apostles to keep Him company as He began His Agony in the Garden. But they fell asleep.

Let us resolve to keep Him company. One of the most beautiful places to do that is in Eucharistic Adoration.

Have no anxiety at all, but in everything, by prayer and petition,
with thanksgiving, make your requests known to God.
—PHILIPPIANS 4:6

People often ask me for ways to improve their prayer life. Although I'm flattered that they come to me with that question, my reply is that many of us spend too much time asking for tips on prayer, buying books on prayer, and talking about techniques in prayer.

My suggestion? We just gotta do it! In many ways, we think it's beyond us. But the fact of the matter is, it's within us. Once we learn that it is the most natural thing in the world, prayer becomes easier.

If you listen to the way kids pray, you notice that they don't have any problem at all.

"Jesus, we thank you because it's so nice outside." Or "Oh, Jesus, my grandma just died, but I know she's with you in heaven for all eternity." Or "I had a fight with my brother today, and I'm sorry about that."

When we talk to God as a child does, we become like little children. That is why Jesus tells us, "Amen, I say to you, unless you turn and become like children, you will not enter the kingdom of heaven."

As Nike says: Just do it.

JANUARY 28

Feast of
Saint Thomas Aquinas

Saint Thomas Aquinas, perhaps the Church's greatest philosopher, taught that "actions flow from being." What we do springs from who we are.

We are not defined by our wealth, nationality, color, sexual attraction, urges, popularity, grades, health, age, possessions, background, or political party.

We have an inherent identity—a dignity from God. And everything we do or don't do—our morality—flows from the belief about who we are and is provided by our faith.

Furthermore, Aquinas agreed wholeheartedly with Aristotle that every person wants to be happy. He believed that the pursuit of happiness is basic to our nature. He was, however, quick to point out that happiness is not the same as pleasure. In fact, he observed that one of the ways we humans get into big trouble is by confusing the two.

Today we often hear, "I sure appreciate all the things the Church does—its charities, schools, healthcare, even its worship, feast days, sacraments, and traditions. But I couldn't care less about what the Church teaches, and I can't understand why our religion is so hung up on all that doctrinal stuff."

I'm afraid those who claim that have it backward: All the good things the Church does flow from who we are. The faith we have provides our very identity. We do those good works precisely because of our faith.

God made us for happiness—now and in eternity. That desire for happiness drives us. But our actions and our faith define us.

JANUARY 29

Humbly regard others as more important than yourselves.
—PHILIPPIANS 2:3

Some years ago my brother, Pat, his wife, Mary Theresa, and my nieces, Grace and Kathleen, came to spend some time with me. Grace was three, Kathleen just one. Suddenly, the quiet house was hopping! And as soon as they'd leave, I would enthusiastically reaffirm my promise of celibacy.

Gracie was talking up a storm, but Kathleen was just learning to speak clearly. You could make out only a few words. One word, though, came across with dramatic clarity: "MINE!" No mistaking that word as she grabbed something she wanted or as you tried to take something from her she shouldn't have.

Therein is a profound lesson about human nature. All of us have a very potent drive deep within to be selfish, to grab, to cling, to possess, to hoard, to keep for ourselves.

As Pat and Mary Theresa—and every parent—can attest, it is a real battle to teach a child to share, to let go, to let others benefit from what we want only for ourselves. The dark side of us wants to clutch and grip things for ourselves, others be darned!

This is what Saint Paul talks about when we read passages from his Letter to the Romans. The Spirit prompts love, life, hope, sharing, and reconciliation, whereas the flesh pushes selfishness, hate, death, and despair. The Spirit whispers "OUR" while the flesh yells "MINE!"

As Christians, we are at our best when we promote the culture of "OUR" over the rule of "MINE!"

JANUARY 30

Come, you who are blessed by my Father. Inherit the kingdom
prepared for you from the foundation of the world.
—MATTHEW 25:34

A concentration camp survivor told a story of his search for hope and meaning in the midst of daily horror. A man of strong Jewish faith, he continually asked himself, "Where is God?"

He and his fellow prisoners lived on the verge of starvation, fed only a chunk of bread in the morning and a bowl of weak gruel each evening. One evening he watched as one of his group, who had been feverish and faint, began to pass out. On his lap was the bowl of gruel. The inhumanity of the situation caused all the prisoners to lock their eyes on the food, each wanting it for himself.

The man next to the dying prisoner did grab it, but instead of eating it, he slowly and gently fed it to the dying man, coaxing him to eat.

"Ah, there is my God," whispered the searching man.

This man perfectly exhibited the compassion of Christ, who loved the sick, the hungry, the beggars, the forgotten, and the suffering. We have a king who rode a donkey, endured a crown of thorns, and ruled from a cross. We have a king who would spoon-feed a dying man when He himself was achingly hungry.

In the face of the starving, hurting, struggling, sick, forgotten, and rejected, we recognize the face of God, for we have a king who taught, "Whatever you did for one of these least brothers of mine, you did for me."

JANUARY 31

Feast of
Saint John Bosco

As you probably know, every day of the year on the Church calendar is a celebration of a saint.

Today is the day of one of my favorites: John Bosco. He was an Italian priest in the nineteenth century who was known for his loving, effective work with young people. It was a tough time for Italy: With the industrial revolution, there were a lot of street kids, kids without parents, and even human trafficking.

To remedy this, Don Bosco (Italians usually call their parish priests "Don") started clubs. He started what would be akin to today's Boys & Girls Clubs. He founded industrial schools. He established orphanages. And with this loving embrace of kids in trouble, he became the patron saint of young people.

I tell you this because, look, this isn't any secret: The Church is maligned today because of its past abuse of kids. And rightly so. Anyone who's not nauseated by that ought to get his or her head examined. But we can never let that eclipse the fact that, to my knowledge, no organization in the history of the world has done more loving, positive good for kids than the Catholic Church.

So what Don Bosco did for troubled kids on the streets of Turin, the Catholic Church is still doing throughout the world. And I'm proud of it.

Saint John Bosco, pray for us.

FEBRUARY 1

I continue my pursuit toward the goal,
the prize of God's upward calling, in Christ Jesus.
—PHILIPPIANS 3:14

At the beginning of the new year, many of us make resolutions. Perhaps it is eating healthier, or working out, or, for that matter, working less. Come the first days of February, I'm sad to say, we've given up on those resolutions and will wait to try again next year.

With this in mind, here are a few promises we can still make for the new year:

NUMBER ONE: I'd recommend that the first thing you do, every day, is make a *morning offering*. Our first thought daily should be of the Lord. We wake up because of Him; we got through the night because of Him; we'll make it through this new day only because of His grace and mercy. It makes sense, then, that as soon as we awake, we should think of Him in prayer: Tell Him we love Him, we need Him, we thank Him, we trust Him. Offer the new day to Him.

NUMBER TWO: Commit yourself to *Sunday Mass*. It's the Lord's Day, our Sabbath, the day of His Resurrection. We catch our breath from the just concluded week and place the coming week in His providential hands. There's no better way to do that than by joining our spiritual family, the Church, in the most sacred Sunday meal of all, the Holy Sacrifice of the Mass.

NUMBER THREE: First Friday, every month, we approach the *Sacrament of Penance*. Let's revive the beautiful custom of *First Friday*. Jesus died on the cross to save us on a Friday. The first Friday of every month we tell Him we're sorry for our sins and ask for His mercy with a good confession.

We have a God of *newness*; we have a God always eager to give us a fresh start.

Candlemas Day
(Feast of the Presentation of the Lord)

This ancient feast comes forty days after Christmas. In traditional Catholic homes in Europe, the Christmas decorations, including the tree, did not come down until yesterday. As faithful Jews, Mary and Joseph took their firstborn son, Jesus, to present Him in the temple in Jerusalem. There the holy man Simeon held Him and proclaimed the Baby Jesus the long-awaited Savior, *the light* to the dark world.

Now, stay with me here. Today's feast comes at the halfway point of winter. December 21 to March 20. Get it? The darkness (and for those of us in cold climates, wind and cold, ice and grayness) of winter is on the run. *The light* (and warmth and breezes and new life and color) of spring is slowly, ever so slowly, but surely on the way. The secular calendar has reduced this sacred drama of winter versus spring, darkness versus light, to Groundhog Day. Oh, for the Middle Ages again!

Of course, the message is clear: What spring is to winter in nature, Jesus Christ, the *Light* of the World, is for us supernaturally.

Jesus Christ is not the s-u-n but the S-o-n. He is *the light* that edges out darkness, the life that conquers death, the warmth of love and mercy that triumphs over the cold of sin.

FEBRUARY 3

*I pray not only for them, but also for those who will believe in me
through their word, so that they may all be one, as you,
Father, are in me and I in you, that they also may be in us.*
—JOHN 17:20-21

We praise Jesus simply because He and He alone is Lord. He is our source of unity. We unite not just with others in our faith but with Him on the cross. Faith in Him saves us.

Those of us who are humbled to claim membership in His Church constantly risk knowing about Him but never really knowing Him; talking about Him while rarely talking to Him; listening to others speak of Him while hardly ever allowing Him to speak to us; and admirably trying to make our churches His home while not heeding His words from John to make His Word our home.

Our Lord dominates, triumphs, and reigns in His weakness precisely through His Passion and death. We, too, are weak. Each of us wrestles with internal brokenness. From a human point of view, it embarrasses us and discourages us; from a supernatural perspective, our weaknesses only move us closer to Jesus on the cross, believing that when He was weakest, He accomplished the most. By dying He destroyed our death.

I submit to you that we renew our faith and our unity with Christ, for the foundation of our unity and the means of realizing it lie only in Him.

Today the nails that pinned Him and the nails we bear in suffering can unite us with Christ if in our weakness we seek His grace and if we let those nails place us on the cross with Him.

Go, eat your bread with joy and drink your wine with a merry heart, because
it is now that God favors your works.
—ECCLESIASTES 9:7

Have you ever heard the great jingle attributed to G. K. Chesterton:

Wherever a Catholic sun doth shine,
There's plenty of laughter and good red wine.
God grant that it ever be so.
Benedicamus Domino!

That is: *Let us bless the Lord!* I'd like to think I say this often because, boy, am I ever grateful to God for the gifts He's given
me. I hope—I pray, dear reader—you can feel that way, too.

And that brings us back to Chesterton's point of gratitude
about Catholic joy.

Once I was taking a trip through Germany with my first
pastor in St. Louis after he retired. We started in the north of
Germany, and by day three we had entered the south, Bavaria.
As we came into Bavaria, our guide said, "You'll notice a big
change now. Up north, there is a lot of industry, the folks are
more somber, and life looks drab. Down here, look at the flowers, the painted homes, the chubby smiling people, lots of kids,
good food, dancing, song, and lots of beer. She concluded, "The
north is Protestant; the south is Catholic."

She knew they were Catholics by their joy.

Joy is what most often attracts people to the Church. Catholics are not Puritans. I remember once preparing a young
couple for marriage; she was Catholic, and he was Presbyterian.
He at first showed absolutely no interest in the Church, but
after a couple of months, he stopped to see me and told me he
wanted to find out more. "Why?" I asked him, wondering what
teaching or practice of the Church was attracting him.

"I've gotten to know Deidre's family so well since we got
engaged, and, well, they seem to enjoy life, they are so happy."
Good Catholics usually are.

Yet I live, no longer I, but Christ lives in me.
—GALATIANS 2:20

I had been a priest for only eight months when I got the toughest convert I've ever had. The parish was holding a mission, and on the third evening a man in his middle to late twenties approached me.

He introduced himself as a professor of mathematics from nearby Washington University, and he expressed an interest in Catholicism. Well, for six months I intellectually wrestled with him, going through instructions, with knockdown, drag-out fights to all hours of the night during our weekly sessions. Finally, after I had completed all the instructions, at our last meeting, he said to me: "You know, there's one point of Catholic teaching I still struggle with."

"What is it?" I asked, assuming it was going to be one of the regulars, like the Real Presence of Jesus in the Eucharist, the Sacrament of Reconciliation, the role of Mary, or the teaching authority of the pope.

How surprised I was when he explained: "Way back at the beginning you taught me about something called 'sanctifying grace.' I must have misunderstood you because I thought you explained that sanctifying grace means that the very life of God actually dwells in the soul of the believer, that we literally share in God's life. I obviously misunderstood you, because that would be just too good to be true."

"You understood me perfectly well," I replied. He was a man who fully appreciated the gift of sanctifying grace. And it's not too good to be true. In fact, it's good that it *is* true!

FEBRUARY 6

Make known to me your ways, Lord; teach me your paths.
—PSALM 25:4

The gift of wisdom has such a burning significance for Christians that we symbolize it with a glowing red tongue of fire. It is associated with the gifts of the Holy Spirit.

That we all have knowledge is a given, but we must humbly admit that we need the wisdom only Christ can give.

Concentrate for a moment on the observation of Saint Paul that "the world in its present form is passing away."

We can't help but detect urgency in God's Word, can we? It is an urgency seen in the preaching of the prophets, in the exhortation of Saint Paul, and certainly in the ministry of Jesus as He bellowed, "This is the time of fulfillment! The Kingdom of God is at hand!"

Thus, since "the world in its present form is passing away," we clamor for the wisdom to conform our judgments not to the fading trends of this transient world but to the eternal truths revealed by Christ and placed into the rational nature of the human person.

The exigencies of this world that is passing away can make the attention we must give to these eternal truths—truths that themselves will never pass away—controversial and difficult, but that never justifies ignoring them.

This is why we humbly acknowledge that we need a wisdom that this world cannot give but that can come only from the Spirit we call "Holy."

Nor do they light a lamp and then put it under a bushel basket; it is set on a lampstand, where it gives light to all in the house.
—MATTHEW 5:15

Scholars of religion report that exterior marks of membership help make a religion cohesive and attractive. Catholic external markers—such as holy days, fasts, genuflection, holy water, candles, bowing one's head at the Holy Name of Jesus, First Fridays, First Saturdays, frequent confession, novenas, devotions—are important to our faith. Yet they don't seem as popular today. Have we lost some spice from Catholic life with their departure? Have we tossed too many external markers of our Catholic identity out the window?

One of my friends once told me that we're too much into "Catholic lite." Are Church leaders trying to attract people by making things easier? If so, I'm afraid it's backfiring. I hear Catholics tell me, "We don't want Catholic lite; we want to be 'lights to the world'!"

Many Catholics are leaving the Church. Why? Studies report that many who leave to join another religion end up as members of a church considered stricter or more conservative!

We should all be yelling: "We don't like 'Catholic lite.' Call us to greatness! Call us to heroic virtue! Remind us that following Jesus calls for sacrifice and that we must long for ways to let ourselves and the world know that we are different. Don't cater to convenience!"

Jesus summoned us to be a "light to the world." Have we put this lantern under a basket? Have we turned light into lite?

FEBRUARY 8

My soul, be at rest in God alone.
—PSALM 62:6

Before becoming archbishop of Milwaukee, Wisconsin, I'd always heard about that city's ferocious ice storms and snowstorms. After my fourth winter there, in vain had I been waiting for a "snow day," one of those unexpected free days when the ice and snow close everything down. Finally, in February 2006, it arrived. And where was I? In sunny Southern California giving a talk! I missed the longed-for snow day.

But growing up in Missouri, I loved those snow days. To get out of bed and see the drifts of white, then hurriedly turn on the radio and hear the good news that Holy Infant School would be closed. Alleluia! A day inside, hot cocoa, reading the Hardy Boys books, playing games, hidden away from the rest of the world.

The eagerness I had for a snow day, I would suppose, came from a deep-down longing we all have for periodic quiet, solitude, and seclusion. A desire very important in the life of discipleship.

I bring this up in February because Catholic tradition dedicates this month to the hidden life of Jesus.

Between His presentation in the temple forty days after His birth and the beginning of His public life thirty years later, the only event we know of in the life of Christ is when He was lost in the temple at twelve years of age. In other words, Jesus spent over 90 percent of His time on earth hidden away. In seclusion. In quiet.

I contend that Our Lord wanted to tell us that quiet, seclusion, silence—a hidden life—has immense value. And that we all need some of it. Prayer, study, silence, relaxation, seclusion: Those were values for the Savior, and they are good for us, His followers.

Whoever sins belongs to the devil, because the devil has sinned
from the beginning. Indeed, the Son of God was revealed
to destroy the works of the devil.
—1 JOHN 3:8

The forces we face in today's world are not just those we can see. I'm afraid we also battle an axis we cannot see, whose powers are stronger than any in creation save one—Our Lord and Savior Jesus Christ.

There are powers of darkness in our culture. Pope Francis often reminds us that we are fools if we dismiss the power of Satan.

But Satan is scared because there is one mightier than he. And as Saint Paul taught, this mighty one "delivered us from the power of darkness."

Our weapon is prayer! And we can take refuge in a home that the powers of darkness are scared of—a house where Mary is our mother, where Jesus dwells, and where we are with family.

We are here on this earth not as warriors but as apostles of life, apostles armed not with money, hate, or destructive words but with love and joy. We are apostles of life who, like those first twelve, believe in the power of Christ and who see, as recorded in the Gospel, "unclean spirits fall down before Him and shout, 'You are the Son of God.'"

Let us never cease in prayer, always giving thanks to the Father, who delivered us from the power of darkness.

*If we say, "We are without sin," we deceive ourselves,
and the truth is not in us.*
—1 JOHN 1:8

The Bible is clear about God's mercy, but it is also clear about God's command to avoid sin. We see evidence of this in the words of Jesus to the woman caught in adultery: "Neither do I condemn you [but] go and do not sin any more!"

Jesus always gives us His mercy, but He also always calls us to change, to stop sinning, and to recognize the truth of a new life in Him. It's a delicate balance. As a wise bishop once said, "The same God who is mercy incarnate gave us the Ten Commandments." This bishop also noted that although it's soothing to meditate only on the parables about mercy, we cannot overlook the parables that describe the "narrow way" or the guests excluded from the banquet because they were not properly dressed. Sin has consequences.

Many pastors report that the problem today is not that people feel they do not deserve God's mercy but that people feel they don't need it!

Indeed, what some people want is not mercy for their sins—that's theirs for the asking—but approval of their decision to live in opposition to what God has taught. We can assure them of God's mercy. But His approval? Sorry. God's forgiveness does not mean His approval.

A wise spiritual director told me years ago: "God loves you where you're at, but He loves you so much that He doesn't want you to stay there!"

FEBRUARY 11

Feast of Our Lady of Lourdes

Water is a powerful baptismal sign.

As God destroyed sin in the waters of the flood in Noah's time, He destroys Original Sin at baptism.

As God saved the dehydrated Israelites in the desert with water from the rock, He saves us through the waters of baptism.

As Jesus saved us on the cross with the blood and water flowing from His pierced side, so He saves us now with the waters flowing at baptism.

Think about February 11, 1858. A beautiful woman appears to a young French girl named Bernadette in a cave right outside the little village of Lourdes in the Pyrenees mountains of southwestern France.

This radiant woman introduces herself as "the Immaculate Conception" and invites Bernadette to renewed prayer, penance, and charity. She tells Bernadette that she wants people to receive the healing, soothing, cleansing, and salvation that only her Son can give.

She instructs Bernadette to dig in the mud to unearth a spring of miraculous water that will symbolize baptism and help bring about the healing, soothing, cleansing, and saving that can come only from Christ. Bernadette obeys, and Lourdes becomes the world's largest baptismal font, with millions of people who are sick in soul, mind, or body visiting there annually.

Mary tells us now what she told Bernadette at the grotto: Pray, repent, love, and be saved by my Son, who gives us the waters of eternal life!

He will not allow your foot to slip; or your guardian to sleep.
—PSALM 121:3

Those of faith profess, "We believe in God, the Father Almighty," knowing it is actually a profession of dependence. We admit that every breath we take, each day we have, and every opportunity we are given come from an omnipotent God, and we bask in the fact that we are totally dependent on Him.

But many people today feel that it is chic to throw off any sense of obedience to God or to His basic code of right and wrong.

It's not that we do not believe in God; it's just that we consider ourselves to *be* gods. We claim dominion over life itself, as we accept abortion, euthanasia, and capital punishment.

We defend freedom as the right to do whatever we want, whenever we want, wherever we want instead of believing that freedom is really the liberty to do what we ought.

The Ten Commandments have become a list of suggestions, the Bible mere literature, and the Church unnecessary.

The real task in life is to be independent of earthly and selfish tyranny while at the same time confessing an utter dependence on God and His eternal law.

Welcome one another, then, as Christ welcomed you,
for the glory of God.
—ROMANS 15:7

Iraq is home to an ancient Christian community that probably is traceable back to Pentecost. So, by the way, are Iran, Syria, Lebanon, Egypt, and many other places in the Middle East. True, they are small Christian communities, but after what they've gone through the last two millennia, it's a shock there's even one believer left. Some of the worst persecution these people have faced, however, is happening right now. Our government has called it *genocide:* a systematic, coordinated, fanatical drive to extinguish Christians.

Mosul and the historic plains of Ur had been home to many Christians for millennia. In 2014, 110,000 of them walked sixty miles to a sanctuary in Erbil, Kurdistan, where they were welcomed heroically by Archbishop Bashar Warda and his small but loving Christian community. In 2015, I had the honor to go to Kurdistan, where I met Archbishop Warda. For almost a week, we visited the churches, schools, clinics, and camps he had put up for the refugees. There we saw courageous men and women charged with caring for the "internally displaced persons"—IDPs—in the spirit of the Bible, of the Corporal and Spiritual Works of Mercy . . . and of Jesus.

When I asked Archbishop Warda what we could do to help, I figured he would, understandably, seek funds for those camps, clinics, and schools. And he did. But what he most urged was *solidarity*! What would mean the world to him and his beleaguered people is the assurance that they are not forgotten, that we know of them and what they have been going through, that we love them and pray with and for them.

Can I promise him that? Can we all promise him that?

FEBRUARY 14

Saint Valentine's Day

The iconic symbol of Saint Valentine's Day is the heart—the representation of love, especially the romantic love between a man and a woman. On this day we often send heart-shaped greetings or heart-shaped boxes of chocolates to someone we care about. We do this because we want those we love to know what we feel, what's in our hearts. We want to give an outward sign of an inward love.

Yet when we think of a heart—a heart that holds a love so powerful and so strong—we must return to the one who created us out of love. This heart—a heart called sacred, a heart wounded by unreturned love, a heart broken by callousness and selfishness—is the heart of Jesus.

Christ's heart is on fire with love for us, but it is surrounded by a crown of thorns. Though it was broken on that weirdly termed "Good" Friday on a cross on Calvary, it nevertheless still beats for us.

It is through this heart that all true love flows. It is this Sacred Heart we trust. It is this heart we turn to through our repentance and acts of sacrifice and atonement. It is this heart we must vow to embrace, to love, and to never betray.

And he gave some as apostles, others as prophets, others as evangelists,
others as pastors and teachers, to equip the holy ones for the work of ministry,
for building up the body of Christ.
—EPHESIANS 4:11-12

We call our priests "Father." In our tradition, a priest is married to the same stunning bride to whom Jesus Himself is wedded: the Church.

And he's a father with children, whom he tenderly brings from the waters at Baptism, feeds in the Eucharist, forgives in Reconciliation, soothes in Anointing, and sends off in Marriage. He is a proud father who often laughs and cries with his family, who corrects and encourages, who leads them in prayer, who loves them to death, all in partnership with his bride, their mother, the Church.

I love my brother priests: They have stuck to it through some of the toughest years of change in the history of the Church. Those my age and older have seen the priesthood go from a position of prestige to one of derision and decline. They've watched their best friends leave active ministry.

Yet our faithful priests keep at it. They smile, they pray, they trust, they persevere.

When all is said and done, our priests do it because they are *in love.* They are hopelessly in love with a Lord whom they cannot see but who is as real as can be. And hopelessly in love with a Church.

Let's pray for all priests today.

Now, why delay? Get up and have yourself baptized
and sins washed away, calling upon his name.
—ACTS 22:16

"I want to be baptized." They are words I will never forget hearing. They came out of the mouth of a man dying in Gift of Peace, an AIDS hospice run by the Missionaries of Charity. It was Good Friday 1989, and I was the priest assigned for the liturgy of the Lord's Passion. Every year on Good Friday, Catholics venerate the cross, typically kissing Our Lord Jesus as depicted on a crucifix. Not all of the patients could get out of their rooms to participate in the liturgy, and so two sisters led me upstairs to visit patients who wanted to participate in the sublime prayer.

In the corner was a man, emaciated, clearly agitated, and motioning for me to go over to him. As I headed his way, a sister intervened, warning me that this patient was known to be violent. The man was insistent. As I approached him with the crucifix, he took it into his hands and kissed the face of Jesus on the cross.

The next day the sisters called me to come back to the hospice at this man's request. He wanted to be baptized. He admitted to me that he'd spent most of his life hating religion. But now he found himself unable to resist. "These sisters are always happy!" He recounted to me his three months in the hospice, clearly on his deathbed. "When I curse them, they look at me with compassion in their eyes. Even when they clean up my vomit, bathe my sores, and change my diapers, they are smiling. All I know is that they have joy and I don't."

Bewildered and desperate, he asked why on earth they were so happy. Their answer? Jesus. "I want this Jesus," the man said to me. "I want this Jesus. Baptize me and give me Jesus! Give me joy!"

What a gift it was for me to baptize, anoint, and give First Holy Communion to this man, who died the next day, on Easter morning. In those sisters, he encountered the presence of God.

Behold, now is a very acceptable time; behold,
now is the day of salvation.
—2 CORINTHIANS 6:2

One of my favorite characters in American literature is Scarlett O'Hara of Margaret Mitchell's *Gone with the Wind*. Do you remember her response to any problem or difficulty that came her way? It was always "I'll think about that tomorrow." "I'll worry about that tomorrow." "Tomorrow is another day."

We are all like Scarlett O'Hara when it comes to our spiritual life, aren't we? Don't we all say: Do I need to pray more? Yes, but I'll think about that tomorrow. Do I need to get closer to God? Sure, but there's plenty of time to worry about that later. Do I need to turn away from sin and follow the gospel more faithfully? Absolutely! Maybe I'll start sometime soon.

Tomorrow is not a given; we cannot live as if there will be one. God calls each of us to prayer, self-sacrifice, and works of charity. We must not wait until tomorrow to heed His call.

This is the day we begin to convert our lives and follow the gospel more closely. As Pope Benedict XVI said, "Conversion means changing the direction of the path of our lives. . . . It is going against the current when the 'current' is a superficial, incoherent, and illusory way of life that often drags us down. . . . Nevertheless . . . we trust in the living and personal gospel who is Jesus Christ. He is the final goal and the profound path of conversion."

FEBRUARY 18

*Then Jesus approached and said to them, "All power in heaven
and on earth has been given to me."*
—MATTHEW 28:18

The headline is so familiar to us: Another group "challenges"
the Vatican on something.

The Vatican is a plot of ground the size of an eighteen-hole
golf course on the banks of the Tiber River in Rome. The Vatican has absolutely no authority to alter the teaching of the
Church. Its sacred duty is to preserve and hand on the deposit
of faith we have received from revelation, from the Bible, from
Jesus, and from His Apostles.

The Vatican does not "make up," "change," or "issue" new
doctrines. It inherits them—receives them—by tradition.
Those timeless teachings are not ours to alter.

Yes, the Vatican may rethink how the truth entrusted to it
might be explained better, presented more credibly, or expressed in a more contemporary way. And yes, the Church does
have some "policies" that can be changed, for instance, abstinence from meat on Friday or even priestly celibacy. These indeed are part of its discipline—still not to be dismissed
lightly—and can be modified.

There are many other areas of pastoral strategy in which we
need vigorous discussion and fresh ideas, but not in the area of
doctrine and not as part of the Church's received tradition.

In the end, our challenge is not to change the teachings of
Jesus and His Church to conform to our whims but to change
our lives to conform to His teaching.

For where two or three are gathered together in my name,
there am I in the midst of them.
—MATTHEW 18:20

"Mass is so boring!"

How often have you heard that common complaint about the celebration of the Eucharist? How often have we said it to ourselves?

What do we say to that unfortunate and almost sacrilegious statement?

Well, for one thing, we simply reply, No, it's not! *You* may find the Mass boring, but that's more your problem than the fault of the Mass.

An event's value does not depend on whether it sometimes "bores" us. The Mass does not exist to thrill us.

We believe that every Mass is the renewal of the most important, critical event that ever occurred—the ultimate sacrifice of Jesus on the cross.

We go to Mass not to be entertained but to pray. It helps if the music is good, if the heat or air-conditioning is working, if the sermon is short and meaningful, and if folks are friendly. But the Mass works even when all those things are missing.

It works because the Mass is not about us but about God. And the value of the Mass comes from our simple yet profound conviction that for an hour on Sunday we're part of the beyond, lifted up to the eternal, a participant in a mystery, as we unite with Christ in the love, atonement, sacrifice, and thanks He offers His Father.

What Jesus does always works and is never boring. The Mass is not some tedious chore we do for God but a miracle He does with and for us.

Jesus said to him in reply, "What do you want me to do for you?"
The blind man replied to him, "Master, I want to see."
—MARK 10:51

Prayer is very common in the human experience. What is also common is our humble admission that we really could use some help. I think we learn something very important from the blind beggar Bartimeus, who was on the side of the road as Jesus and a large crowd were going to Jericho. When Bartimeus hears that Jesus is near, he cries out to the Lord.

And look at what Jesus says to him: "What do you want me to do for you?"

That's a little strange, don't you think? Everybody knew what Bartimeus was looking for. He was blind. And Jesus could see that. What's the lesson here? Why did Jesus want Bartimeus to tell Him?

We need to exercise our faith muscles. And our faith muscles, like other muscles, can get flabby if we're not using them.

Thus, Bartimeus says, "I want to see." And the Divine Physician answers that prayer. But more than the physical healing, Jesus was allowing Bartimeus to say: "Lord, I need you."

And in a real way, Jesus wants to hear us all say: "I need you. Dear Jesus, I need you."

When we say to God in our prayer "I need you," the Lord smiles. And Jesus responds. It's the beginning of all healing. And it's an answer to all prayer: I need you, Lord, that I might see.

Tell the Israelites: On the first day of the seventh month you will have
a Sabbath rest, with trumpet blasts as a reminder, a declared holy day.
—LEVITICUS 23:24

A few years ago, on the evening after Rosh Hashanah, the New Year in the Hebrew calendar, I had the pleasure of an enjoyable evening out at an Italian restaurant. Among the many people at the table, there was a delightful woman at my side. At my urging, she described to me the way she and her family observed the Jewish High Holy Days together.

On Rosh Hashanah, she explained, her people entered a period of reflection and examination of the just-concluded year and made some resolutions about the year ahead. Then, with sundown on Yom Kippur, the Day of Atonement, she and her family began an intense twenty-four-hour period of prayer and fasting from all food and even water. Part of it, she pointed out, was repentance for past sin through prayer and mortification. And, she concluded, it entailed a sense of bodily hunger, thirst, and emptiness, which was but a mirror of the interior hunger and thirst we all have, an emptiness only God can fill.

She then asked me, "Do you Catholics have such an experience?"

Sure, I was able to reply. Every Friday is supposed to be a day of penance for us. Lent, I went on, is a forty-day experience of what she described, with special penance on Ash Wednesday, Good Friday, and the other Fridays of that season.

As we left, I thanked her for what I described as an "evening of recollection," listening to her elaborate on her Jewish faith.

"But I worry," she concluded, "because I fear we Jews might be losing our tradition of sacred times of reflection, prayer, and penance."

"You're not alone," I assured her. "I fear we Catholics are, too."

Feast of the
Chair of Saint Peter

The Feast of the Chair of Saint Peter is the liturgical feast of the office of Peter in the Church. It commemorates Peter's role as the head of the Apostles, the one designated by Christ to be the universal pastor of the entire Church.

It is a suitable feast to give thanks for the gift of Peter's mission, carried out from the time of Jesus to our own day by Peter and his successors. Even secular historians marvel at the papacy's endurance. The eyes of faith see in that a testimony to the Holy Spirit's guidance of the Church from the day Peter himself preached on that first Pentecost until now.

Peter is the gift of Jesus to the Church, a teacher to hand on the deposit of the faith and to be a sign of unity. From the Acts of the Apostles to today, Catholics of every time and place have recognized the gift of Peter and his successors in their midst. The Latin phrase *ubi Petrus, ibi ecclesia*—"where Peter is, there is the Church"—states the importance of this gift.

We need Peter among us. Without his charism, we would be tossed about by every gust of wind, every false doctrine, and every silly trend. As Christ said, "You are Peter, and upon this rock I will build my Church."

Peter is the rock to be sure, but it is Our Lord who is the cornerstone and the sure foundation of the Church.

Behold, the Lamb of God.
—JOHN 1:36

"What makes this place tick?" I quizzed the exuberant pastor as he showed me around the parish, which was renowned for its high rate of Sunday Mass attendance; its first-rate school and excellent religious education for kids, teenagers, young adults, and adults; and its remarkably effective stewardship and successful initiatives of social justice, pro-life efforts, evangelization, and neighborhood presence.

I wanted the recipe so that I could bottle it and send it around.

"Follow me, I'll show you," Father replied.

He brought me to a chapel where perhaps six to eight people of diverse ages were in quiet adoration before Jesus, really and truly present in the Holy Eucharist, there in the monstrance on the altar.

"We've had perpetual Eucharistic Adoration now for four years," the pastor whispered. "We started slowly, about seven years ago, first with a day a week, then seven days, twelve hours a day, until we had a well-oiled system in place. For the last four years, it's been 24/7, with at least two people assigned every hour, all volunteers, and with many, many more during the waking hours. I'm convinced this Eucharistic Adoration is the key to the vitality, growth, and effectiveness of our parish."

"Pray always!" the Good Book tells us, and Jesus exhorted us to make sure that our prayer was patient, persistent, and persevering.

Eucharistic Adoration accomplishes this. It tells the world that "we can't give what we don't have" and that if we do not constantly turn to God in prayer for His grace and mercy, we're finished. The best thing people of faith can do is *pray*. . . . I can't think of a better place to do that than before Our Lord in the Blessed Sacrament.

FEBRUARY 24

We know that our old self was crucified with him, so that our sinful body
might be done away with, that we might no longer be in slavery to sin.
—ROMANS 6:6

Scriptures, which we cherish as God's revelation, teach eloquently the communal nature of sin. Yes, sin is personal, but it
also affects others, with an oil spill effect that poisons all of society, even all of the earth and its peoples.

We Catholics believe in the necessity of acknowledging
one's sins, asking the Lord's mercy, making reparation for transgressions, and renewing our covenant with the Lord.

Atonement, sorrow, and begging forgiveness are especially
urgent today as we hang our heads in shame for the sins we
commit.

But because we believe in redemption, the Church consists
of a people of hope. We do not give up. Daily we confront sadness, tragedy, injustice, trouble, and sin. And daily we take a
deep breath and keep going, counting on interior belief, the
support of great people, the nobility of our cause, and God's
grace and forgiveness.

Our friends see this. Our children see it, too. God shines
through us, and we become examples to those around us. Just
as our sins have that oil spill effect, so do our kind words; so do
our loving actions. Remember that light always trumps darkness. Hope always beats despair. Spring comes after winter.
And eternal life overcomes death.

We learn these lessons at church. We learn this through
Christ.

We are a people of grit who believe and belong, who dream
and dare. The bigger the problem, the more expansive the
hope.

So yes, the Church is in the business of hope. And Christ is
in the business of forgiveness.

For you are dust, and to dust you shall return.
—GENESIS 3:19

Unfailingly, I'll eavesdrop on a familiar conversation every Ash Wednesday.

One year I heard: "I didn't know it was Ash Wednesday until I saw Nick come into the office this morning with ashes on his forehead. I didn't even realize he was a Catholic. It makes sense, though. He's always happy and helpful and has an upbeat word of encouragement for the rest of us when we're down."

See how it works? Nick is actually an apostle, an evangelist. The ashes on his forehead reminded others in the office that Jesus has been beckoning them to "come back." His gospel-like behavior all year gave those ashes credibility.

By our words, our actions, and our very lives and persons, we invite others to Jesus and His Church. That's what we call evangelization.

Ash Wednesday is a day that has become a microcosm of what every day should be: Catholics reminding each other—and the world—of the Christ saying, "Come back to me; spend eternity with me!"

The allure of Lent is that we really should have the Sign of the Cross smudged above our brows every day, not with ashes but by who we are, what we do and don't do, and how we act. Then, as people look at us, they will be reminded of Jesus and His ever-gracious invitation to "come to me."

*Jesus answered, "Amen, amen, I say to you, no one can enter
the kingdom of God without being born of water and Spirit."*
—JOHN 3:5

Today is an anniversary I cherish. It's not the kind of day on
which you light candles on a cake or pop champagne corks. It's
not the kind of celebration most people in my life even know
about. But it's still the anniversary of the most important event
in my life.

On February 26, 1950, at Immaculate Conception Church,
in Maplewood, Missouri, I was baptized.

Obviously, since I was not yet three weeks old, I recall nothing of the sacred event. But what happened to me that winter
day in a suburb of St. Louis was a pure gift from a lavishly loving
God.

What happened to me that cold day in the corner of a parish church? *Everything.*

I became an adopted child of God. The lack of God's life
with which we all enter this world—we call it Original Sin—
was washed away by the waters of the sacrament, and my soul
was flooded with the radiance of God's very own life—grace!
Jesus Christ claimed me as His own. I became a member of a
supernatural family, the Church. Jesus told Satan—who wanted
me badly—to get lost, since I now belonged to Christ. The gifts
of faith, hope, and charity were instilled in my heart.

Not bad for a wintry day in Maplewood.

Do you know the day you were baptized? If so, celebrate it.
If not, I encourage you to find out!

*And, like living stones, let yourselves be built into a spiritual house
to be a holy priesthood to offer spiritual sacrifices acceptable
to God through Jesus Christ.*
—I PETER 2:5

All of God's people are called to priesthood; this is what we call "the priesthood of all believers." This is a call that does not depend on ordination but on baptism. As the Letter to the Hebrews elaborates, the old priesthood of the first covenant ended with Jesus Christ, the Eternal High Priest. In the new covenant, we are all called to the triple office of priest, prophet, and king.

Saints and laypeople of the Church such as Saint Francis de Sales, Saint Thérèse of Lisieux, Saint Josemaría Escrivá, and Dorothy Day insisted on the inescapable call to sanctity for all baptized persons wherever, whenever, and however they were living. But it took the Second Vatican Council to shake us back to the reality that there is a *universal call to holiness.*

Saint Paul, writing to the Galatians, claimed, "I live, no longer I, but Christ lives in me; insofar as I now live in the flesh, I live by faith in the Son of God who has loved me and given himself up for me."

We are indeed all called—as beloved of the Father, as chosen child, as lover of humanity, as healer of wounds, as one sent to bring the good news, and as reconciler—to act in the person of Christ.

FEBRUARY 28

For I was hungry and you gave me food, I was thirsty and you gave me drink,
a stranger and you welcomed me, naked and you clothed me, ill and you
cared for me, in prison and you visited me.
—MATTHEW 25:35-36

I try to visit prisons four times a year: Thanksgiving, Christmas, Easter, and sometime during the summer.

I always find it very inspirational, particularly the prisoners' sense of thanksgiving. Now, you may be asking yourself, How could men in a maximum-security prison be thankful to God? Well, they tell me, in part it's because everyone in their lives has let them down: lawyers, judges, friends, family, old gangs. And certainly they themselves. But the one person who is always there for them? The Lord.

We gather together for Mass. They pray well; they're sincere. Afterward, I get to visit with them and the staff. They always thank me for coming. And then I get to thank them. Some of them are surprised at first to be thanked, and so I explain: "Well, fellas, I'm grateful to come. Because when I stand before Jesus and He says, 'Timothy, when I was in jail, did you come and visit me?' I'll be able to say, 'Yes, Lord, I did.' So, guys, I'm here helping you get to heaven and you're helping me get to heaven. We're all in this together."

Recently, after Mass, one of the men presented me with a gift. It was a pencil sketch of Jesus on the cross on Calvary. It was just magnificent, and I now have it in my room. He said to look closely, and I did. To the right of the Lord was Dismas, the "Good Thief," and I realized that he had sketched himself on the cross next to Jesus.

He encouraged me to continue to study the drawing and began to point out that the Roman soldiers and onlookers were about two dozen of his fellow inmates. "We're all there with Christ on the cross," he said. And boy, was he right.

MARCH 1

Sing to the Lord, all the earth, announce his
salvation, day after day.
—I CHRONICLES 16:23

I was raised to think of missions as something "way far away," and though we must never forget those foreign missions, we must realize that every diocese is a mission territory and every committed Catholic is a missionary.

Maybe we have gotten smug. Maybe we want to coast on the clout, buildings, numbers, size, money, and accomplishments of the past. As a matter of fact, maybe it's dulled us to the truth. So let me challenge you: No more taking our Catholic faith for granted!

No more relaxing in the great things the Church has done. Let us now look to what God is calling us to do.

Replace cynicism with confidence. Replace hand-wringing with hand folding. Replace waiting for people to come back with going out to get them. Replace keeping our faith to ourselves with letting it shine on others.

The whole world is our mission territory. And you and I are missionaries.

MARCH 2

*If we acknowledge our sins, he is faithful and just and will
forgive our sins and cleanse us from every wrongdoing.*
—I JOHN 1:9

What is Lent? Lent is the forty days of preparation for Holy
Week and Easter.

Why do we celebrate Lent? To accept in a more intense way
the invitation of Jesus to be more closely united with Him on
the cross, thereby dying with Him to sin, selfishness, Satan, and
eternal death, so to rise with Him on Easter Sunday to a more
radiant life of grace, mercy, and spiritual rebirth.

During this magnificent season of Lent, we all are called to
prayer, self-sacrifice, and works of charity as we meditate on
and look forward to celebrating the Passion, Death, and Resurrection of Our Lord. In his Second Letter to the Corinthians,
Saint Paul said: "Behold, now is a very acceptable time; behold,
now is the day of salvation."

Someone once asked me if I had any practical counsel for
Lent. "Yes," I replied. "Get back to confession."

The Sacrament of Penance is most closely associated with
the season of Lent, because there is no better time to approach
this sacrament than before Easter.

We are all called to be saints, but we're sure not there yet.
That is why great help getting there is provided by a good confession. Our sins are forgiven and our souls returned to that
perfect day of our baptism.

Feast of
Saint Katharine Drexel

What was one of the events that helped significantly decrease early America's suspicion of the Catholic Church?

The episode that most dramatically motivated Americans who grew up with only negative perceptions about those "ignorant, superstitious Catholics" was the heroic charity of Catholic nuns on the battlefields of the Civil War as they selflessly tended to the wounded and dying.

Those brave religious women seemed to be everywhere, unafraid of cannons or bullets, unconcerned about whether a bleeding man was from the North or the South, and caring for those on both sides with competence, compassion, and faith.

Thousands of those men returned to their homes telling all who would listen, "Hey, those Catholics aren't bad. In fact, some of them, those women they call 'sisters,' saved my life."

We Catholics love nuns. We Americans love nuns. Sisters have sharp minds, soft hearts, radiant souls, and indomitable wills. They have an uncanny charism of sensing where God's people are most in need.

Saint Katharine Drexel was one of those women. She used her family's wealth to benefit others, and then she worked with Native Americans and African Americans, building dozens of missions and schools. In addition, she founded the Sisters of the Blessed Sacrament and the first Catholic college for African Americans in America.

In Saint Katharine, as in all nuns, we see personified the two great commandments that we all must strive to follow: Love God and love your neighbor.

Behold, the virgin shall be with child and bear a son,
and they shall name him Emmanuel.

—MATTHEW 1:23

Emmanuel means "God is with us."

To a world that has concluded that God is incomprehensible and aloof, we say, "Emmanuel: God is with us!"

To a world that wonders if God even cares, is concerned, or can console or cry, we reply, "Yes, He is with us!"

What unites our faith is not simply the deep-down conviction that He is with us but the imperative that we show the world that He is with us not just in churches but in our lives.

A good chunk of our world attacks this message and concludes that God does not dwell within us. Such doubt is understandable, because our individual sin prompts people to consider our claim of Emmanuel as hollow.

The God who is Emmanuel has revealed that His will is for peace, healing, mercy, love, and reconciliation.

Our sacred duty—those of us who dare to claim that our religion is Emmanuel—is to welcome, never turn away; to raise up, never knock down; to act with mercy, never violence; and to offer bread and wine, not instruments of destruction.

So [then] each of us shall give an account of himself [to God].
—ROMANS 14:12

We hear a lot these days about accountability. And that is a good thing, as it affects all aspects of our lives.

We are accountable to ourselves. As people of integrity, we hold ourselves to the high standards coming from morality, a properly formed conscience, and the expectations of Christ and His Church. Sometimes we say things like "I just couldn't live with myself if I did that." That's a good indication that we are a people of character. And often we examine our consciences to hold ourselves responsible, apologizing to God or to another person when we have let them down.

We are accountable to others as well: spouses, family, brothers and sisters in the faith, friends, coworkers, countrymen, teammates, classmates. Others rely on us, and we can't let them down.

We are accountable to nature. If we pollute or abuse nature, it will catch up with us, and we or our children will suffer the results.

We are accountable to history. Those who come after us will bless us or curse us for the choices we make now, and we will have to live with the consequences of our actions—good and bad.

Most significantly, we are accountable to God. As the Bible tells us, one day we shall stand before Him in judgment. On that day no excuses, no rationalizing, no denying, and no hiding will do us any good.

MARCH 6

*For the wages of sin is death, but the gift of God is
eternal life in Christ Jesus our Lord.*
—ROMANS 6:23

There is a Latin phrase *memento mori*—which means "remember
that you will die."

Now, maybe this insight and its implications will strike
some as morbid. On the contrary: It is life-giving and liberating.

My mentor and friend, the late Church historian Monsignor John Tracy Ellis, used to remark that the secret to life was
to view everything *sub specie aeternitatis,* that is, "with the outlook
of eternity." In other words, with every choice in life, I ask,
How will this help me reach my goal of eternal union with
God? If it will hinder my ultimate destiny, it's got to go; if it will
help me get there, I embrace it.

That is why some of the happiest, freest, healthiest people
around are those who know they are dying, as any of you involved in the beautiful hospice movement can attest. As Cardinal Joseph Bernardin said in his final public address, "a dying
person does not have time for the peripheral or the accidental.
He or she is drawn to the essential, the important—yes, the
eternal."

And as Saint Benedict said in his Rule, "Remember to keep
death before your eyes daily." Doing this allows us to live our
lives joyfully and fully. As God intends.

And the two shall become one flesh. So they are no longer two, but one flesh.
Therefore what God has joined together, no human being must separate.
—MARK 10:8-9

In a world that has grown cynical and skeptical about pure love, commitment, genuine romance, and self-giving, we must look to faithfully married couples as a wonderful example.

Those of you who are married or who one day may get married recognize that the most important person in your marriage is God. It does, indeed, take all three—husband, wife, and the Lord—for a successful marriage. It was no accident that Jesus worked His first miracle for a married couple at Cana.

Share with each other the most sought-after commodity you have: time! Give one another the gift of your time, your attention, your interest.

Suffer the crosses together. The world tells us we deserve constant bliss, satisfaction, pleasure, and excitement. Jesus tells us, "Love one another, as I have loved you!" which, of course, refers to the cross. When the cross comes into your married life—through tension, misunderstanding, sickness, struggle, money problems—you will find that you will grow closer to each other and to the Lord if you use these adversities as occasions to grow in trust.

Accept wholeheartedly the Church's wonderful teaching on marriage—that the love you have for each other is actually a reflection of the passionate love God has for us. Thus, it is lifelong, it is faithful, and it is fruitful.

I want you couples to know that I love you, I pray for you, and I thank God for your vocation.

MARCH 8

Then Jesus said to His disciples, "Whoever wishes to come after me must deny himself, take up his cross, and follow me."
—MATTHEW 16:24

The catechumens who enter into full communion with the Church on Holy Saturday bring an exuberance, a joy, and a devotion that can help reignite the flame for Christ in our lives. They frequently speak about Catholic doctrines, practices, and traditions that they find "awesome."

For instance, they love Sunday Mass and receiving the Eucharist. They enjoy the Sacrament of Penance. They rejoice in the teaching authority of the Church as it is personified in the pope.

They appreciate Mary and the saints. One woman told me that the most powerful moment of the Easter Vigil came during the chanting of the Litany of the Saints, when it dawned on her that she was joining a spiritual family with older brothers and sisters.

They speak eloquently about the power of conversion. They have left their "old selves" behind and are a "new creation."

Converts are a booster shot in the arm for our faith. May the light they shine flow through us as well.

MARCH 9

Do not fear: I am with you; do not be anxious: I am your God.
—ISAIAH 41:10

One of the many gifts the Lord lavishes on us is the chance to begin all over again.

Regrets? We've all had a few. But we can always begin again.

How grateful we are that we have a God of second chances who is never quite finished with us. He has told us that it makes Him happy when we take a deep breath and whisper to Him, "Lord, I'd like to come closer to you."

Even our ability to utter that phrase is a gift from Him—a result of His grace. "Let my mercy take care of your regrets," He consoles us, "and concentrate now on a fresh start."

So we humbly renew our commitments again: a few moments of prayer daily; fidelity to Sunday Mass; attention to a habit of sin; a return to the Sacrament of Penance; opening the Bible; an outreach to a friend; or an act of tenderness to one broken or in need.

Jesus told us, "Seek ye first the Kingdom of God," and all else will come.

He is always there for us. He always opens the door when we knock. His line is never busy, and He always answers with a live voice. Christ didn't send an email but came in person. He *is* Emmanuel—"God is with us."

MARCH 10

So Jesus said to them, "Untie him and let him go."
—JOHN 11:44

Not too many years ago, I was visited by a young man who had just been through treatment for opioid addiction. After we spent some time chatting, he asked if we could pray together. I was honored and happy to do that.

He said, "Can I read my favorite passage of the Bible to inspire us in prayer?" and of course I said yes.

He chose a dramatic episode in which the divinity and humanity of Jesus are very visible. The story describes how Jesus raised his good friend Lazarus from the dead. When Jesus arrived, Lazarus had been in the tomb for four days. After Jesus cried out, "Lazarus, come out!" the dead man did so. There's a line that's easy to overlook. When they roll back the rock and Lazarus comes out, he's bound up by his burial garments. Jesus said to them, "Untie him and let him go."

After this young man read that line, he said, "You know, in my addiction, I was all tied up. I was all bound up. When I was taking opioids, I thought I was as free as a bird and didn't have a care in the world. But I was dead. I was straitjacketed. It's only now that I have the freedom to know that I've been untied and let go." He attributed that to his faith. He attributed that to the grace and mercy of Jesus.

Although some of us may not be tied up as dramatically as that cured young man was, the truth is that we all have some bondage in our lives. All of us are tied up. Maybe some old sins. Maybe some addictions. Maybe some old faults. Maybe we feel that we're in a cycle of helplessness and can't get out of it. We hear Jesus today say "Untie him." Untie her. Let him or let her go. He releases us from being bound up.

God is Spirit, and those who worship him
must worship in Spirit and truth.
—JOHN 4:24

It is eloquent testimony to its pivotal place in the foundation of our republic that the right to the free exercise of religion is listed as the first in our Bill of Rights.

Today, though, freedom of religion is being reduced to "freedom of worship"—a personal hobby on one's Sabbath, tolerated as long as the values expressed in that hour of worship have no impact at all on society.

This view is contrary to the genius of the American experiment. Historians tell us that our most exalted moments—the abolition of slavery, the peace movement, opposition to world tyranny, the pro-life movement, the civil rights crusade, and even the Revolution itself—have been expressions of faith, unfettered by government.

My fears about an aggressive erosion of religious freedom arise from my desire not only to defend the faith I love but to preserve the country I love.

The restriction of religious liberty not only inhibits the practice of faith but has dire consequences for society. Faith provides a foundation for the dignity of the human person, representative government, the separation of powers, and the civility essential to a vibrant commonwealth.

Daily we Americans thank God for the freedom of religion at the heart of the inalienable rights our country was founded to protect. Our sense of gratitude and pride as citizens of a nation that respects religious liberty is high.

But never can we take this freedom for granted.

For God so loved the world that he gave his only Son, so that everyone who believes in him might not perish but might have eternal life.
—JOHN 3:16

When I was a boy, on every birthday and every Christmas, my Aunt Sissy would send a card with a quarter and two sticks of Juicy Fruit gum taped inside.

Mom, of course, would quickly remind me that I had better write Aunt Sissy a thank-you note, which I did. Guess what would always happen? Aunt Sissy would reply to my note with another card that had another quarter and two sticks of Juicy Fruit inside it. So I would write another note of gratitude, and back would come another card from Aunt Sissy. It would have gone on forever if Mom had not made me stop!

What was beautifully clear to me was that I could not outdo Aunt Sissy in generosity. Even my thank-you to her would only result in another gift.

This taught me something about God. We can never outdo God in His generosity and goodness.

Every time we thank Him, we open ourselves to receiving yet more blessings from Him. We cannot beat Him at giving!

This is most obvious at Mass. Every Sunday, we go to Mass to worship God. We try our best to let Him know how grateful we are. We offer Him our lives, in union with the eternal sacrifice of His Son. There, we've finally thanked Him sufficiently. Then He turns around and gives His Son back to us in Holy Communion!

What an awesome, wonderful God we have! Outgiving God is just not possible.

MARCH 13

I will give you the keys to the kingdom of heaven.
—MATTHEW 16:19

It's called *Domus Sanctae Marthae,* Latin for "Saint Martha's House," and it was my home at the Vatican for forty-eight hours, along with 114 of my brother cardinals, in 2013. We were there as part of our sacred duty as cardinal-electors to elect the next Successor of Saint Peter.

You remember Saint Martha, don't you? She, along with her sister, Mary, and her brother, Lazarus, were among Our Lord's best friends, and he often enjoyed their company and hospitality at their home right outside of Jerusalem.

We came to Saint Martha's right after the magnificent "Mass to Elect a Pontiff" in Saint Peter's Basilica on Tuesday morning. Each afternoon and each morning, we took a little bus the quarter-mile distance to the courtyard of San Lorenzo in Damaso to disembark and walk into the Sistine Chapel.

The gardens and corridors of the Vatican were eerily empty. After all, the pope was no longer there. We had the place to ourselves. I'd always dreamed of spending some uninterrupted hours looking upon the walls and ceilings of the celebrated Sistine Chapel. Never did I think I'd be doing it this way.

One of the older cardinals, who had gone through the conclave of 2005, assured me I would sense the presence of the Holy Spirit in all of this. He was right. No, not in any brilliant rays of light, sound of wind, or tongues of fire but in common and private prayer; oaths taken; words of inspiration, information, and encouragement exchanged; art and song working their charm; promptings sensed; and discernment going on.

And then the world knew the result of all this, as we cheered the announcement "We have a pope!" It was all worth it. It is His (Jesus's) Church—not mine, not the cardinals', not the Vatican's, not ours, not even Pope Francis's. It is *His* Church! And upon the rock of Peter's (and his successors') faith, He will build His Church.

MARCH 14

For you are a people holy to the Lord, your God; the Lord, your God,
has chosen you from all the peoples on the face of the earth
to be a people specially his own.
—DEUTERONOMY 14:2

Lent makes us marked men and women.

Certainly, when it comes to Ash Wednesday, we are all marked dramatically with ashes. It is a visible sign of being marked that says publicly that we are sinners in need of forgiveness. And as the weeks pass from that beginning of Lent, let's not forget that living out our faith each day marks us as well.

We were marked by God at our baptism. When a person is baptized, he or she is marked with the Sign of the Cross on the forehead. Be it a little baby or an adult convert to the faith, with water and with sacred chrism, we are set apart.

We are also marked—and this is what Lent asks us to work on—by the quality and character of our lives. We are called to make the virtue of our lives as obvious and dramatic as were those ashes on our forehead.

The world marks us as well. We are marked by our membership in the Church. We are marked by others when they say to us: "You profess to be a person of faith, so prove it." The world pays us a compliment because it expects more of us and looks to us for virtue and faith.

Is it always easy? No, it assuredly is not. But Jesus is with us every day of Lent, strengthening us as marked men and women of faith.

Yet even now—oracle of the Lord—return to me with your whole heart,
with fasting, weeping, and mourning.
—JOEL 2:12

Mortification, or putting to death our sinful nature, is an essential part of Jesus's teaching. Some sort of self-denial should always be part of our spiritual regimen.

Jesus doesn't tell us exactly what we should do for penance, but He insists that we undergo some form of self-sacrifice. It may be eating less, giving up certain foods, or doing laudable acts that we find difficult. This is done for many reasons.

For one thing, when we give up something we enjoy, especially over an extended period, we create a craving, an emptiness within. This is valuable because it reminds us that we all have an emptiness deep down that only God can fill.

Penance brings us closer to those who suffer all the time. Our little sacrifices put us in solidarity with those who have to do without every day.

In addition, our acts of penance bring us a little closer to Christ's suffering on the cross. Sure, His was infinitely greater and we could never approximate it, but we want to unite ourselves more intimately to Our Lord on Calvary so that we can be with Him in glory for all eternity.

When we mortify ourselves, we remind ourselves that following Jesus is not easy and being faithful to His teaching and loyal to His Church will always entail some sacrifice.

MARCH 16

*If there is any encouragement in Christ, any solace in love, any participation
in the Spirit, any compassion and mercy, complete my joy by being of
the same mind, with the same love, united in heart, thinking one thing.*
—PHILIPPIANS 2:1-2

Lent does for the spirit what spring training does for baseball players: It helps us get back to basics. During Lent, we concentrate on the essentials of the most sublime contest ever: the quest for the goal of heaven. We sweat and sacrifice our sins away to be ready to do battle against the most dangerous rivals of all: sin and Satan.

Yet, as with spring training, we want the season to begin already. Bring on the main event.

Bring on Passover! The oppressive slavery in the bondage of Egypt is overthrown by the blood of a lamb and by God's deliverance of His chosen people to the Promised Land. The angel "passed over" the homes of God's people, which were marked by the blood of a lamb. God's light guided His people to "pass over" from chains in Egypt to freedom in Israel.

Bring on Easter! Death is now defeated by the precious blood of the one John the Baptist called "the Lamb of God." Our Lord "passed over" from the horror of the cross on Good Friday—a drama colored by violence, hate, lies, betrayal, earthquakes, and an eclipse of the sun—to a new Easter life. The "light of Christ" leads God's people not through the waters of the Red Sea but out of the waters of the baptismal font.

Sin is on the run. Christ is victorious. By dying, He destroyed our death. By rising, He restored our life.

Lent gives us a chance to evaluate our lives and make the necessary changes that will lead us away from the sin and selfishness that sometimes choke our very being and toward the mercy and love of Christ.

MARCH 17

Feast of Saint Patrick

Saint Patrick probably was born in England, but he was kidnapped as a boy and sold into servitude in Ireland. There he came to know and love the people of that verdant, tiny island, as rough and contentious as they were, and longed to teach them the faith he had learned as a child.

Even when he escaped and returned home, he could not get Ireland out of his mind. He eventually returned to the damp turf that now claims him as its patron. To Ireland he took Jesus, His message, and the one, holy, catholic, and apostolic Church.

During the years 1845–51, blight and famine hit Ireland and resulted in the starvation of approximately two million people. Many left, searching desperately for a new home.

Those emaciated sons and daughters of Saint Patrick came by the hundreds of thousands to the United States with nothing of earthly value but the clothes on their backs and fond yet tearful memories of the people and the land they cherished.

But they had something of heavenly value: their Catholic faith. Although Lady Liberty was not yet in the harbor to welcome them to America, another woman was, one called the Holy Mother Church.

In a way, those Irish were missionaries. Through humble, simple ways, they built the Church here in America and passed the faith brought to them by Patrick on to their children. And every day the Church welcomes us, too.

Clear out the old yeast, so that you may become a fresh batch of dough. . . .
For our paschal lamb, Christ, has been sacrificed.
—1 CORINTHIANS 5:7

The classical definition of the paschal mystery is the dying and rising of Jesus and our absorption into it.

On Good Friday, Jesus will pass over from evil, hate, sin, and death to goodness, love, grace, and new life of Easter.

In this way, He invites us to pass over, leaving our selfishness and old ways on the cross and rising with Him to a new life.

Holy Saturday night, the Easter Vigil, will find thousands of people passing over into the new life of Christ in His Church. What about us?

Will we be like the thief on the left of Jesus on Calvary and ignore Him on the cross, or will we be like the "Good Thief" and look to heaven?

Will we profess our faith and embrace the sacraments or just remain bystanders?

Will we just wave at Jesus as He passes over from Good Friday to Easter Sunday, or will we accompany Him?

The pivotal question for each of us is: Will I simply look at Good Friday and Easter Sunday and say, "How nice! Let's dye eggs and buy candy"? Or will I unite with Our Lord in passing over from spiritual death—sin—to a new life of grace?

MARCH 19

Feast of
Saint Joseph

On this Feast of Saint Joseph, we reflect upon the man whom God chose to be the foster father of Jesus, and we look to him as an example of piety, obedience, and love.

Saint Joseph was a man who dealt with numerous emergencies with calmness, trust in God, and responsibility. Think of his virgin wife's "untimely" and embarrassing pregnancy, the birth of Jesus in a stable, the flight to Egypt to escape a murderous tyrant, and the three-day loss of his boy. What an example he is as we see so many emergencies in the Church and the world today!

Saint Joseph—ever attentive to God's will, placing Jesus and Mary at the heart of his life, reliable in his duties to care for and protect his wife and adopted son.

Saint Joseph—the patron of workers, himself a carpenter.

Saint Joseph—with a special care for the poor, always approached in prayer by those in want and need.

Saint Joseph—the chaste spouse of the Blessed Virgin Mary.

Saint Joseph—the protector of the Holy Family, leading them to safety in Egypt.

Saint Joseph—the man closest to Jesus, the man who knew Him first, loved Him most, and held Him closest.

Saint Joseph—the patron saint of a happy death, who died with Jesus and Mary by his side.

No wonder we call him the Patron of the Church Universal. No wonder he is the perfect example of a father. Saint Joseph, pray for us!

*Then the Lord will guide you always. . . . And you shall be like
a watered garden, like a flowing spring whose waters never fail.*
—ISAIAH 58:11

Picture Lent as a beautiful garden in progress. About this time
of year, many of us will begin preparing the plot of land that
will become our summer garden. We clear away rocks, sticks,
and weeds. We fertilize the soil. We take care to prepare the
best possible foundation for our plants to grow.

When we prepare ourselves properly, Lent does the same
thing for the garden of our souls. It clears away sin and selfishness so that our souls can blossom with new life at Easter.

The image of spring itself is also a beautiful image for Lent.
Winter, with its barrenness, cold temperatures, and dreary
skies, gradually gives way to the light, warmth, and new life of
spring. But it's a battle. That struggle between winter and
spring roaring outside is always going on deep down inside as
well.

If we are honest, we have to acknowledge that in our souls
and in our hearts there is a struggle between winter (darkness,
sin, death, coldness) and spring (light, grace, life, warmth). The
winter of our spirit dies as the new life of Christ rises within.

Lent gives us a chance to evaluate our lives and make the
necessary changes that will lead us away from the sin and selfishness that sometimes choke our very being and toward the
mercy and love of Christ, who wants nothing more than to receive our souls in full bloom.

The Mighty One has done great things for me, and holy is his name.
—LUKE 1:49

We have a mighty power to enlist whenever we need help—our Blessed Mother. Like the brave warrior women of ancient Israel—Deborah, Judith, and others—Mary was the one promised in the Garden of Eden to crush the head of the serpent. Catholic wisdom tells us that even the mention of her name brings a chill wind to hell. Lucifer could not damage her from the moment of her Immaculate Conception to the time of her Assumption into heaven.

We can assault the Prince of Darkness with Mary's weapon—the holy rosary. It is a simple, repetitive biblical prayer. We take seriously Our Lord's imperative that persistence characterizes our petitions as we repeat over and over again the Ave Maria—Gabriel's salutation to Our Lady.

Our perseverance continues as we lace the Ave with the Pater Noster, straight from the Master Himself, and let our minds reflect on the epochal events of the life, death, and victory of Jesus and His mother as we recite the mysteries.

Each bead weakens Satan. He tries to convince us that the rosary is childish and superstitious, a talisman of the past best saved as an ornament for our cold hands in the casket. And he hopes we'll give up on it.

But you and I know that this mighty weapon works. Take it from the nightstand drawer and begin again to thread a spiritual bulletproof vest. Satan's wiles are complicated; defense against them is rather simple.

And no one can say, "Jesus is Lord," except by the holy Spirit.
—I CORINTHIANS 12:3

If you look at the Latin word for "Lord"—which the Romans and early Christians would have used as they spread out through the Roman Empire—that word is *Dominus*.

If we're wondering about the solidness and reliability of our salvation, a good question to ask is: Who or what dominates? Because the word *dominates* comes from the word *Dominus*.

Who or what dominates, has dominion over our lives? Is it Jesus? Or is it someone or something else?

If we're honest in our answer to that question, we must admit that very often other things or other people dominate our lives. At times, someone or something other than Jesus has dominion over our lives.

Yet, though our sins may be diverse, we have one thing in common. We need to say: "Jesus, I need a Savior. I can't save myself. I want you to dominate and have dominion over my life. But you know me well, you know me better than I know myself. I've got other things that put in a strong bid for dominion over my life, and I want to get rid of them. I want to say with you, 'Be gone, Satan,' for I believe: Jesus is Lord."

Lent becomes the time when we do this so that, come Easter Sunday morning, we will renew our baptismal vows. When we are asked "Do you reject Satan?" we answer full-heartedly: "I do."

Allow Jesus, the Lord, to dominate our lives this Lent.

"This is my beloved Son, with whom I am well pleased;
listen to him."
—MATTHEW 17:5

You've heard of the Charles Dickens novel *A Tale of Two Cities,* right? I'd like to share with you a tale of two mountains.

The first is Mount Tabor, the site of the Transfiguration. We always have this tale on the Second Sunday of Lent. Peter, James, and John were with Our Lord when He became dazzling white. Moses and Elijah appeared. A voice came down from heaven saying, "This is my beloved Son." Faith in Jesus was easy at that time, I think you'd agree. It was, as they say, a mountaintop experience.

Then there's another hill, or mountain, called Calvary. It was there that Jesus was transfigured not into something radiant and glorious but something broken and bruised and bloody. Was it dazzling bright that day? No; the sun hid in shame as there was an eclipse. Does God the Father say anything about His Son? He is strangely silent. In fact, the Son asks, "Why have you forsaken me?" Faith is not as easy on Mount Calvary as it was on Mount Tabor.

The lesson, of course, is clear. For us as believers, both mountains are necessary. In our lives of faith, there will be moments on Tabor and moments on Calvary. The message Jesus drives home is that He is there with us at both of them.

MARCH 24

For I was hungry and you gave me food, I was thirsty and
you gave me drink, a stranger and you welcomed me.
—MATTHEW 25:35

Many of our readings from the Bible during Lent remind us of
our moral obligation to treat immigrants with dignity and respect.

Remember Saint Patrick's Day just last week, when the
Irish gratefully recalled America's open door given to their
starving and hopeful ancestors when they arrived here? Remember the recent Feast of Saint Joseph, where we discussed
the fact that Jesus was born away from home to parents "on the
move" and that soon afterward the Holy Family had to flee the
wrath of Herod?

In addition, we frequently see news about immigrants on
television, and we see many politicians who are unable to deal
effectively, fairly, and comprehensively with immigration reform. Probably because I reside in New York City, under the
shadow of our welcoming Statue of Liberty, I think about immigrants often. Here in New York I greet on an almost daily
basis those who have arrived recently. They are some of our
most reliable and hardworking neighbors. Welcoming them is
an essential part of our religious and patriotic heritage.

When we die and meet Jesus, He will ask: "When I was a
stranger, did you welcome me?" I feel certain that we Catholics
will be able to look Him in the eye, smile, and reply: "Yes!"

Annunciation

At the middle of the human drama is a pregnant woman. All of history is dated from the birth of her baby.

No one is more patient than an expectant mother. The baby cannot be rushed. Waiting is all she can do.

God's will, God's ways, and God's plan cannot be hurried. His time is not our time. God does not wear a watch or keep a daily agenda.

God takes the long view. In the Garden of Eden, when His design of life and love was thwarted, He dreamed of a "New Eve," a woman who would crush the serpent. This woman, to carry the Savior in her womb, would, of course, be free from Original Sin.

We hail that dream, that woman, the New Eve, and her baby, the "Second Adam." We serenade her, the one "clothed with the sun," carrying the Son in her womb.

No one has transformed history more than the One conceived by the Holy Spirit in the womb of the Blessed Virgin Mary. We adore Him! We love her!

We're back in the Garden of Eden, after the Original Sin, cherishing the New Eve, herself immaculately conceived, pregnant with the Second Adam, a fresh start. Her yes to the good angel Gabriel trumps Eve's yes to the evil angel Lucifer. The Second Adam's yes to the tree of the cross cancels out the first Adam's no to God's will in the Garden of Eden.

Good news indeed. She's pregnant! Get the baby's room—our hearts—ready! Life will never be the same.

Hail Mary, full of grace!

MARCH 26

See, I am creating new heavens and a new earth.
—ISAIAH 65:17

Anthropologists tell us that all great peoples and all great civilizations have two things that keep them going: memories and dreams.

If you go to daily Mass (something that, I may add, I highly encourage during Lent), you'll often hear the first reading dealing with memories of the people of Israel. Those memories are filled with faith in the great things that God had done for them in the past and that inspire them in the present.

You also will often hear a prophet such as Isaiah leading the people to dream what the New Jerusalem will be like. We know, of course, that the prophet is speaking of the New Jerusalem, which we call heaven, a place where "no longer shall the sound of weeping be heard . . . or the sound of crying."

It's so beautiful to reflect on the dream in which all strife, tears, and adversity will be washed away. And the dream of living with God in heaven—as well as with the people we love—for all eternity in complete happiness.

Allow yourself today to reflect on all the times God has been there for you. And allow yourself to dream of the future God has in store for you.

Memories and dreams. We need them both.

Watch carefully then how you live, not as foolish persons but as wise,
making the most of the opportunity.
—EPHESIANS 5:15-16

In what ways do you find yourself wasting time?

Perhaps you can admit that you waste time on social media. Maybe you find yourself wasting time watching Netflix. I hope you won't say that you've wasted time reading this book. But the truth is, we all waste time.

Today I encourage you to waste time with Jesus, for it's been said that that's what prayer can feel like sometimes. It's possible that your friends and coworkers think you're wasting time attending Mass. Or perhaps you've found yourself saying that confession is a waste of time. Why confess my sins, that little voice in our heads may say, when chances are those same sins will be right back in my life next week?

You could be exercising. Or doing something productive around the house. Or spending time with loved ones.

But I say: Waste time with the Lord!

As Christians, we sometimes are called to waste something for Jesus. Do you remember the story about when Jesus was in Bethany with his friends Lazarus, Mary, and Martha? Mary took a liter of oil and nard and anointed the feet of Jesus. But Judas called it a waste, pouring 300 days' wages away. Yet Jesus congratulates her. He's moved that she would "waste" something so precious on Him. And He's moved when we "waste" our time with Him in prayer.

*In this is love brought to perfection among us, that we have confidence
on the day of judgment.*

—I JOHN 4:17

Palms play an important role during our Lenten journey.

The custom at the time of Jesus was that people would wave palm branches to salute returning heroes and victors of wars. Thus, when the people in Jerusalem on that Sunday before Passover waved palms at Jesus, they were saluting him as a possible victor and conqueror. Of course, they were wrong in thinking of Him as a political hero who would drive the Romans from the Holy Land.

Jesus eventually would be a conqueror: The next Friday on the cross and Sunday with his Resurrection, He would triumph over sin and death. His would be not a political victory but a victory of eternal value. First the victim. Then the victor.

The palm tree is celebrated for its sturdiness and strength because it has roots that sink deep. It's hard, if not impossible, to knock it down. And in that way, Our Lord is like a palm tree: He is rejected by His friends, lied about by false witnesses, condemned and scourged at the pillar, crowned with thorns, forced to carry the cross. Yet He will not be deterred from the path He knows His Heavenly Father wants Him to take. He is like a palm tree: Yes, at times He will bend to the earth as He falls under the weight of the cross, but He will get back up.

He dies on the cross, but Easter Sunday tells us that He will rise to new life. He will be vindicated. He is a victor because, like the palm tree, He was never uprooted. What a lesson for you and me.

We all go through those periods in life of struggle, rejection, unfairness, and sickness. But we must stay sturdy and strong, continuing on the path down which God guides us. For even at times when it seems that loss and defeat are near, we know that with Jesus, victory and triumph are ours.

"Take courage, it is I; do not be afraid."
—MATTHEW 14:27

"Be not afraid," we're told, is the most frequently repeated exhortation in the Bible.

Naturally, there are lots of times in our lives when we're afraid. I think of one small example: In 2012, I was asked to address my brother cardinals and Pope Benedict XVI in a Consistory in Rome. Upon receiving the request, I was flattered. Upon hearing that I would be asked to give the address in Italian, I was naturally worried, because I speak Italian like a child.

But then I recalled that when I was a newly ordained parish priest, my first pastor said to me as I went over to school to teach the six-year-old children their catechism, "Now we'll see if all your theology sank in and if you can speak of the faith like a child."

We need to speak again like a child the eternal truth, beauty, and simplicity of Jesus and His Church.

After the Second Vatican Council in the 1960s, the good news was that *triumphalism* in the Church was dead.

The bad news was that so was *confidence.*

We are convinced, confident, and courageous in the New Evangelization because of the power of the person sending us on mission—who happens to be the Second Person of the Most Blessed Trinity—and because of the truth of the message and the deep-down openness in even the most secularized people to the divine.

Confident, yes!

Triumphant, never!

We must not be afraid of the truths of Jesus Christ. Or afraid of His Church.

MARCH 30

Enter his gates with thanksgiving, his courts with praise.
Give thanks to him, bless his name.
—PSALM 100:4

My mother lives in an assisted care facility. She is happy there except for one thing. Her worry? That she's become a burden to us! She spent her life caring for us, and now it weighs on her that we have to care for her.

Yes, she listens as we assure her that we love her and want to care for her as tenderly as she looked after us. She hears us and thanks us, but she is still bothered.

In a way, this is a tribute to her sense of responsibility. Mom grew up and lived out her vocation as a mother and wife in a time when one welcomed one's duties and did one's best in meeting those responsibilities.

Things seem different today. A lot of folks no longer embrace a culture of duty but one of entitlement.

When we assure her that she need not worry, she sighs and replies, "I'll try. I guess all I can do is be grateful."

Precisely! All any of us can do is be grateful—to God, family, and friends and for all the blessings we have.

We do things for others out of love. As the Prayer to Saint Francis of Assisi teaches, "It is in giving that we receive." Saint John Paul II called this "the law of the gift."

We are at our best, and we are acting the way God intended, when we give ourselves away in selfless love to another.

For, if you confess with your lips that Jesus is Lord and believe in your heart that God raised him from the dead, you will be saved.

—ROMANS 10:9

This teaching of Saint Paul is so pivotal and significant because we all want salvation. We all need salvation. If you didn't, I'm guessing that you wouldn't be reading this book.

If we admit we need salvation and want to be saved, it naturally brings up a few important questions:

Who is our Savior? From what do we need to be saved? How do we get salvation? Let's take them in order:

Who is our Savior? Jesus is Our Lord and Savior. His very Holy Name means "God saves."

From what do we need to be saved? We need to be saved from sin. From Satan. And from eternal death.

How do we get salvation? Saint Paul provides the answer: "If you confess with your lips that Jesus is Lord and believe in your heart that God has raised him from the dead, you will be saved."

Saint Paul gives us what's probably the earliest creed and act of faith. Yet even answering these three questions may make us a bit anxious, particularly when we see him writing to the Philippians and he exhorts the faithful to "work out your salvation with fear and trembling."

Thus, we are believers who know our Savior, yet we work out salvation with fear and trembling. Let both of these truths sink in.

APRIL 1

If anyone hears my voice and opens the door, then I will enter his house and dine with him, and he with me.

—REVELATION 3:20

Are you with Christ or against Christ?

That's a question we are faced with in our lives.

On Palm Sunday we sing, "All glory, laud and honor to you, Redeemer King." We join the crowds waving palm branches on the Mount of Olives and claiming Jesus as Messiah as we acclaim "Hosanna to the Son of David."

Yet just five days later we say, "He deserves to die. Crucify Him! Crucify Him!"

Religiously, it seems, you and I are bipolar. We claim Him as Lord one day and shout "Crucify Him" another day.

That seems to be the affliction that all of us have. There are moments in our lives, thanks be to God's grace and mercy, when we feel very close in our friendship with Jesus. Sin seems to be on the run. Grace and mercy and virtue seem to be in the ascendancy. Our prayer isn't too bad, and we're faithful to the sacraments. It's those moments when we shout out "All glory, laud and honor to you, Redeemer King."

But you know the flip side, right? Don't we all. There are other times in our lives when we seem at enmity with God. When sin seems in the ascendancy. When we are flippant in our religious obligations. We don't put God first or take Him seriously. We have to admit that both of those are part of our religious odyssey.

Where are you today?

APRIL 2

Know, then, that the Lord, your God, is God: the faithful God who keeps
covenant mercy to the thousandth generation toward those who love him
and keep his commandments.
—DEUTERONOMY 7:9

Mercy is the trait of God most often mentioned in scripture. God is slow to anger and rich in mercy. God also expects us to have mercy for others.

We ask mercy from the Lord when we have hurt Him by our sins; we ask mercy from others when we apologize for hurting them; and we show mercy to others when they ask pardon for harming us and we forgive them.

Yet there are two problems with mercy.

The first is when we conclude that our sins are so ugly, so nauseating, or so wretched that we could never receive God's mercy. Such people feel alienated from God and wallow in guilt, figuring they deserve God's scorn. We call this *despair*.

Judas Iscariot felt despair, remember? When he realized what he had done, he took a rope and hanged himself.

The second obstacle to God's mercy is called *presumption* and is the opposite of despair. We take God's mercy for granted, ignore it, or figure we don't need it.

If Judas Iscariot personifies despair, the Pharisees represent presumption. They were smug, content, and self-righteous in their dismissal of Jesus's invitation to receive mercy.

In the healthy middle is someone like Saint Peter, who sinned viciously yet repented and accepted God's mercy.

Saint Peter, then, is our model. Let's walk that road to salvation, avoiding the ditches—despair and presumption—on either side!

*Jesus said to them, "Amen, amen, I say to you, before Abraham
came to be, I AM."*
—JOHN 8:58

It's said that reading or listening to the Bible is never the same after a pilgrimage to the Holy Land. I'd agree.

Of the multiple spiritual fruits of a pilgrimage there, one stands out for me: We have a God who has intimately and powerfully inserted Himself into our history. As the old saying has it, it actually becomes "*His*-story."

Our God revealed Himself personally to people whose names are still revered: Abraham, Isaac, Jacob, Moses, David.

And for us Christians, God actually entered history in His only begotten Son, Jesus Christ, who walked this sacred ground.

This is important for us. We Americans live in a culture formed by the Enlightenment. In many ways this is very good.

Part of the Enlightenment is *deism,* which holds that although there is indeed a supreme being, it is distant, aloof, impersonal. This divinity has set creation, and our lives, in motion and now leaves us alone, to greet us one day when it's all over.

We Christians (and Jews) do not have a deistic approach to God. For us, God is personal. He has revealed Himself to us, entered into covenant with us, called us, formed us, and He is intimately part of history.

We Christians dare to take it a step further as we profess that this God took flesh in Jesus Christ, the mystery we call the *Incarnation.*

It is tough to settle only for deism at Bethlehem, Nazareth, the shores of the Sea of Galilee, the Mount of Beatitudes, Cana, Capernaum, Bethesda, and Jerusalem.

APRIL 4

So, as you received Christ Jesus the Lord, walk in him.
—COLOSSIANS 2:6

During the happy years I spent in Rome, I grew fond of the Italian custom of a *passeggiata:* a casual evening stroll, always with a friend and usually after a good meal. If someone asks you to go on a *passeggiata,* it is a compliment. It means that he or she enjoys your company and wants to get to know you better. The conversation on this walk is usually substantive.

In a way, Lent is like a *passeggiata.* We are walking with the Lord in the desert.

Even more so, Holy Week is a *passeggiata.* Christ invites us to take a walk with Him, to accompany Him on the way to His death and Resurrection. He wants us near because He has important matters to confide in us.

We begin on Palm Sunday, walking with Him on His entry into Jerusalem, waving palms and acclaiming Him Our Lord.

Throughout the week, we might walk with Him again as we make the Stations of the Cross, stopping fourteen times to reflect on His Passion.

We'll take a *passeggiata* with Him again on Holy Thursday, after the Mass of the Lord's Supper, as we process with the Holy Eucharist to the altar of repose.

On Good Friday we walk with Him again, on the Way of the Cross.

On Holy Saturday, at the Easter Vigil, we process with the paschal candle from the new fire into the darkened church, proclaiming Christ as the Light of the World.

And on Easter Sunday, this annual *passeggiata* that we have taken with Christ ends at the beginning of a new life in Him.

And whoever does not provide for relatives and especially family members has denied the faith and is worse than an unbeliever.
—I TIMOTHY 5:8

The Church's rich tradition of prayer and devotion is a powerfully providential way to keep families united, strong, healthy, and holy. We have a treasury of simple, tried-and-true acts of prayer and devotion that keep marriages and families strong, in love, and close to God.

If you are not doing these things, I challenge you to incorporate some of them, or some of your own, into your family life:

- Joyful yet simple celebrations of Baptisms, First Communions, Confirmations, weddings, and jubilees of marriage
- Faithfully worshipping together as a family at Sunday Mass and preserving the gifts of quality time and a meal together
- The presence of holy water, the crucifix, the Bible, and images of Christ, Mary, and the saints in our homes
- Asking a priest to bless a new home
- Rallying around relatives who are sick and dying
- Remembering parents and family members at Mass on the anniversary of a death

Maybe one of the reasons we no longer do a lot of these things is precisely that pastors never talk about them or encourage them. In these days of tension, turmoil, and challenge, we need all the help we can get.

APRIL 6

Paul, a slave of Christ Jesus, called to be an apostle and set apart for the gospel of God . . .
—ROMANS 1:1

Back in 2008, Pope Benedict XVI proclaimed the Year of Saint Paul. All the Holy Father was asking was for us to pay special attention to that towering figure for a year.

The case has been made that after Jesus Himself, no figure has had a more profound impact on Christianity than Paul.

Hardly a Sunday goes by that we do not hear from him in the Liturgy of the Word. Think about it: Unlike Peter and the Apostles, Paul did not know Jesus while He was with us physically here on earth.

Paul knew Jesus only by *faith*. True, Paul had a genuine, personal encounter with Christ while on the road to Damascus that literally "knocked him off his high horse," changing his name and his life forever.

But Paul accepted Jesus as his Lord and Savior by *faith*. That gives Paul immense credibility, because he's just like us: None of us were with Jesus during His three years of public life, were we?

Yet we are expected to put our life on the line for this Christ, to believe He is the Son of God, Our Lord and Savior, the Way, the Truth, and the Life, without ever seeing Him, touching Him, hearing Him in His bodily form.

Paul is our ally, our patron, our apostle. His faith, hope, and love in and for Jesus are passionate, personal, transforming, life-changing, life-giving, now and in eternity.

There is no fear in love, but perfect love drives out fear because fear has to do with punishment, and so one who fears is not yet perfect in love.
—1 JOHN 4:18

A loving, lifelong, faithful, life-giving marriage takes sacrifice, hard work, and heroic virtue.

Perhaps this is why many of our young people do not get married. Recent studies in the United States tell us that only 50 percent of our young people now approach the Sacrament of Marriage. Live together? Yes. Marry? Not yet.

Many in the Church have pondered the reasons. A bishop I know suggested that our young people have lost a sense of dream and dare. After all, a lifelong love is a *dream* everyone has; to attempt one is nothing less than a *dare*.

I once witnessed the marriage of a man who explained that he had dated many women and even lived with one. He had felt that no deeper, more permanent union was necessary for him until he attended the wedding of a good Catholic friend. There, he saw a man and a woman dream together; there, he heard his friend and the woman he loved dare to say: "You're the only one I want for the rest of my life."

It was then that he understood that he was hardly loving his partners at all but enjoying them, using them, possessing them. He realized he wanted more.

In the Church—which is often caricatured as stale or out of date—he had found the freedom to dream and dare.

I firmly believe that today's poets, today's romantics, today's bold dreamers unafraid to take a dare happen to be faithful married couples.

APRIL 8

Believe me that I am in the Father and the Father is in me, or else,
believe because of the works themselves.

—JOHN 14:11

"Do not let your hearts be troubled!"

Jesus spoke those words to a troubled Church and to very troubled and confused disciples. They were at the breaking point. Everything they knew was changing. They had an ominous sense of disintegration and loss. It was dark, and they were in a dark night of the soul themselves. In many ways, we are those disciples and we are that Church now.

But Jesus showed a path to them in this time of darkness. He began by giving them a forthright commandment: "You have faith in God; have faith also in me."

This is not an exhortation. It is a command. As the Lord unfolded His message, He explained that in the trouble and crisis they confronted, in which disaster seemed inevitable and without a solution, He would always be with them. The basis of their trust was not that everything would turn out well. The basis of their trust and their power to persevere was the unshakable truth that Christ would never leave them.

This perseverance comes from the deep inner springs of living water found only in a life of faithful prayer. This perseverance comes from the conviction that the Father, the Son, and the Holy Spirit give themselves to us in eternal and infinite love.

In times of trouble, just as He did 2,000 years ago, Christ holds out His loving arms to us, reminding us to have faith in Him, for He will never leave us.

APRIL 9

*Is anyone among you sick? He should summon the presbyters of the church,
and they should pray over him and anoint him
with oil in the name of the Lord.*
—JAMES 5:14

At the annual Chrism Mass during Holy Week, when I bless
the oil used throughout the year during the conferring of sacraments, I think about the fact that the oil is all about consolation. Two thoughts come to mind.

First, I am deeply grateful for the men and women who
bring this oil of blessing, healing, soothing, protection, and
selection—literally and figuratively—to God's people. Rightly
do we renew the sense of mission and ministry charted by Isaiah to "bring good news to the afflicted, to bind up the brokenhearted, to proclaim liberty to the captives, . . . to comfort all
who mourn."

Second, I understand that we all need it, too. Therefore, I
invite you to let the Lord anoint you. Maybe we are brokenhearted, mourning, or suffering in some way. But Jesus is here
right now, and He asks us to set our eyes upon Him. He in turn
looks back at us and says, "These have been rough days for you.
Let Me anoint you. Let Me pour My oil upon you."

A priest once confided in me that when he was going
through a very difficult time, he felt the comfort of Christ during Mass. At the Eucharist, as he elevated the host, he imagined
Jesus lifting him up. Instead of him lifting up the Lord, Jesus
was holding him up. What a consolation that was!

Let the Lord be our consolation, too. Let Him anoint us and
hold us up!

APRIL 10

I am the first and the last, the one who lives. Once I was dead,
but now I am alive forever and ever.
—REVELATION 1:17-18

Some years ago, I was asked to toast the most influential person in my life. The occasion was a banquet hosted by *Time* magazine honoring "The 100 Most Influential People in the World."

When the extraordinarily gracious folks from the magazine came to visit with me in preparation for this happy occasion, one of them asked who I would consider the most influential person in my life. "That's a no-brainer," I replied. "Jesus Christ is the most influential person in my life."

The kind journalist clarified: "I'm sorry; I should have been more precise: The person has to be alive now."

"Same answer!" I came back. "Jesus Christ!"

Jesus Christ is alive; that's the significance of the feast on the Sunday called Easter.

"Why do you seek the living one among the dead?" the angel asked those faithful women at the empty tomb down the slope from a hill called Calvary where He had been executed three days earlier, on a Friday strangely termed Good.

I admit He is a Person of bewildering paradox:

True God, yet true man; God's Son, yet born in a stable; architect of the world, without a home of His own; a king whose throne was a cross, whose crown was of thorns; dead at a mere thirty-three, yet alive forever; a man of peace whose followers have tragically waged violence in His Holy Name; a man of love whose heart is broken by the sin, hatred, and division in the members of the Church He founded, even in its leaders, including me.

Yet He never gives up on us, asking only our love, faith, and trust. I toast Him as my Lord and Savior. I toast Him as my best friend. I believe He's always with us, He who invites each of us to enjoy with Him a future banquet of eternal life in heaven.

APRIL 11

Have among yourselves the same attitude
that is also yours in Christ Jesus.
—PHILIPPIANS 2:5

We encounter them in classrooms and hospitals, feeding our elderly and bringing Holy Communion to the infirm; I meet them in prisons and in boardrooms; they are cooking and serving meals in our soup kitchens; they pastor parishes and administer universities; they advocate for peace and push for justice; you'll find them welcoming immigrants and running shelters and daycare centers. Then again, you may never see them, but their presence is powerful as they pray constantly in cloisters and monasteries; often you'll recognize them by their distinctive dress or familiar titles like "Brother," "Sister," "Father," or "Mother"; at other times you'll notice them only by the serene, selfless, faithful spirit they exude.

I am speaking, of course, of the consecrated religious women and men who serve Jesus and His Church. What is *encouraged* of all Christians—the evangelical counsels of poverty, chastity, and obedience—is *expected* of our religious, who present themselves totally and radically to Christ.

We owe them a lot. There's no way our Catholic faith would be as vibrant and deeply rooted as it is if those sisters, brothers, and order priests had not been part of our heritage. And we are all the better for it. Would you join me in taking a moment to thank God for the gift they have been, and still are, to our faith?

APRIL 12

Amen, I say to you, whatever you did for one of these least brothers
of mine, you did for me.

—MATTHEW 25:40

Visiting prisoners, one of the Corporal Works of Mercy, can be difficult to do or even to want to do. Jesus taught us to look for Him in everyone, and that includes those who are incarcerated. These men and women are hurt; they are injured by those who should have loved them, by a harsh and selfish society that scorns them, and by acquaintances who have led them astray and abandoned them behind secured walls.

Prison is the womb of sadness, a place where joy is left on the doorstep and happiness is barricaded away. Feelings of hopelessness and despair easily overwhelm these men and women.

Broken people forget how to have faith. Haunting memories of abuse, violence, and anger overtake the hidden sparks of light that are burrowed in one's heart. Doubt prevails. There is no light, no hope, no chance to change and become anything more than a locked-up criminal.

It is the compliment, the pat on the back, the genuine smile, and the warm hug that a prison ministry offers that lead a despairing soul to stop and recognize that spark of hope within a tomb of darkness. And when an inmate feels so far down that there is nowhere else to go, a prison ministry offers the little bits of "perfect joy" that we all crave. Compassion and caring teach these "numbered" men and women that forgiveness is real and, indeed, possible in the midst of deep pain.

Jesus said to him, "I am the way and the truth and the life.
No one comes to the Father except through me."
—JOHN 14:6

Jesus's final mandate was "Go, teach all nations!" This is the sacred duty of evangelization—of teaching others about Christ.

It is "ever ancient, ever new." The how of it, the when of it, and the where of it may change, but the charge remains constant, as does the message and inspiration: "Jesus Christ, the same yesterday, today, and tomorrow."

The entire Church is defined as missionary, meaning that all Christians, by reason of Baptism, Confirmation, and the Eucharist, are evangelizers of Christ.

No Christian is exempt from the duty of witnessing to Jesus.

God does not satisfy the thirst of the human heart with a proposition but with a Person. His name is Jesus. We are charged to know, love, and serve not a something but a Someone. Our Lord tells us He is the way and the truth and the life.

The way of Jesus is in and through His Church—a Holy Mother who imparts to us His life. This impels us to think about the Church in a fresh way: as a mission.

We, as missionaries and evangelists, must be people of joy, for the mission is about love.

As Saint John Paul II taught in *Redemptoris Missio,* the Church does not "have a mission," as if "mission" were one of many things she does. No, she is a mission, and each of us who names Jesus as Lord and Savior should measure ourselves by our mission effectiveness.

Then He took the bread, said the blessing, broke it, and gave it to them, saying,
"This is my body, which will be given for you; do this in memory of me."
—LUKE 22:19

The Eucharist is the hallmark of our Catholic identity. It is integral to our spiritual health and even to our mental and physical health. The weekly gathering as a spiritual family at Sunday Mass sustains us and offers a peaceful and joyous beginning to the week.

Over the years, I have received many letters from people telling me that prayer, solidarity, and a sense of Catholic cohesion surrounding a specific bishop, pastor, or cardinal have inspired them to return to Sunday Mass.

Alleluia! God is good. He uses us to draw you close and help you feel a sense of community.

The beautiful passages from the Gospel describing Our Lord's visits with His disciples after His Resurrection tell us that most of the time Jesus ate His meals with His friends. That still happens every Sunday at Mass: We hear the Lord's Word, and we are fed and nourished with the bread of life.

The earliest recollection of the first years of the Church, found in the Letters of Saint Paul and the Acts of the Apostles, makes it clear that the first Christians considered Sunday Eucharist essential.

It's the greatest prayer we have, for we are literally "in holy communion" with Christ.

I ask you to renew your resolve to begin each week, on the Lord's Day, with Sunday Mass.

It defines us as Catholics; it makes us His Church.

APRIL 15

The Lord, your God, is in your midst, a mighty savior, who will rejoice over you with gladness, and renew you in his love.
—ZEPHANIAH 3:17

We find Christ's presence everywhere.

A man once told me: "I believe we have to discover the Lord's will and His presence in whatever situation we find ourselves. Right here, I've made Jesus the center of my life. I find Him in our weekly Mass, in our weekly Bible study, in my singing in our choir, in my daily prayer, and in just everyday struggling to get through life."

Profound? You bet it is, especially when you consider who said it. That perceptive comment came from a prisoner, a man incarcerated for a serious crime. He articulated a startling insight about Christian discipleship: that Jesus comes to us wherever we are, that the Lord can be found anywhere, everywhere, even—perhaps especially—in difficult situations in which we may be tempted to think He is absent.

Christ comes to us gently, softly, simply, every day, in the people, events, challenges, and struggles of life.

He comes in clumsy attempts at prayer, in bread and wine at the Eucharist, in endless meetings, in tensions at home, in financial woes and sick kids, in handshakes and apologies, in acts of kindness and smiles, in sandwiches wrapped for street people and kids taught to read, in wheelchairs pushed and coffee poured for another person, in blood drives and food pantries, in His Word proclaimed and the words of absolution, and in so much more.

God comes to us always. It's up to us to recognize Him, serve Him, and discover Him.

APRIL 16

Feast of
Saint Bernadette Soubirous

Lourdes is the renowned shrine in southwestern France where Mary appeared to Saint Bernadette in 1858. On this Feast of Saint Bernadette, we contemplate the impact that Lourdes has had on our faith.

At our Blessed Mother's direction, Bernadette dug in the mud of the grotto of Massabielle and discovered a spring. This ice-cold spring water still flows at Lourdes, and pilgrims take Our Lady's advice and bathe in and drink the healing waters.

The ritual of the water reminds us of the life-giving waters of the Sacrament of Baptism, and pilgrims readily describe their physical, emotional, and spiritual renewal.

Lourdes means light! Candles are everywhere, and God's Holy Word echoes throughout the shrine!

Lourdes is the scene of conversion as pilgrims repent of sins and seek the powerful inner healing of the Sacrament of Penance. More than crutches and wheelchairs, sins are left behind at Lourdes.

Lourdes is about love, as it is the village where the sick, broken, searching, twisted, and tortured in soul, mind, and body are embraced and consoled by our spiritual mother.

Finally, Lourdes is all about Christ. Yes, Mary is tenderly present there, but she is there only to bring us to her Son. Think of her words at Cana: "Do whatever He tells you!"

She wants us to meet Him anew, to let Him live in our souls through a transfusion of His grace, and to allow that life to spill out to others.

So whoever is in Christ is a new creation:
the old things have passed away.
—2 CORINTHIANS 5:17

I was so happy to see him, a man I had met while he was in prison who was now on parole. He came to find me at church and explained, "I have a job, a little apartment, and a wife. Now she's expecting our first baby, and she's going to become a Catholic at Easter. God has been so good!"

What an inspiration.

That young man, an ex-convict, had risen to new life!

The Risen Jesus invites us all to rise with Him. He shares with us His triumph over the cross.

The man I met at the prison had died. He had put to death a life of crime. His faith, his restitution, his rehabilitation, and his good intention and resolve had all led to a fresh start. He has risen and now has a new life. And he would be the first to tell you he never could have done it without Christ.

We hear such resurrection stories all around us. We see them inside of us. We are partakers in the Resurrection of Jesus. In and through Him, we have the power to die to our sins, anxieties, heartaches, and suffering. Through Him, with Him, and in Him we rise to a new life of virtue, peace, and fidelity. Yes, the cross is still there and always will be, but with Him we can conquer it.

Just ask the cancer survivor, the recovering alcoholic, or the married couple struggling and persevering. The Resurrection goes on!

Consider it all joy, my brothers, when you encounter various trials,
for you know that the testing of your faith produces perseverance.
—JAMES 1:2-4

Why would a person of faith be cheerful even in the face of tragedy? Our reason for joy is the cross of Christ.

When Jesus suffered and died on the cross, the sun hid in shame. The earth literally sobbed with convulsions of sorrow as an earthquake occurred.

Jesus, pure goodness, seemed to have been bullied to death by undiluted evil. But then came Easter Sunday!

The sun came up, and the Son came out as He rose from the dead.

Guess who had the last word? God! Hope, faith, and love triumphed, and we believers have not stopped smiling since.

Therefore, as the Bible teaches us, if God loves us so much that He didn't spare His only Son, "nothing can separate us from the love of God."

Good Friday does not have the last word. Easter does! That's why we must laugh even in the face of darkness. We must believe that everything is in God's providential hands and that "all will work out for those who believe."

Lord knows there are plenty of Good Fridays in our lives, but they will not prevail. As we Irish claim, "Life is all about loving, living, and laughing, not about hating, dying, and moaning."

That's why a crabby, griping, whining believer is an oxymoron. That's why we say, "Joy is the infallible sign of God's presence." Faith in the cross of Christ and hope in His Resurrection give us that joy.

Jesus said to them, "I am the bread of life; whoever comes to me will never hunger, and whoever believes in me will never thirst."
—JOHN 6:35

Jesus wanted to tell us that He was the bread of life from the moment of His birth in a manger in a little town called Bethlehem—a word that means "House of Bread."

He was born in a manger—a feed box—because He came to be our food.

The night before He died, at the Last Supper, He took bread, broke it, gave it to His disciples, and said, "Take and eat; this is my body."

This bread—Jesus Christ—comes to us at Mass in the Eucharist.

If we ever really understood the awe, power, beauty, grace, and mercy of the Eucharist, we wouldn't be able to build churches big enough or fast enough. As a matter of fact, that's precisely what's happening in the developing countries of the world, in Asia and Africa, where churches are jammed and people walk a day's journey for the bread of life.

An old proverb claims: "No Eucharist, no Church." Yet scholars tell us that most Catholic people in America no longer go to Sunday Mass. We'd better do something about that.

Anyone who admits that he loves and needs the Jesus who was born in a little town called "House of Bread," who called Himself "the bread of life," and who gave us this bread on the night before He died realizes humbly that you can't love and need Him if you ignore Him in the Eucharist.

APRIL 20

A glad heart lights up the face.
—PROVERBS 15:13

I'll never forget the opening Mass for the academic year in my first year as a seminarian in Rome. The cardinal celebrating Mass looked out at the thousands of priests, sisters, and seminarians and asked a favor of us during his homily. I'm sure I was not alone in expecting a big request for heroic holiness or excellence in scholarship. Instead, he said: "As you walk through the streets of Rome, please smile." Smile? That was all? He asked it, of course, because a smile goes a long way. It can be the difference between people seeing a closed door and an open door to faith.

"If the world saw our happiness," wrote Saint Madeleine Sophie Barat, "it would, out of sheer envy, invade our churches, houses, and retreats, and the times of the Fathers of the Desert would return when the solitudes were more populous than the cities."

Joy, you see, brings people to God.

When you think about joy, what do you have in mind? When Catholics talk about joy, we're not talking about something giggly and Pollyannaish. Joy is not a hyperpositive mania about everything and seeing the world through rose-colored glasses. That would tend to be very annoying, wouldn't it? (A person like that, by the way, probably does not have interior peace. And this wouldn't be telling the truth about life.)

By joy, I'm talking about interior peace. This, Saint Paul teaches, gives rise to exterior happiness. Joy gives us freedom but doesn't make us reckless. True joy won't get on your nerves.

That is why I am eager to preach the gospel also to you in Rome.
—ROMANS 1:15

Rome: the "Eternal City," the *Caput Mundi* ("capital of the world").

The city of Romulus and Remus.

The city that gave its name to one of the most sustained periods of peace the world has ever known, the Pax Romana.

Rome, whose edicts could summon Joseph and Mary to Bethlehem for the Nativity of their firstborn and whose appointed governor, Pontius Pilate, would sentence Him to death on a cross thirty-three years later.

Rome, whose roads, language, and law allowed the Apostles to spread the message of Jesus, bringing Peter and Paul to the Tiber.

Rome, whose emperors unleashed three centuries of persecution of the Church founded by Christ.

Rome, whose emperor Constantine would finally not only tolerate the Church but allow it to become the cohesive influence holding his crumbling empire together.

Rome, whose bishops would become the unifying force in the Western world upon the collapse of the ancient empire, providing science, art, music, charity, and universities—a culture drawing people to God.

The Church in Rome brought Jesus and His message to the world, giving us peace, human dignity, compassion, education, charity, and saints.

The city is a living Advent, with the Lord usually just around the corner, hidden, unexpected, lurking, and at times obscured by earthiness and mustiness but always waiting for us to discover Him anew.

*For this reason a man shall leave his father and mother and be joined
to his wife, and the two shall become one flesh.*
—MATTHEW 19:5

Usually, as we watch a couple preparing for marriage, we call them "beautiful," or "so in love," or "happy."

Pope Francis calls them brave.

Why? Because to marry according to the Lord's will is becoming countercultural.

First, fewer and fewer couples actually even approach the sacrament. We have a crisis of vocations to lifelong, life-giving, faithful, forever marriage! To go against the norm is brave.

Second, a good number of those who do marry end up in divorce. It used to be observed that Catholic couples do not divorce. To marry now, when a couple sees so many failed marriages all around them, is brave.

Third, our culture wonders about anyone's ability to say "forever" and entrust oneself to another. Those who choose to commit themselves in sacrificial love to another for the rest of their lives are brave.

Fourth, the Holy Father notes that couples who marry in the Church are especially courageous, because they dare to claim that their marriage is not only one of human love but one of divine love. They desire to love each other as God loves us. To dare that is brave.

With all that going against them, our newlyweds today deserve our love, admiration, prayers, and gratitude more than ever. They are brave!

APRIL 23

Everyone shall be saved who calls on the name of the Lord.
—ACTS 2:21

The glorious Easter season often presents daily Mass readings from the Acts of the Apostles, the inspired book of the New Testament written by Saint Luke.

It is a bracing message indeed, and its main point is that Jesus Christ, Our Lord and Savior, who was crucified and who has risen, is alive and active, here and now, in His Church!

In Acts, Saint Luke describes some characteristics of the early Church as examples for us. Although they were in the world, the first followers of Christ also realized that they were not of it; they knew they had to nurture their communal togetherness if they were to fulfill Our Lord's will. They looked to the Apostles as authentic teachers of the faith. They gathered together frequently, most often on Sunday, to listen to the Scriptures, to praise God, and to do what Christ did the night before He died: celebrate the Eucharist.

Their faith in Him was strong, their hope in His assurances was durable, and their love for God and for one another was tender.

Reflecting upon the Acts of the Apostles during Paschaltide is an examination of conscience to see if we are loyal to the characteristics of our first-generation Christian ancestors.

If we're lucky, we have attractive models today who base their daily lives on the gospel and the paradigm of the Acts of the Apostles and who show us that the Church of the Acts of the Apostles is still very much alive!

APRIL 24

So we, though many, are one body in Christ and individually parts of one another.

—ROMANS 12:5

Monsignor John Tracy Ellis used to introduce his courses on Church history by saying, "Ladies and gentlemen, be prepared to discover that the Mystical Body of Christ has a lot of warts."

Yet we passionately love our bride with wrinkles, warts, and wounds all the more.

The Church is a communion, a supernatural family. Most of us, praise God, are born into it, as we are into our human families. Thus, the Church is in our spiritual DNA.

In Graham Greene's novel *The Power and the Glory,* when the young girl asks him why he doesn't just renounce his Catholic faith, the unnamed "Whisky Priest" replies: "'That's impossible! There's no way!... It's out of my power.'"

Greene narrates: "The child listened intently. She then said, 'Oh, I see, like a birthmark.'"

To use a Catholic word, bingo! Our Church is like a birthmark. Founded by Christ, the Church had her beginning at Pentecost, but her origin is the Trinity.

Yes, her beginning is in history, as was the Incarnation, but her origin is outside of time.

But they did not listen to me, nor did they pay attention.
—JEREMIAH 7:24

Sometimes we complain to God.

Why is this happening to me, why do I have to go through this, why do other people seem to get off so easy, and so forth. We like to lament and complain and gripe, and that's understandable. In fact, it's a form of prayer you find in the Psalms.

When I'm tempted to complain to God, I like to think of it from God's side.

If anyone's got a right to complain, it's God. He has the right to complain about us! And we hear from Jeremiah, as he's speaking for God: You people won't listen. I've taught you, I've sent you prophets, I brought you out of slavery in the land of Egypt, I've made covenants with you, I protected you, I guided you, I brought you this far. All I ask is your fidelity, and you don't listen and you don't obey.

Therefore, a great antidote when we're tempted to complain about God is, just for a second, to put ourselves in God's place. He has every right—infinitely more right—to complain about us. But His mercy never stops. And we stand in utter need of God's mercy. So as we wait for God's mercy constantly, God waits for us. And He does everything possible to see if we will respond to His invitation of salvation and eternal life through conversion of heart.

APRIL 26

*The heart of the intelligent acquires knowledge, and the ear
of the wise seeks knowledge.*
—PROVERBS 18:15

Saint Francis of Assisi is often credited with saying, "Preach always. Use words if you have to."

The Church does preach always, and we do so by both actions and words.

Our growth in the faith—soul, mind, and heart—should never stop. Sure, it's intensive and consistent for children and youth, but it does not come to a halt when we graduate.

Outside of our Catholic schools, religious education is essential for our children. Our parishes do heroic work in offering weekly catechesis for our children who do not attend Catholic schools.

Preparation for the sacraments is a classic part of Catholic life. Parents prepare for the christening of their new baby; children are tenderly and intensely prepared for confession and First Holy Communion; our young people take the months leading up to Confirmation seriously; and our engaged couples know they should spend at least as much time preparing for a marriage license as they do for a driver's license!

Now, more than ever, our Catholic people are called upon to explain and defend their faith. If you're not well grounded in it, get ready to have it taken away from you by bestselling atheists, by the high priests of secularism, by op-ed pieces that distort our faith, or by people from other religions who are indeed well versed in their own.

We call this learning our "lifelong faith formation." It never stops. It's not a luxury but a duty.

APRIL 27

I urge you therefore, brothers, by the mercies of God, to offer your bodies as a living sacrifice, holy and pleasing to God, your spiritual worship.
—ROMANS 12:1

Happy Easter!

Yes, we can still say that. Even when Easter Sunday itself has come and gone, the joy and hope and promise of Easter is so expansive that it can't be limited to Easter Sunday. In fact, in the Church calendar, we have seven Sundays of Easter. And actually, in the Catholic belief, every Sunday is a little Easter as we celebrate the Resurrection of Jesus.

I think you'd agree with me: The Resurrection of Jesus Christ from the dead is something worth celebrating.

We praise God the Father for raising God the Son from the dead. We praise Jesus for conquering sin and death. We thank God that darkness and hatred have been conquered by His Resurrection.

Furthermore, the celebration of Jesus is not just for what God did for His Son but for what God has done for us. It was not just a personal victory on Easter Sunday. God wants to share it with us and give us part of the triumph that was His on Easter Sunday.

If that's not good news and not something worth celebrating, I don't know what is!

Feast of
Saint Gianna Molla

How many of us know physicians who don't just live but proclaim their faith in their practice of medicine?

How many of us have heard the erroneous claim that the Catholic Church is against science and progress in helping couples conceive and bear children? Probably quite a few.

It was my joy and privilege years ago to visit and bless the Saint Peter's Gianna Center of Manhattan.

The Gianna Center is named for Saint Gianna Beretta Molla, an Italian physician, wife, and mother. When Gianna was pregnant with her fourth child, doctors found a dangerous tumor that put her life at risk. They urged her to abort. Instead, she had surgery to remove the tumor but demanded that the baby girl be kept safe even at the risk of her own health. Gianna died in 1962 at the age of thirty-nine, shortly after giving birth to a healthy baby girl. Hers is a profound story of strength and trust in God.

The Gianna Center is dedicated to Saint Gianna and is operated by young, dedicated, and faithful physicians determined to practice their faith and their medical skills in the field of NaProTechnology. They offer a unique service, as they are specially trained in helping couples in the noblest quest of all: the procreation of human life! They practice morally licit, technologically savvy, and successful ways for couples who have difficulty conceiving a child to bring about new life.

Saint Gianna inspired them, as she continues to inspire us.

Lord, you are our father; we are the clay and you our potter:
We are all the work of your hand.

—ISAIAH 64:7

Console, love, pardon, give of yourself. Proclaim the good news, for it is the magnet that draws so many diverse kinds of people to the heart of Christ. See goodness in the midst of evil, embrace joy during moments of pain, suffer with those who despair, and offer peace to those imprisoned in hurt.

Listen to others, hear them, fight for justice, unearth mistreatment, and demand change. Touch hearts and speak the truth at any cost. Find the best in the worst and lead others to share in that vision. Convert tears to smiles and show people God's true nature. Rejoice when they find Him deep within their own scarred being.

Be the affirming presence that draws others to trust you, to open their hearts, and to understand that someone wholeheartedly and unconditionally cares for them. Respect others for who they are and for the stories they tell, and gently lead them to believe in the beauty within. Fight for those who have no one to fight for them and who retreat into isolation.

It is a rare gift in this world to find someone who genuinely understands, loves, and comforts people, especially those who seem lost in confusion or who feel alone, misunderstood, or unlovable.

There is a beautiful sculpture hidden within the stone of rejection and hurt. It is our job to become the instrument that chisels until we uncover the beauty.

Strive to enter through the narrow door, for many, I tell you,
will attempt to enter but will not be strong enough.
—LUKE 13:24

Our Catholic family has been through tough times, with the scandals and the nauseating details of the horrific abuse of minors by priests. This has left many of you bewildered, frustrated, and angry. It has left our good and faithful priests demoralized. Many of you have told me more than once how let down you feel by your bishops. You feel angry, confused, and disappointed. So do I.

Tremendous shame has come upon our Church because of the sexual abuse of minors. I have asked before and ask again for forgiveness for the failings of those clergy and bishops who should have provided safety to our young people but instead betrayed the trust placed in them by God and by the faithful. We can't express our sorrow and regret enough, particularly to the victim-survivors and their families, who have suffered so deeply.

But I want you to know that I hear you. You want accountability, transparency, and action to combat this evil. And you deserve it.

I pledge again that I will do all in my power to ensure the safety of our young people and to react with sympathy, understanding, and respect toward those who come forward with an allegation of abuse.

Please join me in praying that the Church can bring peace and consolation to victim-survivors and their families who have experienced the horror of abuse. I ask your sincere prayers for victim-survivors and their families. I once again urge anyone who has an allegation of abuse of a minor to go immediately to the district attorney to report it.

Jesus, risen from the dead, shatters the darkness of evil and death and brings us to new life. It is my heartfelt prayer that together we as a family of faith may be healed and so bring the light of the Resurrection to the darkness of our world.

Feast of
Saint Joseph the Worker

It was a cold February day, and I was to celebrate Mass at one of our Catholic schools. Before I got vested, I ducked into the boys' bathroom, there to find the janitor scrubbing the floor. The smell of disinfectant almost knocked me over.

"Oh, come on in," the janitor said. "It's just that I try to keep these bathrooms as clean as I can. With all this flu and stuff going around, I want our kids to be as safe from germs as possible."

The Lord was protecting His children and tending to their well-being through the toil of this humble janitor.

This feast speaks volumes: The only begotten Son of God had an earthly father who was a carpenter and grew up in a home where labor enriched, nourished, and was looked upon as noble and virtuous.

Work, as Saint John Paul II would later teach, is an opportunity to cooperate with the Creator in His ongoing care for His creation and His creatures. Our toil, no matter how tedious, is thus filled with meaning and purpose.

Jesus learned that lesson by watching His earthly father, Saint Joseph, saw, hammer, and build. I absorbed that same lesson by seeing my own dad labor day in and day out so that he could nourish, sustain, and care for us.

And I saw it again as that janitor mopped the bathroom floors to keep those kids healthy.

Like a shepherd he feeds his flock; in his arms he gathers the lambs, carrying them in his bosom, leading the ewes with care.
—ISAIAH 40:11

Jesus as the Good Shepherd has to be one of the most magnetic names given Our Lord.

If Christ is the Good Shepherd, guess who are the sheep. You and me! The poetic image of Jesus as a strong Good Shepherd tending to us—leading us to clean water and lush pastures; protecting us from cliffs, briars, and wolves; searching for the ones who stay or fall behind—is very consoling.

Sheep look innocent, pure, cuddly, and docile, but they are some of the stupidest animals around. They think they are smart, but they like to wander off independently, figuring that on their own they'll discover freedom and happiness. But they learn the hard way that away from the shepherd and the fold, there await cliffs, sticker bushes, wolves, and butcher blocks.

Sound familiar? We are like sheep, aren't we? We are often coaxed into thinking we really don't need the teachings of Jesus or His Church. So we wander, we assert our autonomy, we drift away, we experiment. We listen to "smart" voices telling us that we can get along fine without Him.

But real freedom, security, happiness, and verdant pastures come only in sticking with the Good Shepherd and His flock.

The good news is that Christ is our Good Shepherd and that we admit we're sheep and not very smart, and so we stick ever more closely to Him as one of His flock. And therein lies the greatest wisdom of all.

MAY 3

Jesus Christ is the same yesterday, today, and forever. Do not
be carried away by all kinds of strange teaching.
—HEBREWS 13:8-9

How often have you heard this: "That old-fashioned, dusty, out-of-it, stuck-in-the-mud Church has to get with the times or she is going to lose folks"?

The Church's divine mission is not to alter her teaching to keep up with the times but to deepen her conformity to what God has revealed in the Bible, through the teachings of Jesus, in the natural law, and through the Magisterium.

As is clear from Saint John XXIII's moving address solemnly opening the Second Vatican Council, the council was called to determine how the timeless deposit of faith could be transmitted more effectively without compromising or diluting its integrity. According to the teaching of the council itself, it is the pope, united with the bishops of the Church, who is to give and provide the genuine interpretation and implementation of the council's meaning.

Our challenge is not to change God's revelation to conform to our whims or the changing times but to change our lives to conform to His designs.

The Church is not "out of it" but is actually right in the middle of it and really way ahead of us, as she has her eyes on the eternal.

She is a seasoned, wise, loving mother founded by Our Lord and Savior. The Church hardly has to change her wisdom; we need to change our lives. Forget "keeping up with the times" in faith and morals. Rather, "keep up with the timeless"!

MAY 4

You will receive power when the holy Spirit comes upon you,
and you will be my witnesses in Jerusalem, throughout Judea and Samaria,
and to the ends of the earth.

—ACTS 1:8

Forty days after Jesus's Resurrection, we celebrate His Ascension into heaven.

Do you recall what the Apostles did upon Christ's return to His Father in heaven? They stayed together in constant prayer awaiting the gift of the Holy Spirit.

The Apostles could have bidden each other farewell and taken off on their own to follow the command of Jesus, but they stayed together—and the Church was born. We are in this together, they tell us; our lives will never be the same, and now we are profoundly united as a spiritual family.

They prayed. Jesus had charged them to teach, to evangelize, and to introduce Him to the world. And, of course, they did. But He also had taught them "first things first," so they inaugurated the mission with intense prayer.

How long did they pray? They prayed for nine days! (The Latin word for "nine" is *novem*. This is the first novena!)

For what did they pray? They prayed for the gift of *someone*— the supreme gift of the Holy Spirit. Nine days later, their prayers were answered when the Holy Spirit came on Pentecost.

Jesus Christ, although no longer with us physically, is indeed alive, present, powerful, and still personally with us. He is Lord; He has dominion over time and space. "I am with you always," He assures us as He ascends.

MAY 5

*For he has looked upon his handmaid's lowliness; behold,
from now on will all ages call me blessed.*
—LUKE 1:48

Our Blessed Mother Mary bore the One who would proclaim, "I am the way, the truth, and the life!" Without her Son, our lives and our souls would be in constant winter. The Author of Life called her "Mother." We who gratefully share in His life can tenderly call her "Mother" as well.

From the very first moment of Mary's life in her own mother's womb, she—by a privilege given to her by God the Father in anticipation of the redemption of His and her Son—was preserved from sin. We call this her *Immaculate Conception*.

We honor our mother in a moving tradition at baptisms and at weddings. At baptisms, the new parents will take their just-christened baby to the statue of Our Lady and present the infant to her. At weddings, the newly married couple will carry a floral tribute to Mary, who interceded for the young couple at Cana so many years ago, and ask her help as they embark on a new life together.

We honor our mother when we pray the rosary, reflecting upon the events from her life and the life of her Son.

We honor our mother during the month of May with joyful songs and crowns made from flowers.

We honor our mother when we place statues of her prominently in our homes.

In the Church's art, liturgy, poetry, and feasts, Mary stands highest among mortals.

MAY 6

Then the peace of God that surpasses all understanding
will guard your hearts and minds in Christ Jesus.
—PHILIPPIANS 4:7

A few years ago, during a daily Mass, we read about a group in the earliest days of the Church whose members griped because they felt neglected. Someone after Mass later pointed out to me that complaining seems to be a constant in life not only in the Church but in our lives as well.

Constant griping and complaining can get to us, can't it? Constructive criticism is good, welcome, and helpful. Continual whining is not.

Many psychologists tell us that not to complain can be unhealthy and allows matters to get worse. The same experts advise that constantly complaining—in a bitter, judgmental way—is also toxic.

At times, it may feel that our lives are a huge mess, with a lot of divided opinions and ideas and a lot of reasons to lament. But the Holy Father believes that the Holy Spirit can bring unity and a sense of direction out of complaining, disagreement, confusion, and division. A mess can be an invitation to discern a direction from the Holy Spirit!

A man who did more than his share of viciously attacking the Church, Saul, urges us to reflect on what can bring about peace. Writing as Paul, he said: "I urge you to live in a manner worthy of the call you have received, with all humility and gentleness, with patience, bearing with one another through love, striving to preserve the unity of the spirit through the bond of peace."

MAY 7

The covenant I made with you, you must not forget.
—2 KINGS 17:38

Simply put, if we forget God, all hell breaks loose. And without getting apocalyptic here, I fear that as a nation we have forgotten God.

Historian that I am, I know that this spiritual amnesia is not unique to our times. The Old Testament reminds us that God's chosen people, Israel, continually stumbled. As long as they grounded their lives in God, kept their covenant with Him, and remembered His mercy and grace, they were on the right path. But they were continually tempted to forget Him, ignore Him, and deny Him—and that's when tragedy strikes.

I'm not the first to suggest that something is severely awry in our country and that it's because we have forgotten the Lord.

During America's fight for independence, John Adams was asked if America had a chance. He whispered, "Yes, if we fear God and repent our sins."

Debate about the role of religion in our national life has always been a bit contentious. However, a cherished part of American wisdom is that faith, religion, worship, and biblical morality are essential to a civil society. My apprehension is that what's promoted today is an America "free of religion" instead of a "freedom of religion."

Our currency says "In God We Trust." But do we trust in Him, or have we forgotten Him? For when we forget Him, all hell certainly does break loose!

*Your light must shine before others, that they may see your good deeds
and glorify your heavenly Father.*
—MATTHEW 5:16

On the morning it was announced that Benedict XVI had nominated me a cardinal, a journalist asked if I had ever "wanted to be a cardinal."

"Yes," I readily replied. "When I was six years old, I wanted to be Stan Musial!"

Stan, of course, was one of the greatest baseball players ever, to this day the most renowned player on my beloved hometown St. Louis Cardinals.

In fact, when I was ten, I had gone to the airport with my dad and brother, Bob, to meet my grandma, who was returning from a vacation.

And who did we see walking through the terminal? "The Man!" "Dad," I exclaimed. "Is that Stan?" He was so famous, a first name was all it took.

"It is!" Dad replied. "Go over and say hello."

Sure enough, Bob and I did. "Hi, Stan," we blurted out.

The Man looked at us. "Whaddaya say, sluggers?" I've never forgotten it.

Stan was a man of faith who was not embarrassed to be a light to the world. His Catholic faith was deep, sincere, and simple—a part of his fiber. He rarely spoke of it, argued about it, or hit people over the head with it. But he lived it. He radiated it.

After Stan's funeral Mass, a prominent baseball player told me that he had fallen away from the Church but that Stan's example had led him back.

Stan would blush at being called an evangelist, but his example changed lives. And that is what Jesus calls all of us to do: be an example that changes lives.

MAY 9

Do not be afraid, Mary, for you have found favor with God.
—LUKE 1:30

Mary, God's work of art, is what the Creator intended all of us to be. Never has a religion so elevated a woman as has Christianity.

Historians of the Roman Empire document how much the Church's elevation of women threatened the status quo. In an empire that treated women like chattel, the Church declared woman equal in dignity to man. In a culture that declared that she could be dismissed from a marriage by a selfish husband, the Church taught that marriage was forever. In a culture in which women were viewed as objects of pleasure for men, Christianity objected, raising sexuality from just the physical to a very icon of God's love for us: personal, passionate, faithful, forever, and life-giving.

Women became saints; women founded monasteries; and women began schools, orphanages, and hospitals.

In the development of the history of the United States, women in the Catholic Church were university presidents, hospital CEOs, and the most effective professional social workers decades before the rest of the culture caught up.

Every Catholic fifty-five and older can recall the days when the most influential, effective, and beloved people in the parish were "the Sisters."

It is the Church that believes that the omnipotent God of the universe awaited the free consent of a woman before His plan of salvation could proceed.

Best of all, the Church protected and exalted the most noble vocation of all—that of a mother.

Feast of Saint Damien de Veuster
of Molokai

Saint Damien was born in 1840 in Belgium. From a young age, he knew he wanted to become a priest. When he was old enough, he joined the Congregation of the Sacred Hearts of Jesus and Mary. At the age of twenty-four, he volunteered to serve at a leper colony on the Hawaiian island of Molokai. He was ordained there, and there he would live until his death in 1889.

Damien understood what Christ meant when He said to "do to others as you would have them do to you." When Damien arrived in Molokai, he found a group of discarded outcasts whom no one wanted. Those unloved people were forced onto the island, cut off from friends and family. They had no dignity and no hope. Damien ate with them, talked with them, helped them build houses, brought the Word of God to them, showed them the love of Christ, and baptized many. He eventually would contract and succumb to the disease.

Before Damien arrived, those lepers were like the Samaritan woman at the well—sinners, outcasts—who found in Christ the Savior for whom she so longed.

They were like the man born blind in the Gospel who realized he was in the dark until he met the "Light of the World."

They were like Lazarus, who realized that without Jesus he was dead, lifeless, and without hope.

Through Damien, they came to know Christ. Through Damien, they found salvation.

MAY 11

Be strong and steadfast; have no fear or dread of them, for it is the Lord,
your God, who marches with you; he will never fail you or forsake you.
—DEUTERONOMY 31:6

When tragedies happen in our lives, we are sometimes tempted to cry: "My God, why have you forsaken me?"

It's easy to feel alone, isolated, and unloved when tragedies occur. God wants us to seek shelter with Him when we are suffering, to find relief in His loving embrace. Whether that shelter is in the physical house of God or in the spiritual house of prayer, we know that spending time in communion with Christ will calm and soothe our upset hearts and minds.

After experiencing the loss of a job, a divorce, or the death of a child or a spouse, or if we are suffering from a physical or mental ailment, picking ourselves up and building a new life can be challenging. But Christ gives us the strength we need to rebuild. We are a people of faith, and we know that whenever we need Christ, He is there—in the Mass, in the crucifix, in Holy Communion, and in prayer. He listens and guides us.

Even during those times, we thank God for His blessings, for we believe in God, we believe in His Son, and we believe in His mother, Mary. We draw our strength from them.

Through prayer, God gives us the grace and the perseverance to rebuild our shattered lives. He gives us many examples of resilience—so evident in the saints, whose faith is an inspiration to us all!

Nothing is impossible with Christ.

And coming to her, he said, "Hail, favored one!
The Lord is with you."
—LUKE 1:28

There's an inherent beauty in the rosary. Not only is the rosary a wonderful prayer, it's an effective means of evangelization.

Think about it: If we know and pray the rosary, we become familiar with the story of the life of Jesus and Mary—the enchanting mysteries that are part of "the greatest story ever told."

Furthermore, we then know the most basic prayers of our tradition: the Sign of the Cross, the Apostles' Creed, the Lord's Prayer, the Hail Mary, and the Glory Be.

No wonder Saint Paul VI called the rosary "the school of the gospels."

My grandmother loved praying the rosary. She would tell me: "When I pray the rosary before I go to sleep, I feel close to Our Lord. I think of all He did for me, and I almost feel as if I'm holding Mary's hand and she's praying with me."

That's what I mean about the basics of our faith. My grandmother couldn't talk much about the Trinity or the more complex moral issues of her faith, but she sure loved Jesus; knew His life, death, and Resurrection; and held fast to His mother and His bride—the Church—as she struggled through each day.

What if we all knew and trusted the rosary as she did? Not only would we comprehend the mysteries of the life and the teachings of Jesus, but the strength we would gain would bring us closer to Him.

MAY 13

But if we walk in the light as he is in the light, then we have
fellowship with one another.
—I JOHN 1:7

The parish is an amazing place! Parishes are the front lines of the Church. We Catholics are grounded where we live. The Church is not some cerebral, amorphous ideal or the 108 acres in Rome called the Vatican. It is where our babies are baptized, our grandparents are buried, our children are educated and catechized, our young couples are married, our sins are forgiven, God's Word is proclaimed, His very body and blood are consumed, and the sick and poor are embraced.

Parish life is where it's at.

As I travel around the Archdiocese of New York, I meet thousands of people. Usually, after telling me their names, they let me know which parish they call their spiritual home. When I meet former New Yorkers during my travels around the country, odds are they will tell me not that they're "from the Bronx" but that they're "from Saint Francis," not that "I'm from Staten Island" but that "I'm from Blessed Sacrament."

That's the pride we have in our parish identity.

People love their parish; people are loyal to their parish; people do not want to lose their parish!

As essential as our parishes are, they are at the service of the entire Church. Parishes are a means to an end, with the goal of furthering the Kingdom of God in our own souls and in our community.

Stay close to your parish. Become a part of it. We need you.

MAY 14

Be mindful of prisoners as if sharing their imprisonment,
and of the ill-treated as of yourselves, for you also are in the body.
—HEBREWS 13:3

Every Eucharist is special because we relive the Last Supper. But near the top of the list of my most memorable venues for offering Mass has to be prison. I savor celebrating the Eucharist there.

One of the Corporal Works of Mercy is visiting prisoners, and I have done this many times. Each Eucharist in jail never fails to move me, and I want to explain why.

The prisoners actually want to be at Mass, and they participate enthusiastically. The inmates cherish serving, singing, leading the petitions, bringing up the gifts, and taking care of their chapel. They acknowledge that they really need the Mass and a Savior. When they look up at the Sacred Host and proclaim, "Lord, I am not worthy that you should enter under my roof; but only say the word and my soul shall be healed," they truly mean it.

They have discovered that there is a Lord, a friend, a Savior who will not disappoint them and who shows up even when it's not visitors' day.

Some ancient Christian writers compared life on earth to a prison. There is a bit of truth there. Actually, we were all on death row until Jesus took our sentence upon Himself. We were guilty, but He paid the price for our sins. We think we're innocent, but He is the innocent one—and He paid our ransom with His blood.

*All good giving and every perfect gift is from above, coming down from
the Father of lights, with whom there is no alteration or shadow
caused by change.*
—JAMES 1:17

I find myself incredibly grateful for spiritual gifts. We often praise God for natural gifts—our health, our freedom, our family and friends—and we should. But we glorify God as well for His abundant supernatural blessings.

We have a God who listens to our prayers.

We have a Father who sent His Son to save us and His Spirit to abide in us.

We have Jesus with us in the Eucharist.

We have a God who always forgives us.

We have a Church that is our spiritual family.

We have a tender, loving mother in Mary.

We have God's Word in the Bible.

We have a Lord who is near us when we are sick or struggling, whose power and grace often are not recognized until the crisis is past.

This lavishly generous God wants us to praise Him not because He craves it, not because He needs it, but because it's good for us to do so.

As we gratefully acknowledge the abundant gifts that flow from Him, we open ourselves to receive even more—and we have a God who likes to spoil us by giving us more.

We are ever so thankful that He takes care of our bodies and our lives here on earth.

MAY 16

What profit would there be for one to gain
the whole world and forfeit his life?
—MATTHEW 16:26

Here is a refreshing surprise: The Church's so-called old-fashioned ideas are actually more timely, urgent, and ahead of the curve than ever! Let me give a couple of examples.

The Church teaches that couples should save living together and sexual intimacy until marriage. Such a moral approach is scoffed at as silly, impractical, and repressive. In fact, "up-to-date" thinking posits that it's good for a couple to cohabitate before marriage. Not only does it save money, but the couple get to know each other better and grow more compatible, leading to a happier, more permanent marriage! Right?

Wrong! Turns out the Church is wise. *The New York Times* reported on the somber findings of a study that showed that living together before marriage leads to high rates of marital unhappiness and divorce. So much for the wisdom of keeping up with the times.

A man in hospice once told me his deepest regrets. He had left his wife and kids. His drive was money, prestige, property, and a younger, prettier wife. An old priest friend once had tried to talk him out of his "jet-set lifestyle," warning him that a life without faith and morals would destroy him. The man had dismissed him then, saying that "times have changed" and that the Church should "get with it."

He died alone, recalling the words of Jesus about gaining the world but forfeiting your life.

As he lay dying, he admitted that the old priest and the Church had been right after all.

MAY 17

So we are ambassadors for Christ, as if God
were appealing through us.
—2 CORINTHIANS 5:20

All citizens, especially those in positions of leadership, are called to reclaim respect for the sanctity of human life. Thus, every person becomes a missionary, an ambassador, and an evangelist of the good news of human dignity.

Our attitude toward the sanctity of life says volumes about our true character as individuals, as a community, and as a nation. We're talking here not about a religious conviction peculiar to any individual creed or church but about a human right—about civil rights.

Although it is true that men and women of faith have an even more enhanced motive for defending life—namely, our belief that the Creator alone is the sovereign over everyone—all men and women committed to civil rights, of any or no church or religion, know deep down what Saint John Paul II taught in his prophetic encyclical *The Gospel of Life:* "It is impossible to further the common good without acknowledging and defending the right to life, upon which all the other inalienable rights of individuals are founded, and from which they develop."

Thus must the gospel of life be proclaimed and promoted in all places and times, especially in print, TV, radio, and schools, where minds are formed and hearts are changed, and in the halls of government, where the power to enact laws to protect this civil right rests.

Christ commands us to have the courage and honesty to speak the truth.

Rend your hearts, not your garments, and return to the Lord, your God,
for he is gracious and merciful, slow to anger, abounding in steadfast love,
and relenting in punishment.
—JOEL 2:13

I tried my best to read everything that Saint John Paul II wrote, and in so doing I noticed that one word appears over and over: *return*. He exhorts priests to return to the Upper Room where Jesus gave the Church the gift of the priesthood. He tells young people to return to their inner dignity, for they are made in the image and likeness of God. He summons the sick to return to Calvary to share in Christ's cross, which gives meaning to their suffering. He tells married couples to return to the radiance of their sacred bond—a bond that mirrors God's love. And to America, he tells us to return to the protection of life and welcome those in need.

He asks us all to return to what is most decent, noble, and uplifting in our makeup as children of God. He asks us to return to Jesus—to come back to Palestine and be saved.

Saint John Paul II wanted to return the Church to the way Jesus intended it, and he wanted all of us to experience again the excitement, the invitation, the conversion, the promise, the miracles, the teaching—the Person who walked in Palestine 2,000 years ago and who lives now in His Church.

MAY 19

*Behold, I am coming soon. I bring with me the recompense
I will give to each according to his deeds.*
—REVELATION 22:12

We know that this life on earth is not all there is. The sense of eternity—the innate impulse that our very person is immortal—can be found ingrained in the heart of the human person.

We ponder this as we think about Christ's love for us.

Christ dwelled among us bodily on earth for three decades. In His preaching He assured us that whoever believed in Him would never die. Not only did He teach us about immortality, He leads us there and empowers us to live life to the fullest by His own death and Resurrection.

His coming, though, is not limited to that first arrival two millennia ago, because He will come again at the end of time. When this second coming will take place, we don't know. We do know that Jesus will come to us personally, at the moment of our death, but we don't know when that will occur either.

Since we don't know when either day will arrive, it's important to be prepared. Thus, we relish every moment, living it to the fullest for Christ.

We know that all that we cherish in this life is but a hint of an eternity in heaven united with the God who did come, does come daily, and will come at the end of our earthly life and at the end of the world.

He said to them, "Come away by yourselves to a deserted place
and rest a while."
—MARK 6:31

The first time I ever saw a pope was in August 1972—and Pope
Paul VI talked about vacations.

Yes, vacations. The Holy Father spoke warmly about vacations: time off from work, school, and our daily routine. I can
still recall him saying that a vacation was a wonderful gift from
God, a time to savor family, friends, nature, art, song, food,
good laughs, and company—and a time to grow closer to Jesus
through prayer, meditation, and spiritual reading.

The Holy Father concluded by saying that a vacation can be
an occasion of grace and holiness. Almost as an afterthought he
added, "Be careful, because a vacation can be at times an occasion of sin, too."

With summer inching closer to us, I recall those uplifting
words, as many of us will soon take vacations. Our wonderful
schools are letting out for some welcome weeks of respite, our
parish programs are winding down a bit, and all of us can take
a much-needed break.

Our best friend, of course, is Jesus, and so I recommend
that He be part of our vacations, too. Thinking of Him, listening to Him, and speaking to Him would be a great vacation
resolution.

Our vocation in life is to be a child of God, a follower of
Jesus, a faithful member of His Church, united with Him by
grace, prayer, and the sacraments.

Our vacation is a time to deepen, enjoy, and strengthen that
vocation.

*See that you do not despise one of these little ones, for I say to you
that their angels in heaven always look upon the face of my heavenly Father.*
—MATTHEW 18:10

I know it is not easy for anyone, especially young people, to go against the prevailing culture, but we must not be afraid to be *countercultural*—to go against what society insists is correct. The good news is that we are not alone, especially when it comes to cherishing preborn life.

We have come to expect almost annual revolutionary technological breakthroughs that change the way we live and work. We have seen staggering medical advances that have given doctors wonderful new tools in fighting disease and injury. And we have seen the baby in its mother's womb.

Many of you have seen your little brothers and sisters before they were born in those grainy videos and those photographs often pinned to the fridge. Maybe you have even seen images of yourself or your own baby. You have gasped with wonder at the sight of little arms flailing and legs kicking, heads bobbing and hearts beating, and mouths sucking thumbs.

So many people have tried to convince us that a preborn baby is nothing more than a "clump of cells." College professors, politicians, Hollywood glitterati, and media talking heads have hammered us with the message that the decision to abort has no more moral significance than having a wisdom tooth extracted.

We are rightly skeptical. They may believe what they say, but in this matter they are wrong. We know better. We have seen, and we believe.

But we proclaim Christ crucified.
—I CORINTHIANS 1:23

When we speak of Christ, we must not forget to speak of the cross. I have always found it compelling that the first thing Jesus did when He appeared to His Apostles after His Crucifixion was to show them His wounds. Yes, He did this to let them know it really was Him, the same one who had been crucified just a few days earlier. But I wonder if He did not also show them His wounds because that was what He wanted His newborn Church to do—preach the wounds.

Do you remember what He said after showing them His wounds? "As the Father sent me"—and see what happened? these wounds—"so I send you." You had better get ready for wounds, too.

Maybe the greatest threat to the Church is not heresy, not dissent, not secularism, not even moral relativism, but a sanitized, feel-good therapeutic spirituality that makes no demands, calls for no sacrifice, asks for no conversion, entails no battle against sin, but only soothes and affirms.

The columnist David Brooks once said that people today seem to want a comfortable, convenient, tolerant complacency. They do not ask "What does the Lord expect of me?" but rather "What will the Lord do for me? How will He satisfy my needs?" They aren't looking for orthodoxy but for what Brooks calls "flexidoxy."

We cannot have a life in Christ without the life He gave us by dying upon that cross. To forget the cross is to forget His ultimate sacrifice.

And so I say to you, you are Peter, and upon this rock I will build my church,
and the gates of the netherworld shall not prevail against it.
—MATTHEW 16:18

The office of the Successor of Saint Peter is essential to the Church. We understand that "apostolic" is one of the marks of the true Church. The pope ensures that we stay connected to the Apostles, especially Saint Peter.

Yet—and here's the surprise—the Church is not equated with the pope, and her effectiveness does not depend completely on the Holy Father. The Church counts only on Jesus. Her life is not synonymous with that of the activities of the Bishop of Rome, however much we love him, listen to him, and are loyal to him. The Church is bigger than our Holy Father.

And he'd be the first to tell us that.

Yes, Jesus is radiantly alive in the ministry of the Successor of Saint Peter, whose teaching, governing, and sanctifying are uniquely effective. But the explosive light and life of Christ reaches to the ends of the earth through the Church in her fullness, not just through the ministry of its supreme pontiff.

God's people pray and believe; God's Word is preached and accepted; God's poor are loved and served; God's life is imparted in the sacraments; and Satan is on the run. That's the Church!

Yes, Jesus teaches, serves, governs, and sanctifies in a uniquely effective way through the Successor of Saint Peter, but in the end it's not about them. It's not about the pope; it's all about Jesus and His Church!

When Jesus saw his mother and the disciple there whom he loved,
he said to his mother, "Woman, behold, your son."
—JOHN 19:26

May is a fitting month to honor Our Lady, isn't it?

Nature is alive as Mother Earth brings the new birth of spring. Trees, grass, and flowers are all in bloom. No wonder we reflect on the one who gave birth to Our Lord and Savior!

With marriages, graduations, moves, First Communions, Confirmations, anniversaries, and much more, May is a month of transition.

Our Lady was there at the two most dramatic transitions ever: the birth of Our Lord and His death on the cross. She is with us as we go through life's changes, its ups and downs, and its joys and sorrows.

Mary was there when history transitioned from B.C. to A.D. In fact, it could not have happened without her humble yes! And she was there again, on Calvary, as the world and humanity were transformed from damnation to salvation.

It is radiantly evident that those in need find solace, healing, and protection in her mantle. The pastor of the parish where I grew up had been an army chaplain in the heat of World War II. He often recalled that hundreds of soldiers died in his arms as he anointed them and absolved them. Their final words were usually about their moms back home.

We also have a spiritual mother. Jesus gave us His own as His last gift from the cross.

In moments of crisis, sickness, struggle, and searching, we flee to her and plead, "Hail Mary, full of grace."

So you too should love the resident alien, for that is what
you were in the land of Egypt.
—DEUTERONOMY 10:19

The Catholic Church is universal, and we can learn a lot from our American Catholics from Mexico, Central and South America, and the Caribbean. They bring a vitality, warmth, and promise to our wider Catholic community. We need them; we embrace them; we honor and respect them. We look to them with admiration and reverence as we gratefully recognize that the roots of their durable Catholic religion are centuries deeper than our own.

The welcome migration of Hispanic Catholics from other parts of the Americas to the United States reminds us as well that we still are an "immigrant Church." Just as past generations of Catholics embraced and helped settle our grandparents from Ireland, Italy, Germany, Poland, and Central and Eastern Europe, we continue that tradition and welcome immigrants today. Of course, this gift of immigrants includes people not just from Latin nations but from Africa, Asia, and Europe.

We Catholics in the United States are at times tempted to look at our Church as an institution, a bureaucratic structure, or a distant, cold voluntary organization. Our Latino Catholics who now join us look at the Church as a warm, inviting family—a home. They are right! We can learn a lot from them.

The Catholic Church is our home. We are all one in solidarity—not just with one another but with Christ.

*Always be ready to give an explanation to anyone who asks you
for a reason for your hope.*
—I PETER 3:15

How can each of us help our fellow Catholics grow in their faith?

When speaking to the youth at World Youth Days, our Holy Father reminded the young people that Jesus said, "Go and make disciples."

At the heart of our Church mission is the call for us all to be disciples, to invite others back to and into the Church, and to equip our parishes and ministries to do the same thing.

Very closely related to discipleship is the call to be evangelizers—to spread the gospel that we are a loved, redeemed, and saved people through the life, death, and Resurrection of Jesus. As Saint Paul VI reminded us, "Evangelizing is in fact the grace and vocation proper to the Church, her deepest identity."

We read in the Acts of the Apostles how the first Christians planned the best ways to evangelize, preach the gospel, celebrate the sacraments, and organize communities of faith. The mission of the Church, then and now, is precisely the same: the salvation of souls. This mission is accomplished as the Church and her members teach the coming of the Kingdom of God and, with the help of God's grace, witness to that coming by the quality and character of their lives.

This constancy in mission and service has inspired millions and has renewed the Church for the better time after time. When we lead by example, we become that light beckoning others to Christ.

Thus it will be at the end of the age. The angels will go out and separate the wicked from the righteous.
—MATTHEW 13:49

We are never alone. We are all part of a spiritual family called the Communion of Saints.

We believers here on earth are only part of a bigger picture. Yes, we are members of the Church here and now, but we're just one branch of this supernatural family, sometimes called—since we're fighting sin and Satan—the Church Militant.

Several years ago, I attended the wake for a fourteen-year-old girl who had been killed in an accident. Distressed as her parents were, her mom whispered to me, "She's still with us, and we look forward to being with her again one day."

In other words, those Catholic parents believed in the Communion of Saints. Their daughter, through the mercy of Jesus, was alive forever, awaiting reunion with them in heaven.

Another branch of the Communion of Saints is called the Church Triumphant, and it includes all the saints in heaven. But there are also the other "citizens" of heaven, like the girl I just spoke about and our beloved faithful departed.

Then there's the third branch—the Church Penitent—those souls still experiencing the mercy of Jesus, being purified of their sins in purgatory.

The ultimate family reunion will come only at the end of time, when we will all, we pray, be with the Lord.

Our spiritual family—this Communion of Saints—cannot be destroyed by sin, Satan, or death. That's why Jesus died on the cross and rose from the dead.

Be made clean.
—LUKE 5:13

In Luke 5, we see Jesus in action as He heals a leper and a paralytic. He responds to a genuine human need, answers a prayer, and restores dignity and wholeness.

Jesus did that so wondrously, so uniquely, so dramatically. We are in awe of His power and His mercy.

Sometimes I wish Jesus were here with us right now to teach, to heal, to restore, to make whole, to be with us.

And then it dawns on me: He is! He is alive and active in and through His Church. He gave us His word, "I will be with you all days, even to the end of the world!"

You want to see Him healing? Visit our Catholic hospitals and clinics; sit with our priests as they anoint; accompany Eucharistic ministers as they take Holy Communion to our sick and homebound.

You want to see Him teaching? Visit our splendid Catholic schools, our programs of faith formation, retreats, or Rite of Christian Initiation of Adults (RCIA) classes.

You want to see Him leading us to His Father? Come to baptisms, First Communions, or confession or look around your parish at the amazing work your pastor does every day.

You want to see Him serving the poor? Come to our food pantries, our soup kitchens, our Catholic Charities outreach. See our embrace of immigrants, prisoners, preborn babies and their mothers, Alzheimer's patients, and the homeless.

Right now, you can echo the yearning of the leper, sometimes whispered, sometimes groaned: "Lord Jesus, if you wish, you can make me clean."

Through him the whole structure is held together
and grows into a temple sacred in the Lord.
—EPHESIANS 2:21

What does it mean to rebuild the Church here in America?

Rebuilding always begins with ensuring that the foundations are secure. There is no point worrying about a paint job if the pillars are falling down. Likewise, rebuilding the Church means taking care of our foundations: Sunday Mass, the Eucharist, teaching the faith to our children, serving those in need, solidifying marriages, increasing prayer life, and more. At the very foundation of our Christian life is the friendship offered to us by the Lord Jesus, nourished by His Word and our personal prayer and evident in our charity.

In one sense, it is easier to rebuild a cathedral. That's a matter of money and materials. Rebuilding—or establishing—a friendship with Christ demands more of us. It demands not something of what we have but something of who we are.

Friendship with the Lord demands that we spend time together. We call that prayer and liturgical worship.

It demands that we come to know the Lord and His Church better.

It demands that we meet His family and His friends—the Blessed Mother, Saint Joseph, and all the holy men and women saints of every age.

It demands that we take His call to conversion and change our lives from sin to grace.

It demands that we introduce Him to our friends. We call that evangelization.

When we strengthen our faith and the faith of those around us, that's when we truly rebuild the Church.

Blessing and glory, wisdom and thanksgiving, honor, power,
and might be to our God forever and ever.
—REVELATION 7:12

When it comes to prayer, there's a tendency to complicate prayer and focus on sophisticated, mystical experiences. But it doesn't have to be so tough.

One of the things that's obvious to me is how very often the exclamations we use on a daily basis, without thinking about it, are prayers we may have heard from our parents or godparents.

When we say something like "Oh, my God"—usually at a surprise or a tragedy—it's really a prayer.

Simple things such as "Thank God" and saying "I hope to God that happens" can be a prayer.

And, of course, as Catholics, we have tremendous advantages when it comes to the Holy Sacrifice of the Mass.

If you're at Mass bored to tears and you're thinking "I should be praying," keep in mind that in fact you are. In front of you is the renewal of the greatest prayer of all: the sacrifice of the Son of God to His Father on the cross on Calvary.

Next time you find yourself bored, say to yourself, "Let me unite myself with Him. Let me be absorbed and sucked up into this eternal sacrifice of prayer."

Take advantage of what we've got. We're never by ourselves when it comes to prayer. Especially when we're at Mass.

Feast of the
Visitation

Like many of you, I was raised with a high value placed on visiting people, especially when they encounter adversity. A neighbor a block over had a fire; the next day we visited to see how they were doing and if they needed anything. Uncle Ed had eye surgery; we visited to make sure he was recovering. After my grandpa's death, we visited my grandma frequently.

In the Bible, we read about a special event called the Visitation, which occurred when Mary traveled a great distance to care for her kinswoman, Saint Elizabeth. At the Visitation, a humble virgin, first aware by faith of her rather unique pregnancy and conscious of the fragile divine and human life within her, sets out on a long and arduous journey to encourage and support yet another woman with what we would today call "a problem pregnancy," as Elizabeth, at an advanced age, was pregnant with John the Baptist.

Scripture tells us that John leaped with joy when Mary, carrying Baby Jesus in her womb, approached. He knew that the Son of God was near.

On this special day—this biblical icon of trust, joy, and charity—two women visit with each other and rally around the two tiny gifts of life bouncing within them.

And when we read that story, we feel a kinship with John leaping for joy in the womb, as this is the joy we, too, feel in the presence of Our Holy Lord.

JUNE I

Take my yoke upon you and learn from me, for I am meek and humble
of heart; and you will find rest for yourselves.
—MATTHEW 11:29

June is traditionally dedicated in our Catholic calendar to the
Sacred Heart of Jesus. The Friday after the Feast of Corpus
Christi is the Feast of the Sacred Heart. Since childhood, I've
had a strong devotion to Jesus under this title.

The heart symbolizes love, mercy, tenderness, and compassion. Our God has a heart! His Sacred Heart is literally on fire
with those noble sentiments, and I find that very consoling.

I have found two very practical ways to bond with the Sacred Heart of Jesus.

One is the morning offering. It is easy but profound. Early
each day, right after getting out of bed, dedicate the day to Jesus
and unite all your prayers, works, words, thoughts, and trials to
His Sacred Heart.

Here's what I have prayed every morning since I made my
First Communion:

> *All for Thee, Most Sacred Heart of Jesus!*
> *Sacred Heart of Jesus, I place all my trust in Thee!*
> *Sacred Heart of Jesus, I believe in your love for me!*
> *Sacred Heart of Jesus, have mercy on me, a sinner!*
> *Sacred Heart of Jesus, Thy Kingdom come!*

The second is First Fridays. When Jesus revealed His love
and mercy by appearing to Saint Margaret Mary and showing
her His Sacred Heart, He invited her to encourage people to
approach the Sacrament of Penance and attend Mass on the
first Friday of every month.

Are you looking for a booster shot for a listless, weary spiritual life? Add this easy prayer to your day and attend Mass on
First Fridays.

JUNE 2

Be kind to one another, compassionate, forgiving one another as
God has forgiven you in Christ.
—EPHESIANS 4:32

Love for Jesus and His Church must be the passion of our lives!

The Church loves God's world as His only begotten Son did. She says yes to everything that is good, decent, honorable, and ennobling about the world and says no only when the world negates the dignity of the human person.

Our world would often have us believe that the culture is light-years ahead of a languishing, moribund Church. But of course we realize that the opposite is true: The Church invites the world to a fresh, original place, not a musty or outdated one.

It is always a risk for the world to hear the Church, for she dares the world to foster and protect the inviolable dignity of the human person and human life; to acknowledge the truth about life ingrained in reason and nature; to protect marriage and family; to embrace those suffering and struggling; to prefer service to selfishness; and to never stifle the liberty to quench the innate thirst for the divine that the poets, philosophers, and peasants of the earth know to be what really makes us genuinely human.

Like the Church, we also must say yes to everything that is good, honorable, and decent. And we must understand that we have a sacred duty, arising from our intimate union with Christ, to cherish, care for, protect, and help unite in truth, love, and faith all of our brethren.

JUNE 3

The Father is in me and I am in the Father.
—JOHN 10:38

On Trinity Sunday, the Sunday after Pentecost, we confess our faith in the one true God, who reveals Himself as three divine persons—Father, Son, and Holy Spirit.

The Second Person of the Blessed Trinity, God the Son, became man. And Christ remains really and truly with us in the Sacrament of His Body and Blood.

Soon we will celebrate Corpus Christi, the Feast of the Body and Blood of Christ.

Christ is truly with us at every Mass. We receive Him—body, blood, soul, and divinity—each time we worthily approach Holy Communion.

One year, I attended an annual bishops' meeting where we discussed a vast array of Church matters. But the most productive session came when we gathered and prayed as the Blessed Sacrament was placed in the monstrance on the altar. Seeing nearly 300 bishops on their knees in silent prayer before Jesus was truly a powerful experience.

As I tiptoed out of the room to stand in line for confession, I heard two of the young hotel workers chatting:

"It's sure quiet in there," whispered one of them. "What are they doing?"

"It's weird," replied the other. "They're all just kneeling there quietly, looking at this flat piece of bread in this fancy gold holder."

He almost got it right—except that we believe, with all our heart and soul, that it's not a flat piece of bread but Jesus Christ, really and truly present.

JUNE 4

As a body is one though it has many parts, and all the parts of the body,
though many, are one body, so also Christ.
—I CORINTHIANS 12:12

We belong to the Church. Our Catholic faith is that "pearl of great price" to which we cling, and it has been passed on to us— often at the cost of great sacrifice—by our parents and grandparents. Our great Catholic landscape of America is dotted with churches, parishes, and communities founded by our great-grandparents, who came to this country poor in the eyes of the world but rich in the eyes of faith. They brought with them the treasure of their Catholic faith. Along with family, their Church was of supreme importance.

The Church is Christ. He remains alive, powerful, accessible, and active in His Church!

On her deathbed in 1821, our first native-born American saint, Elizabeth Ann Seton, whispered her last words to her sisters: "Be children of the Church." During Pentecost, I remind you, "Be sons and daughters of the Church!"

JUNE 5

But the day of the Lord will come like a thief, and then the heavens
will pass away with a mighty roar and the elements will be dissolved by fire,
and the earth and everything done on it will be found out.

—2 PETER 3:10

Is the end of the world coming? Absolutely! When? No one knows.

Jesus was blunt about the end of the world, saying that He would come again in glory to judge the living and the dead. That we know.

He was not, however, blunt about when this would happen. In fact, He confessed that even He did not know. Such knowledge belongs only to His Father in heaven.

God's Word teaches us that there will be "signs" of the end of the world. But the ones He lists—war, earthquakes, famines, calamities—apply to almost every era in human history.

Some religions interpret the exhortations of Jesus about the final days with much more precision. We Catholics figure that there's not much use in trying to calculate the calendar and we can better use our time preparing ourselves.

Approach every day as if it could be your last. Make sure that you are at peace with God, are in a state of grace, and have forgiven anyone who has offended you. Ask pardon from those you may have hurt, including the Lord. Go to confession often. Say an Act of Contrition before bed every night. Prepare yourself, as Jesus could call you personally—or the entire world—at any time.

We know that the end of the world is coming; we just don't know when. What we do know for sure is that we must be ready!

JUNE 6

Blessed are the peacemakers, for they will be called children of God.
—MATTHEW 5:9

I will never forget, as a sophomore in high school, sitting in my seat waiting anxiously to hear our teacher answer the question he had posed at the opening of the class: "What was the major cause of World War II?" He went through all the classic reasons for the war—economic depression, German desire for "living space," fascist fanaticism and racialism, the wavering of England and France—concluding after each one that although it was significant, it was not the major cause of World War II.

Well, then, what was it? He finally told us, "The major cause of World War II . . . was World War I!"

War causes war. Even wars in the home and in families cause other wars. One war rarely solves problems but usually causes new ones, which lead to the next horrible war.

It was during World War I that the pope became the most dominant voice for peace, restraint, and diplomacy—a pulpit subsequent popes have eloquently occupied as they have taken their duty as "vicar of the Prince of Peace" with seriousness. As a British historian once observed, "In his work for world peace, the pope has the world as his parish." That world ranges from a global scale to our homes.

In any war, it's the weak and poor who suffer most. Real heroes opt for dialogue, diplomacy, trust, patience, and cooperation.

Christ commands us to "love one another." It is only then that we will find peace.

JUNE 7

All your children shall be taught by the Lord; great
shall be the peace of your children.
—ISAIAH 54:13

It is the time of year when we celebrate graduations. What a joy it is to witness how the spiritual leadership of our pastors and the dedication of our teachers and principals at Catholic schools pass on the faith to the next generation.

Catholic education has a profound and lasting effect on those who are blessed to experience it. Research validates the fact that Catholic schools are the best thing going, with success rates through the stars.

When I attend graduations, I look forward to listening to the student addresses. With different flourishes and styles, those student speakers usually end up with the same themes.

First, they all refer to God. They realize that they could not have achieved graduation without God's grace and mercy and that their Catholic education is indeed a gift from the Lord and His Church.

Second, their thanks spill over to others as they acknowledge their parents and families, who sacrificed to give them a Catholic education.

Third, they talk about virtue, character, and morality. They understand that Catholic education forms the mind, body, heart, and soul. They're looking forward not only to what they can do in life but to who they will be: virtuous people of faith and morals.

Finally, they mention service. They realize that what we get is a gift not to keep but to give away in love to others.

We have an immense treasure in our Catholic schools. As Christ says, "Let the children come to me."

JUNE 8

The land will never lack for needy persons; that is why I command you:
"Open your hand freely to your poor and to your needy kin in your land."
—DEUTERONOMY 15:11

When the at-the-time-agnostic author Malcolm Muggeridge asked Mother Teresa how she could hug, kiss, bathe, and carry the dying, filthy, discarded beggars of Calcutta—people, he admitted, that it made him gag even to look at—Saint Teresa replied, "Because in them I see the face of Jesus."

The Church preaches principles rooted in the Bible, in the teachings of Jesus, in natural law, and in Church tradition. We trust that those principles will enlighten those who look for guidance.

As Saint John Paul II remarked, "The Church does not impose; she only proposes."

A fundamental proposition is that care for the poor, the sick, the vulnerable, and the defenseless has a priority in our lives for what we call the common good.

Far too many across the economic spectrum are struggling, anxious about their next meal or keeping a roof over their heads. Our Catholic faith always turns first and foremost to protecting the poor and most vulnerable. It is often the poor, the babies, the oldest, and the newcomers who are most threatened. But at the same time, we recognize that too many are now "nearly and newly poor" and that anxiety and fear are part of their daily lives.

Saint Teresa saw the face of God in the poor people she cared for in the streets of Calcutta. The dignity of each person as made in the image and likeness of God calls us to do the same thing for the poor in our midst.

JUNE 9

Let us search and examine our ways, and return to the Lord.
—LAMENTATIONS 3:40

More and more people are saying to me, "I'm really thinking of coming back to the Church." Alleluia! That grace is an answer to prayer.

What they're saying is that they are indeed Catholic but that they've drifted, grown lax, or even left, especially after all the scandals in the Church. And now, thank God, they sense a tug back. All I can say is, "The door is open!"

Many ask how they can return. Usually I recommend a few simple steps.

The first is prayer. Your sincere desire to come back to Our Lord and His Church is itself a prayer and an act of return.

The second step back is Sunday Mass. God is wise: He knows we need to give Him His day. His Third Commandment is "Keep holy the Lord's Day." Listen to your Father!

Finally, make a good confession. Don't be scared! Your desire to "get back to the Church" is already a sincere expression of repentance—an acknowledgment that your friendship with Jesus is not what it should be. Any priest worth his salt pops champagne corks when someone comes into the confessional and says, "Father, it's been a while. Can you help me get back on the right track with a good confession?"

Sure, there's a lot more we can do, including increased service and charity and deeper study of our Catholic faith. That will come once you start with the three resolutions above.

Welcome home!

JUNE 10

*Rising very early before dawn, he left and went off
to a deserted place, where he prayed.*

—MARK 1:35

We need silence, don't we? Saint Padre Pio preached, "The language God enjoys most is silence." The psalmist wrote, "In quiet and in trust shall be thy strength."

One wonders if contemporary culture is in a conspiracy against silence. Even when we're alone, we run from quiet, preferring the radio, the TV, or our phones.

Yet the Church encourages silence. Visitors always comment on the atmosphere of reverence and the whispers that fill our churches as we recognize that we're in a house where we speak and listen to God, not to one another.

The Mass itself prescribes moments of silence as we pause to call to mind our sins or we keep quiet after reception of Holy Communion. In years past, we used to become silent between noon and three on Good Friday to recall Our Lord's Passion. And we all have grateful memories of days of recollection and retreats where silence was mandated. Today, more and more parishes offer Eucharistic Adoration, with people simply sitting quietly before Jesus.

Even the Gospels relate that, during His public life, Jesus often would go off to a secluded place to pray in silence.

Saint Peter sometimes talked too much, but the Gospels tell us that at the Transfiguration of the Lord, "He did not know what to say," and simply exclaimed to Jesus, "Lord it is good that we are here." Then he shut up.

Maybe we need to take a lesson from Peter once in a while.

JUNE 11

*We also know that the Son of God has come and has given us discernment
to know the one who is true.*

—1 JOHN 5:20

What's at the core of the universe? What is at the very foundation of existence?

Some have concluded that at the core of creation is . . . nothing! Some scientists call this a "black hole"; some philosophers refer to it as "nihilism."

Others speculate that at the nub of the universe is evil— raw, violent, power-grabbing badness.

We believers don't buy either of those two answers.

Those with faith and hope are steadfast in the conviction that at the center of it all is a heart!

Christians hold fast to the Bible's teaching that God is the deepest power in the universe.

God revealed Himself as a Blessed Trinity: one God in three divine persons. The second person of this Trinity took flesh and became man. We call this the Incarnation. Thus, our God has a name, Jesus, and this Jesus has a heart.

Picture that image of the Sacred Heart: Jesus with His heart exposed. It is on fire with love, compassion, tenderness, and meaning. Yet it is broken, surrounded by a crown of thorns.

When we want to get to the bottom of something contentious, we often ask, "What's the heart of the matter?"

That's what we wonder about life. For us, the heart of the matter is the Sacred Heart. As Saint John Paul II taught, "Jesus Christ is the answer to the question posed by every human life."

After all, He is "the way, the truth, and the life."

But God, who is rich in mercy, because of the great love he had for us,
even when we were dead in our transgressions, brought us to life with Christ.
—EPHESIANS 2:4-5

Of all the many gifts from God that inspire our gratitude, His mercy is at the top of the list.

It's the attribute of God mentioned most often in the Bible. It's the one petition that always caught the ear of God's Son: "My Jesus, have mercy on me!"

God has mercy on us in our sins, our trials, our setbacks, and our worries.

Our beloved Pope Francis has become the "troubadour of mercy." Ever since his address on his first Sunday as our Holy Father, he has reminded us that we have a God who is rich in mercy, that we are never beyond the scope of His mercy, and that the only limit on the Lord's mercy is our reluctance to trust in it and ask for it, never His hesitancy to give it.

Pope Francis has shown a radiant sensitivity to people who feel unworthy of God's mercy, who are burdened by their sins and regrets, or who feel the Church would never welcome them back with the tenderness God promises. The saints and theologians call this awful sentiment despair: a belief that I am so horrible, so unlovable, so sinful, or so unworthy that God could never forgive me or His Church accept me.

Yet God constantly reminds us that His mercy is a lot more powerful than any sin of ours and that the Church is in fact made up of sinners who admit daily their need for God's mercy.

JUNE 13

*For we do not have a high priest who is unable to sympathize
with our weaknesses, but one who has similarly been tested
in every way, yet without sin.*
—HEBREWS 4:15

There are three ancient temptations that we all face. In fact, they are the very same things Jesus faced during His temptations in the desert. What are they?

TEMPTATION ONE: Sensual pleasure. Jesus was hungry, and so Satan dared Him to turn those stones into bread and satisfy His earthly desires. Of course, those of us who are not fasting in the desert for forty days have our own temptations in regard to food. Alcohol. Sex. All the sensory pleasures.

TEMPTATION TWO: Power. Satan says that if Jesus bows down and worships him, he will give Him all the kingdoms of the world. The same thing applies to us, since we all have urges, desires, goals, and temptations to use or trample other people.

TEMPTATION THREE: Pride. Satan tells Jesus to jump from the top of the temple. And the temptation for all of us is to say, "I'm in charge of my own life; I'll be the center of existence."

The three temptations that Our Lord faced and conquered are the same three that threaten to dominate our lives and take salvation away from us. But we don't have to fight these temptations on our own. We can call on the Lord at all times, knowing that when we are weak, He is strong.

JUNE 14

*Do not conform yourselves to this age but be transformed
by the renewal of your mind.*
—ROMANS 12:2

God's revelation to the people of Israel elevated marriage as He compared His love for His chosen people to the passionate, faithful love of a husband for his wife. Children, He taught, were never to be sacrificed. No! Instead, we are called to sacrifice for our children.

This revelation is made even more profound by Jesus, who restored marriage to the way His Father intended it: forever, faithful, and fruitful.

Saint Paul deepens this inspired teaching, comparing the bond between husband and wife to the eternal bond between Jesus and His bride, the Church.

Church historians tell us that the early Christians fascinated the people around them with their deep respect for the noble nature of marriage and family. Their commitment challenged the dominant culture of the Roman Empire, a promiscuous society that treated women as chattel and marriage as less than forever and faithful. Those early generations of Christians were convinced that their task was to transform the world, especially by their example.

Ours is the task of recovering the truth, beauty, and goodness of marriage and family. To a world that wonders if anyone can really say "forever," if fidelity is possible, and if children are a gift and never a burden, we say yes!

We echo what Christ revealed—that the bond between a man and a woman in marriage leads to a healthy, sound civilization, with happiness here and in eternity.

As a father has compassion on his children,
so the Lord has compassion on those who fear him.
—PSALM 103:13

I thank God for the gift of my dad, for he was a loving, responsible, caring man. His faith and his family were his focus, his passion, and the center of his life.

I am convinced that the restoration of fatherhood as an esteemed vocation in the Church and in our society is the key to renewal and the antidote for many of our cultural ills. By their word and their example, dads teach us many important lessons.

When a man fully embraces what it means to be a dad—to be a father—he is in a position to teach us fidelity. Simply put, a dad is a man of his word. He is true to the vows he made to the Lord and to his wife. He keeps the promises he made to his children on the day of their baptism, when he agreed to teach them "by word and example."

True dads are selfless and willing to make sacrifices, including the most seemingly insignificant ones. My dad loved ketchup. No meal was complete without it. Yet when the bottle was nearly empty, he would never touch it. The little bit remaining was for us.

Dads gift their children with time. I remember standing in the front yard, baseball glove in hand, waiting for Dad to come home from work. Though he was hot, sweaty, and tired, he always had time to play a little catch.

Finally, dads teach their kids about God's true nature. What a supreme compliment to every dad: God revealed Himself as a father!

What children think of their dads profoundly influences the way they think of God. If they see their dads as loving, selfless, faithful, and forgiving, this will translate directly to our Heavenly Father.

JUNE 16

Beloved, let us love one another, because love is of God;
everyone who loves is begotten by God and knows God.
—1 JOHN 4:7

The most touching compliment I have ever gotten is that I have shown people Jesus.

As a matter of fact, that's the mission statement for every Christian, every Catholic, every deacon, priest, and bishop, and the mission of the Church herself—to fulfill the request that rises up from God's people: "We would like to see Jesus."

As Catholics, we believe that the Church is the face of Christ.

We all understand the importance of family: parents, grandparents, brothers, sisters, aunts, uncles, cousins. It is through our family that we come to know about Christ.

We have a family in the Church as well, for it is our spiritual family. God is our father, Jesus our brother, Mary our mother, the Apostles, saints, and angels our relatives.

They all show us how it is the job of family—earthly and spiritual—to lead others to Christ.

Years ago, I was in my doctor's office and the nurse related that there was a physician in the office with the last name Dolan. When she asked him if he was related to me, he paused a moment and then replied, "Yes, as a matter of fact, I am related to him, because I'm a Catholic, and so he's my father."

Can you imagine how moved I was by that? Never was the truth of the Church as family more obvious to me. We are family, and I am proud to show you the face of Christ.

Every perfect gift is from above.
—JAMES 1:17

God showers us with millions of gifts: life, creation, faith, salvation, grace, prayer, the promise of eternal life, the sacraments, the Church, and many more. None of them are deserved, none of them are earned, but all are given freely and graciously by a loving, generous God.

It worried Saint Paul that many devout Jews felt that they could earn salvation or merit God's favor, thereby deserving eternity. He believed that salvation and God's favor are free gifts from God. We can do nothing to earn these gifts, for we are totally unworthy of them. We can only have faith and trust in the utter goodness of God. We are saved not by what we do for God but by what God does for us.

Some may ask, "Does this mean that we should just be passive and act indifferently since we can never earn God's gifts?" To this, Saint Paul says no! We must love God. We must worship Him, follow His commandments, pray to Him, and serve Him in our neighbor not to earn His favor, since we can never do that, but because we want to respond to this gracious and good Father who showers us with every good gift.

Religion and faith and moral living are not things we do to merit and earn salvation. We do them because we understand that this is the only appropriate way to respond to such a generous Father.

God showers us with gifts; He gives them freely. We respond with our free gift of love and dedication to Him.

I praise you, because I am wonderfully made;
wonderful are your works!
—PSALM 139:14

Harry Bosch, the detective in Michael Connelly's award-winning books, posits the guiding principle of his life: "Everybody counts or nobody counts."

That is the perfect pro-life declaration.

Everybody counts—both the mother facing a difficult pregnancy and the tiny, fragile baby in her womb; the Israeli and the Palestinian; Grandma in hospice and her healthy, athletic grandson; the double-amputee veteran and the Olympic runner.

In God's eyes and in the wisdom of any enduring culture, every life is sacred.

The basic principles of justice, logic, and civility are dramatically violated in an abortion.

Ronald Reagan said it well: "We cannot diminish the value of one category of human life—the unborn—without diminishing the value of all human life."

Back in 1973, even the most avid abortion supporters thought the lethal and dangerous procedure would be rare and, if done, would be done only in the earliest months of a pregnancy. Now abortion is legal well into pregnancy, government is expected to pay for it, and to refuse to do so on the grounds of conscience is questioned. Any limit on it is looked upon as evil, oppressive, and unenlightened, and any civil discussion about alternatives is politically incorrect.

Pope Francis speaks movingly of the terrors of the "throw-away culture" in which the lives of the poor, the immigrant, the preborn baby, the elderly, the handicapped, and the terminally ill are considered disposable, and he challenges us to defend the dignity of the human person—because everybody counts!

JUNE 19

For it is testified: "You are a priest forever
according to the order of Melchizedek."
—HEBREWS 7:17

On June 19, 1976, I was ordained a priest.

Early in life, one of the ways I viewed my vocation to the priesthood was as an opportunity to help people, especially in tough times. Growing up in those idyllic 1950s (which we now know weren't all that idyllic), the parish priests in my own parish were known as "go-to guys." If you were out of work, you'd go see the priest. If you were having marriage problems, you'd go see the priest. If you were troubled by sin and any sort of difficulty, you'd go see the priest.

I'm not saying that the priests were able to help all the time, but they sure tried. And I liked that. I thought, Boy, I'd like to spend my life helping people. Lord knows there are lots of great ways to do that without being a priest. But that was a defining element of my own discernment of my call to the priesthood.

And then there are the priests who proved their sanctity in even more extraordinary cases. Like Maximilian Kolbe.

Kolbe was held as a prisoner in Auschwitz. After another inmate appeared to have escaped, the commandant said that ten men would be put to death by starvation as a warning to all the prisoners. One of them was a married man with children.

When Kolbe volunteered to take the man's place, the commandant said, "Who is this Polish swine?" Kolbe's answer was, "I'm a Catholic priest." That applies to all of us. A mother or father or a brother or sister, we would all lay down our lives for our loved ones. We have been baptized into the priesthood of all believers.

You are being enriched in every way for all generosity,
which through us produces thanksgiving to God.
—2 CORINTHIANS 9:11

"Let us give thanks to the Lord, our God."

"It is right and just."

We say these words at every Mass. Why does God desire our thanksgiving? He certainly doesn't need it. He doesn't need anything.

Yet the Bible, Jesus, and the saints exhort us to offer God our praise and gratitude.

It's not because God needs it but because we do.

We need to thank God because it reminds us that He is a loving, omnipotent God who revealed Himself to us as a caring Father who cherishes His children. In a way, an act of gratitude is an act of faith, as we confess that all comes from God.

Praising God is good for us because it keeps us humble. Our lives, our talents, and our accomplishments are all due to God. Sure, we develop them diligently, but we admit that we owe everything to the Lord. A grateful person, then, is rarely puffed up or proud but humble.

In addition, gratitude to God inspires us to be more aware of those who may not so dramatically or obviously enjoy God's abundant gifts. When we are conscious of God's gifts to us, we are aware that it all comes from Him, that we did nothing to deserve such gifts, have no right to them, and thus have a duty to share them with those who are not as fortunate.

Go, therefore, and make disciples of all nations.
—MATTHEW 28:19

How can we help more Catholic people grow in their faith?

We must respond to the invitation of Jesus in our time. Pope Francis notes that Jesus does not say "go" only if you would like to or "go" if you have time but rather "Go and make disciples."

Very closely related to this discipleship is the call to evangelize—to spread the gospel that we are a loved, redeemed, and saved people through the life, death, and Resurrection of Jesus. At the heart of our evangelization process is the charge to invite others back to the Church.

The mission of the Church is the same now as it was when Jesus walked the earth: the salvation of souls. This mission is accomplished as her members proclaim the coming of the Kingdom of God and witness to that coming by the quality and character of their lives.

Today's Church calls for a *mission model,* not a *maintenance model.* No longer can we presume that our people will come; no more can we be comfortable that people raised Catholic will live and die Catholic.

Now we must "cast out to the deep." We must step outside our own worlds and our fears and, with our hearts and minds focused on Christ, traverse those turbulent waters into His loving embrace. From time to time we will sink, as Peter did, but Our Lord will always be there, offering His outstretched hand. We simply need to grasp it.

JUNE 22

The Lord will guard your coming and going
both now and forever.
—PSALM 121:8

A few years ago, I awoke to find out that the flight I was supposed to take that morning had been canceled. Figuring that I would catch the next flight, I went to the airport anyway. When I arrived, I found that because of inclement weather, thousands of people were stranded. I stood in long lines waiting to rebook, then waited on standby for a flight. As I did that, I got to know several of the people waiting in line around me.

Instead of anger, impatience, and threats, the folks with me were chatty, hopeful, and helpful. We all swapped stories of where we were headed and why and offered one another tips about possible alternative routes.

Maybe I'm reading too much into this, but we had become a temporary community. We were better off because we stuck together, encouraged one another, and shared triumphs and woes.

It seems to me that that headache of a long morning was a snapshot of life. We're all on a journey—from God, back to God. On the trip, we experience a lot of adversity and heartache, but with the grace and mercy of God and with the community of those making the pilgrimage with us, we get through.

Jesus sets the pattern, as usual. And He tells us the trip is worth it. He encourages us to never lose hope, to help our fellow travelers, and to keep the goal—eternal life with Him—always in mind.

God, you know my folly; my faults are not hidden from you.
—PSALM 69:6

At baptism, Original Sin is washed away and our souls teem with God's very life—the actual indwelling of the Blessed Trinity that we term sanctifying grace.

That's how God always wants our soul to be: free from sin, radiant with His grace, innocent—as it was on the day of our christening.

But what happens when that glow is tarnished by sin? Are we lost? Can we recover it?

You bet we can! How? Through the Sacrament of Penance.

I love hearing confessions. I also love going to confession, and need to, every two weeks or so. Often, "new Catholics"—adults who entered the Church at the Easter Vigil in recent years—tell me that one of the attractions of Catholicism was the Sacrament of Reconciliation.

Tragically, some folks stay away because they think their sins are so ugly and horrible that God wants nothing to do with them. Although a realistic admission of the evil of our sins is good, to stop there is not. The main message of God's revelation—in the Bible and especially in the words of Jesus—is that God's mercy is a lot more powerful than our sins. Don't "play God" with yourself. He's told us over and over that He wants to forgive us. Don't be stricter on yourself than He is!

Pope Francis claims, "The best Christians are those standing in line for confession; the happiest are those who have made a humble one."

JUNE 24

Therefore, putting away falsehood, speak the truth, each one to his neighbor,
for we are members of one another.
—EPHESIANS 4:25

I hear remarks like this a lot today: "I used to be a Catholic"
and "I grew up Catholic."

Sometimes the people making those remarks have fallen
away temporarily and intend to return to the Church. However, most of the time, they do not have warm and grateful sentiments about the Church.

Unfortunately, when I hear personalities on TV or the
radio say, "I used to be Catholic," they imply, "I'm beyond that
now. I'm enlightened and liberated from those silly, superstitious shackles, and now I'm a 'freethinker,' a mature adult."

In his Letter to the Ephesians, Saint Paul urged us not to be
like children "tossed by waves and swept along by every wind of
teaching arising from human trickery."

Pope Benedict XVI once observed that "what takes real
courage is adhering to the faith . . . even when it contradicts the
'scheme' of the contemporary world."

Our faith in Christ and His Church is not childish baggage
that is discarded when we become grown-ups. There's nothing
more adult, enlightened, or freeing than our Catholic faith, no
matter what the in-crowd preens about.

In reality, the truly enlightened, mature, liberated folks are
those who are humbly, joyfully, and gratefully confident in their
Catholic faith and are well aware of the Church's struggles but
who live their faith sincerely and pass it on to their kids. Now,
that's an "adult faith."

JUNE 25

Simon Peter answered him, "Master, to whom shall we go?
You have the words of eternal life."
—JOHN 6:68

I know a group of women who collectively call themselves "Wednesday Women." A couple of dozen strong, these are impressive women, all professional, well educated, leaders in the community. Every Wednesday morning they gather at their parish for prayer and Bible study. Each is eager to deepen her own faith and pass it on to others—especially her children. And here's what really struck me: They make a promise to say something positive about their Catholic faith every day!

The promise, they tell me, is a tough one to keep because everywhere around them they find antagonism toward the Church. These women are told that the Church is "waging a war" on them. They read newspaper articles by editorial columnists who were raised Catholic but who have "moved on."

Yet these women persist in their faith. When tempted to join the crowd and walk away, they find themselves echoing Saint Peter, "To whom shall we go?"

They have become used to snide remarks from "former" Catholics, but they don't take the bait. Instead, they smile and reply with a gentle, positive remark about the Church they love. And they are met with disbelief, a look of pity or condescension, or—occasionally—a look of interest or curiosity that might lead to a worthwhile conversation and a gentle invitation to come back home.

We need more Wednesday Women (and men)—and we need them on Sunday, Monday, Tuesday, Thursday, Friday, and Saturday as well.

JUNE 26

In my Father's house there are many dwelling places. If there were not,
would I have told you that I am going to prepare a place for you?
—JOHN 14:2

Funerals, like everything we do in the Church, are not all about the deceased or us but all about Jesus. We attend a funeral Mass not to celebrate the life of the departed—although that's part of it—but mainly to celebrate the life, death, and Resurrection of Jesus. It is an act of faith in the power of His cross and Resurrection.

While never masking the natural grief and sadness that come when someone we love dies, we concentrate more on eternal life, emphasizing the promise Jesus made when He said: "Whoever believes in me, even if he dies, will live."

Although we rejoice in the gift of eternal life promised us by Our Lord and trust that the one for whom we grieve is now in heaven, we do not take it for granted. There is purgatory, and there is hell. That's why humble prayers for the mercy of Jesus upon the soul of the departed is strong in Catholic tradition.

Several years ago, I was at the funeral Mass of a twelve-year-old boy who had died of cancer. At the end, a classmate of the boy whispered to me, "I'm not a Catholic, but seeing the faith of him and his family through all of this, seeing this church help so much, being here at this Mass with all this talk about eternal life, I think I'm going to become one!"

I was amazed by the child's eloquence, especially during such a sad time. What a wonderful testament to our faith and to the eternal mercy of Christ!

*Were not our hearts burning [within us] while he spoke to us
on the way and opened the scriptures to us?*

—LUKE 24:32

We are not meant to be disciples alone. We are meant to follow Jesus together, and it is a journey. We are not meant to remain where we are but to follow Him to where He wants to lead us—to heaven.

We need only think of Jesus on the road to Emmaus as a model for how He leads us. You recall the story? Two disciples are leaving Jerusalem on Easter Sunday evening, having witnessed the Crucifixion on Good Friday. They are discouraged. They have lost hope. They have heard that Jesus has risen, but they consider that news too fantastic to be true. The Risen Jesus draws alongside them in the guise of a fellow traveler and asks them why they are disconsolate. He then proceeds to restore their hope after opening their eyes to His presence.

Picture this miraculous image. Jesus draws near. He accompanies them with His loving presence. He listens to their experience. He rebukes them for their mistakes. He teaches them about the truth of the Scriptures. He reveals Himself in the Eucharist. He restores their hope and leads them to conversion.

Thus converted, the disciples race back to Jerusalem to take their place with their fellow disciples. They had been going the wrong way, and Christ turned them around!

We have a little bit of those men in us sometimes. And like them, we need Christ to gently turn us around.

JUNE 28

Feast of
Saint Irenaeus

Pope Benedict XVI once articulated that the message of the Church is overwhelmingly positive, not negative, as some often see it. The Church is at her best when she says *yes* to all that is noble, decent, good, and life-giving. And when she does on occasion have to say *no* to whatever threatens to degrade us, that is but an immeasurably greater *yes*.

Our critics say that the Church is against everything and that all she can be counted on to do is condemn things and crush new ideas. Nothing could be further from the truth! She is on the side of life, not death; love, not hate; freedom, not shackles; peace, not war; light, not darkness.

The early Church Father Saint Irenaeus wrote, *"Gloria dei vivens homo"*: "The glory of God is humanity alive."

Saint Irenaeus knew what all the saints know, what Catholic theologians, philosophers, artists, and storytellers know: The Church sees creation and creatures immersed in God's love, God's grace, and God's presence, and the human project is a breathtaking work of art as every man and woman is made in God's image and likeness.

The vocation of the Church, then, is to encourage what is most true and worthy of humanity. She is not wagging a threatening finger but applauding life and seeing in all of life an invitation to affirm in reverent and grateful worship the God whose glory is you and me, fully alive!

Feast of Saint Peter
and Saint Paul

I admit that June 29 is not a big deal here at home, but I invite you to make it one. This is a big feast day in Rome—fireworks and all—and it's not only a holy day but a holiday, because Peter and Paul are the patrons of Rome, considered to be the founders of the Church in Rome. What Romulus and Remus are to imperial Rome, the reasoning goes, Peter and Paul are to Christian Rome.

It was the will of Jesus to build His Church upon the rock of Peter. And it was the will of God to convert Saul and use Paul as a fisher of men. Both were martyred for their faith, and we celebrate them today.

Through all the twists and turns of history, the Church has remained faithful to the primacy of Peter and the words of Paul.

At a critical moment in His preaching ministry, Jesus teaches the people about the Eucharist. After the "bread of life" discourse at the synagogue in Capernaum, many of His disciples decided to follow Him no longer. Jesus asks the Apostles whether they, too, would like to go away. Peter gives a beautiful response: "Master, to whom shall we go? You have the words of eternal life."

Saint Paul reminds us to "be thankful . . . singing psalms, hymns, and spiritual songs with gratitude in your hearts to God."

In the face of difficulties or uncertainty, in the face of unexpected missions, Paul teaches us to remain thankful, for we will "have our true citizenship in heaven."

Jesus told Peter his mission would be to strengthen his brothers in the faith, and what could be more inspiring than what Peter said: "You have the words of eternal life"?

Venerable
Pierre Toussaint

Sometimes, *how* we do things is as important as *what* we do.

Pierre Toussaint was a man of peace. He was born into slavery in Saint Domingue (now Haiti) and then taken to New York by his master's wife and allowed to train as a hairdresser. He earned his own money and, though still a slave, became wealthy. When the family he was enslaved to fell on hard times financially, he helped them. At the age of forty-one, Pierre was freed.

Yellow fever was rampant at that time, and Pierre often searched fearlessly through the quarantine areas for the abandoned, taking the sick into his own home to nurse them. He lived the Corporal Works of Mercy, tramping the streets constantly to feed the hungry and visit the sick.

Children—black and white—received an education they could never have dreamed of without his generosity. Those orphaned by successive plagues found a home built for them by Pierre.

Every day for sixty years he trudged to Mass in Old St. Patrick's Church. Many times, even on bitter cold mornings, he was passed by wealthy Catholics in their carriages who refused to pick him up because he was black. Time after time he was insulted or even refused a seat in the church he had helped rebuild. Yet he went on peacefully, doing endless good.

Pierre was declared Venerable in 1996. I pray that someday he will officially become a saint, for if ever a man was a saint, it was Pierre Toussaint.

While he was speaking, a woman from the crowd called out and said to him,
"Blessed is the womb that carried you and the breasts at which you nursed."
—LUKE 11:27

My mentor used to say that "old heresies never die. They just return under new names." He would go on to remind us that the oldest heresy, or wrong belief, in the Church was a denial of the reality of the Incarnation, doubting that God actually became one of us.

Myth, story, literature, and metaphor are indeed inspired, crucial parts of the gospel. However, the essence of revealed Christianity is that the birth, life, death, and Resurrection of Jesus really did happen. It is historical.

As the English poet Coventry Patmore wrote, Mary is "our only Saviour from an abstract Christ." No creature was more aware of the reality of the Incarnation than Mary. Her Son was hardly just an idea. He was incarnate in her womb, born at Bethlehem, and raised in Nazareth. He cried, He grew, He bled, He died. She held Him as a baby; she held Him as a corpse. You cannot cradle an abstraction. Ideas do not have mothers. Our God does.

That's why the Church maintains that the love of Mary is the best protection against heresy. It's tough to reduce God to an abstraction or an idea if you believe He has a mother. It's hard to deny the reality of the Incarnation if you marvel at the crib and the Pietà.

So join me in renewing your love for, trust in, and devotion to our Blessed Mother.

"The Word became flesh, and dwelt among us." That's the Incarnation.

JULY 2

"Everything is lawful for me," but not everything is beneficial. *"Everything is lawful for me,"* but I will not let myself be dominated by anything.
—I CORINTHIANS 6:12

As we approach the anniversary of the birth of our nation, it's good to remember that God is pro-freedom. When He created us, He gave us free will. Robots, He did not make; thinking, reflective, free people, He did.

God so defends our freedom that He allows us even to reject Him! As we somberly recall, that's what our first parents did—and we've never been the same since.

Why did God give us this freedom? Because, as His Son would teach us, He wants us as friends, not as slaves. All He desires is our love and trust. Friendship, love, and trust cannot be forced, only freely given.

In the Gospel of Luke, the disciples return to Jesus from a Samaritan town that had thrown them out. They are understandably frustrated and furious and suggest to the Lord that they call fire down upon that nasty place.

Jesus rebukes them. That's not the way He or His Father acts! God whispers, He doesn't yell; He invites rather than coerces. He respects our free will even when we tell Him to get out of our lives.

Yet freedom isn't an absolute good, Saint Paul tells us. If we interpret freedom as the right to do whatever we want, consequences be darned, we actually become slaves!

Although God gives us freedom, He also has revealed to us how we need to use our freedom if we want happiness now and in eternity.

We're free to ignore His revelation. But if we do, we risk losing eternal life.

JULY 3

By His dying on the cross and Resurrection from the dead, Jesus conquered sin, Satan, evil, and death itself. And here's the good news: He wants to share that victory with us! If that does not give us hope, what can?

Now, I'm not naïve. There are many natural reasons not to hope. In our world we see the continual threats of violence, terrorism, injustice, and poverty. Many people feel anxious about an uncertain future. Immorality and threats to life itself seem rampant. Personally, we struggle with sin, or sickness, or adversity and occasionally are tempted to wonder where Christ is.

But Jesus brings us hope. Sin, Satan, evil, and death do not have the last word. Grace, mercy, goodness, life, and Jesus have the final say! He wants to take all our worries, sins, and struggles—all our dying—and put them to death with Him so that we can rise with Him to new life.

A big, cosmic argument is going on in the world, and it's been going on since Adam and Eve. As with every other argument, whoever has the last word usually wins. But by dying on the cross, Jesus had the last word. By dying, He destroyed our death; by rising, He restored our life!

For you were called for freedom, brothers. But do not use this freedom
as an opportunity for the flesh; rather, serve one another through love.
—GALATIANS 5:13

Today is the birthday of our nation, and with the rest of you, I thank God for the bountiful blessings He has lavished on our wonderful country. I pray every day for citizens of nations where, instead of peace, prosperity, and freedom, they experience war, violence, hunger, persecution, poverty, and oppression.

For us Catholics, the Bible, the Ten Commandments, the preaching of Jesus, and the morality of the Church all enhance and protect genuine freedom. God gives us freedom and then implants in our hearts and reveals to us the sense of moral duty that allows us to live "in the freedom of the children of God."

Although so thankful for our political independence, we are concerned about a moral autonomy that makes us comfortable living without responsibility to God. Words such as *subjection, lordship, kingdom,* and *servant* are hardly popular in our American vocabulary. In our religious lexicon, though, they are at the core of our relationship with God. We know that America, like any other nation, is at its best when it acknowledges its absolute reliance on God.

Perhaps the most revolutionary words an American can utter today are those that open the Creed: "I believe in one God, the Father almighty." God is sovereign; the Lord, not the state, is almighty; and God's way, not mine, is normative.

To rebel against God, then, brings not liberty but slavery. To obey the Lord leads to genuine freedom. Christ is our king, not King George!

JULY 5

*And they were all filled with the holy Spirit and began to speak
in different tongues, as the Spirit enabled them to proclaim.*

—ACTS 2:4

Jesus was a compassionate friend and the most effective teacher ever. He still is!

He knew His friends—the Apostles and disciples—had been on a roller coaster of emotions. They had savored His presence with them those three years of what we call His public life, when they were with Him daily witnessing His teaching and miracles.

Then they were devastated when He was arrested, falsely accused, tortured, and crucified. So, as a compassionate friend and wise teacher, He prepared them.

"I will not leave you orphans!" He assured them. "I will be with you all days, even until the end of the world."

"How?" they asked.

Through the gift of the Holy Spirit!

God the Father sent us His Son. God the Father and God the Son send us God the Holy Spirit.

The Holy Spirit is with us through grace, the life of God within our hearts and souls. You want wisdom? Courage? Inspiration? Mercy? Salvation? Pray! The Holy Spirit brings us the gifts we need and for which we ask.

Never forget that simple but potent prayer entailing three short words: Come, Holy Spirit!

JULY 6

Therefore, we are not discouraged; rather, although our outer self is wasting away, our inner self is being renewed day by day.
—2 CORINTHIANS 4:16

A marathon is a wonderful paradigm for life.

The marathon has a goal—the finish line. So do we: The goal of life is heaven and the salvation of our soul.

The marathon requires practice. Nobody runs it without a lot of preparation. The journey of life needs practice, too. We have successes, and we have failures. Sometimes we win, other times we lose, especially in our struggle with sin.

The marathon is about perseverance. It's not necessarily the fastest who win but those who stick to it. So it is with our lives. Jesus often told us to persevere in our prayers and in our fidelity to Him.

The marathon takes discipline. Our life of discipleship needs the same rigor. Jesus recommends fasting and self-sacrifice.

The runners rely on the cheers and support from the crowd. In our marathon on the road of life back to the Lord, we are encouraged by that "crowd of witnesses," the Church Triumphant.

If a runner stumbles, he or she gets back up again! So do we when we sin, especially through the Sacrament of Penance.

The competitors have to stay on the course or they're disqualified. Jesus gives us the boundaries of His teaching and His commandments as our map.

Finally, those who reach the finish line get a reward. So do we. As Saint Paul remarked, though, ours is hardly a trophy that will tarnish but everlasting glory—the greatest reward of all!

JULY 7

*I no longer call you slaves, because a slave does not know what
his master is doing. I have called you friends, because I have told you
everything I have heard from my Father.*

—JOHN 15:15

Jesus is my best friend. He wants to be yours, too.

When Pope Benedict XVI was elected as Successor of Saint Peter, he called us all to holiness, just as Our Lord did, and he defined holiness as a "friendship with Jesus."

That's about as down to earth as you can get. Yes, Jesus is my Lord and my Savior, but He is also my best friend and He calls me to union with Him in holiness now and forever.

We get to know our best friend in the Gospels, in the Creed, and through the timeless teaching of the sacred tradition of the Church. This friendship nourishes us and gives us hope in the midst of life's trials. This friendship sustains us during times of despair and times of joy.

Jesus doesn't exclude anybody but invites everybody to the greatest adventure of them all—a life with purpose and eternal meaning, given in love to God and His people, faithful to the inner dignity He has given us—while guiding us to conform our lives to the liberating message of His revelation.

He compliments us for the good we've done and the talents we have while challenging us about the ways we may have drifted and realistically cautioning us about the dangers of sin.

It's rather simple: Jesus Christ invites us to friendship with Him—a friendship that forms and transforms and leaves us never the same. That's holiness.

JULY 8

Certainly sons [and daughters] are a gift from the Lord,
the fruit of the womb, a reward.

—PSALM 127:3

At our family get-together on the Fourth of July, as I watched the children play and felt the joy of family, it dawned on me that the kids were the center of their parents' lives. The parents lived for them; they would die for them.

Catholics traditionally are known for having a lot of kids. When people introduce themselves to me, they often grin and tell me, "I'm one of five"—or more—"kids. I come from good Catholic parents."

To view marriage as intended by the Lord for the procreation of children and to welcome babies as God's gifts is very biblical and very Catholic.

A little over fifty years ago, Saint Paul VI reaffirmed this baby-centered worldview in his encyclical *Humanae Vitae*. When he worried that artificially preventing birth would result in a demographic winter, a diminished regard for the lifelong character of marriage, a lessening of respect for women, and an increase in promiscuity, people sneered that he was an old worrywart.

I'd say he was a prophet. Countries in Europe now have a higher death rate than birthrate, divorce hovers around 50 percent here in America, and there's the "Me Too" phenomenon showing a shocking abuse of women.

History has at its center—when B.C. becomes A.D.—the birth of a baby: Jesus.

Families have as their center the kids. So should culture and society.

Our Catholic view that it's all about the kids is a value worth defending!

JULY 9

I will offer a sacrifice of praise and call on the name of the Lord.
—PSALM 116:17

At the 1976 Eucharistic Congress in Philadelphia, we sang for the first time: "You satisfy the hungry heart with gift of finest wheat."

The very word *Eucharist* means "thanksgiving." Simply put, the Mass—the Eucharist—is the most sacred, effective, powerful way we can praise our astoundingly gracious Father who lavishes countless gifts upon us.

Thus, as we internally profess our faith in the Eucharist, we are moved to manifest that faith externally at Mass. We genuflect as we enter a church. We say out loud, "Lord, I am not worthy that you should enter under my roof," before approaching the altar, publicly indicating a desire to be cleansed of sin. We say "Amen," meaning "yes," when we receive the body and blood of Christ. We dress modestly for the Eucharist, giving a public sign that this is an event more sublime than playing tennis or lounging at the pool.

Our partaking of the Eucharist indicates a communion not only with Our Lord but with His Church. Thus, we would not dare violate its integrity by receiving the Eucharist if we were conscious of mortal sin or dissent from clear Church teaching.

The inspired psalmist asks, "How can I repay the Lord for all the great good done for me? I will raise a cup of salvation and call on the name of the Lord."

That's precisely what we do at Mass.

But scripture confined all things under the power of sin, that through faith in Jesus Christ the promise might be given to those who believe.
—GALATIANS 3:22

Every Mass is an act of faith in the Person, the true God and true man, Jesus Christ. We would not be there without at least a hint of that faith.

This is the Jesus who taught, "Do not let your hearts be troubled. You have faith in God; have faith also in me."

This is the Savior who said, "Everyone who lives and believes in me will never die."

This is the Redeemer who told us, "I have come to bring life, life in abundance, life forever."

This is the Messiah who dared claim, "I am the Resurrection and the life."

This is the Jesus who, by dying on the cross and rising from the dead, opened the gates of heaven and won for us the victory of eternal life, the saving events of His death and Resurrection on Good Friday and Easter Sunday.

Faith in Christ offers us the only hope and consolation we can muster during times when we are tempted to succumb to discouragement, doubt, crushing sadness, and nightmare.

Jesus came to give life and save life, to protect and guide us, to save us from everlasting flames.

"We adore Thee, O Christ, and we praise Thee, because by Thy Holy Cross Thou hast redeemed the world."

JULY 11

Enlighten them in regard to the statutes and instructions, showing them
how they are to conduct themselves and what they are to do.
—EXODUS 18:20

What were the last words of Jesus before He ascended to heaven? "Go, therefore, and make disciples of all nations."

Obedience to that final imperative has been a constant of the Church's identity and mission. In the first days of the Church, we see that the earliest Apostles were indefatigable in their instruction of anybody who would listen. The earliest followers of Jesus were termed disciples, or students, and He was reverently referred to as Teacher.

The Fathers of the Church, in those first centuries, taught others by writing and gathering students around them.

When Saint Benedict established the monastic system, his monasteries became renowned centers of learning. The Church is considered the founder of the university, and religious orders such as the Dominicans, the Jesuits, and the Ursuline sisters were acclaimed as scholars and teachers of the young.

The Catholic Church in the United States is celebrated for its vigorous system of schools, educating children up through high school and young adults in universities.

The obedience to the command of the Teacher continues in our parishes and in our homes.

Many years ago, I visited Ethiopia and met with the president. He told us that the most valuable gift the Church could give his struggling country would be the establishment of a Catholic university.

He was not a Catholic; his country had only a tiny Catholic minority. But he knew the Church's huge contribution in teaching and he wanted in on it, for Catholics still adhere to Christ's command to teach!

JULY 12

Amen, amen, I say to you, whoever believes in me will do the works that I do, and will do greater ones than these, because I am going to the Father.

—JOHN 14:12

My niece Shannon was diagnosed with bone cancer when she was eight. Right after the diagnosis, a well-intentioned neighbor graciously approached my sister with expressions of concern.

"You have asked Jesus to heal Shannon, haven't you?" the neighbor inquired.

"We have," my sister replied, "and we are blessed with a fabulous doctor who specializes in pediatric oncology."

The neighbor protested: "If you have entrusted Shannon to Jesus, you have the best doctor of all. Why are you hedging on your faith? You don't need doctors, hospitals, surgery, chemo. Just pray! Don't you believe the Lord will answer your prayers for healing?"

My sister replied, "I believe Our Lord will answer our prayers. I just believe that one of the ways He'll answer is through good doctors and treatment."

Saint Thomas Aquinas called this "secondary causality," a classic constant in Catholic thought: God acts—heals, loves, cares for, teaches, forgives, reveals Himself—through other persons, places, and things.

Preeminently, God acts in and through Jesus, His only begotten Son. And Jesus continues to heal, love, forgive, instruct, care for, and be present in an abundance of ways. He acts through all of us. We are agents of His love, mercy, care, reconciliation, and healing. He continues to answer prayers through us.

Simply stated, we can put no shackles on the wideness of the Lord's healing powers. He answers prayers in ways we never can imagine.

Blessed are they who are persecuted for the sake of righteousness,
for theirs is the kingdom of heaven.
—MATTHEW 5:10

Throughout the world, especially in areas controlled by radical Islam, Christians are under attack. Each day leads to new reports of Christians beheaded, beaten to death, raped, or forced to flee. In some countries the victims are branded with an N to identify them as followers of Jesus of Nazareth. The ancient churches of the Middle East, which have been in countries like Iraq, Syria, Egypt, and parts of Lebanon since the time of the Apostles, are literally near extinction, as believing Christians have been burned and slaughtered or forced into exile.

It's called "Christianophobia"—a systematic, unrelenting persecution of believers to intimidate them at best, to eradicate them at worst, and it shows no sign of letting up. New cases are reported daily from places such as Pakistan, Sri Lanka, India, Indonesia, the Middle East, and Africa.

Yet in many of these besieged countries, people flock to Sunday Mass, vocations to priesthood are booming, and tens of thousands join the Church each year even though it could cost them their lives!

Here in America we drift along, watching our people walk away, our numbers shrunken, our faith diluted. In our country of comfort, peace, and freedom, we're lax in our faith; in those countries of persecution, bloodshed, martyrdom, and attack, they're rebuilding, and the faith is more vibrant than ever.

Our persecuted brothers throughout the world show fortitude and perseverance that are exemplary models for us all.

For from him and through him and for him are all things.
To him be glory forever.
—ROMANS 11:36

I relish the continuity of the Catholic Church. Part of Catholic wisdom is that Jesus keeps us intimately close to Him in the Church. The Church continues the life, teaching, invitation, grace, mercy, and salvation that Our Lord came to bring. He is the vine; we are the branches.

I can remember being very moved, even as a boy of seven, when my teacher, as she prepared us for First Holy Communion and Confirmation (the two sacraments came only weeks apart then), told us that every Mass was just like being there with Jesus and His Apostles at the Last Supper and that our Confirmation would be as if we were there with the Apostles and Mary in the Upper Room that first Pentecost.

Wow, I thought. I'm part of something big. This goes all the way back to *Jesus*.

That's continuity.

Continuity does not mean the Church is a frozen lake with everything still, stalled, and immobile. Rather, the Church is more like a flowing river: It has one source—Jesus Christ, the eternal spring—with fresh, life-giving water cascading through the centuries, defined by the riverbanks.

The Church is one with Christ. We are loyal to Saint Peter and his successor, and we delight in this continuity with Jesus, His Apostles, and His Church.

Jesus, Peter, Saint John XXIII, Saint John Paul II, Benedict XVI, Francis, you, and me. Jesus continues in His Church.

Which is easier, to say to the paralytic, "Your sins are forgiven,"
or to say, "Rise, pick up your mat and walk"?
—MARK 2:9

Here's an important word in the Catholic lexicon: *holistic.* When looking at the miracle that we call the human person, we take in the whole: body, mind, and soul. This is essential in our works of education; this is necessary in our efforts in healthcare and charity.

Jesus did this. Remember when He was asked to heal the body of the paralytic? He did, but only after tending as well to the soul as He forgave the sick man's sins.

Recall when the people were hungry and He fed their bodies with loaves and fish that miraculously multiplied? But then He also spoke of bread for the soul in the Holy Eucharist.

We have, thank God, made extraordinary progress in treating bodies racked by illness, pain, infections, and cancer. Now there seems a rising hope that we can make similar strides in healing the mind.

The Church has long been on the front lines of treatment for mental illness. Decades ago, when mentally or emotionally struggling people were shunned, straitjacketed, and hidden away as embarrassments, Church agencies, hospitals, and homes were there, run lovingly and professionally by sisters.

Jesus, the Divine Physician, never stopped at the healing of bodily ailments. He saw deep into the soul, the mind, and the psyche. Those literally in chains because of their mental illness were freed, released from bondage.

His Church and His people can do no less.

JULY 16

We love because he first loved us.
—1 JOHN 4:19

Did you know that a significant number of service and military people are Catholic? I believe one of the reasons for that is that the Catholic tradition prepares and encourages our young people to seek a life of service and care for others. Service of another—using our talents, time, and treasure to help the community—has been a constant of Christian life since the first years.

Indeed, we have a sense of vocation about us. There's a big difference between a job and a vocation, isn't there? Yes, we all need jobs. It's how we look at it, though. A vocation is a calling, a way we spend our lives in service of others; there's more to a vocation than punching a time card and getting out of the place we work. Our hearts are in it. We believe that everyone has a calling, a vocation, a way God wants us to spend our lives. A job is something we *do*. A vocation is something we *are*.

Commentators sometimes dismiss today's generation as "in it for themselves." Don't tell that to our Catholic families! They've been formed to be a man or a woman for others.

Christ taught and modeled a life of selfless service. The Gospel says, "No one has greater love than this, to lay down one's life for one's friends." When you grow up seeing the crucifix at home, in the classroom, or at church, that lesson of sacrificial love sinks in.

Why do you notice the splinter in your brother's eye, but do not perceive the wooden beam in your own eye?
—MATTHEW 7:3

What's sadder than sin is to presume we're without any! If we think we are without sin, we reject Jesus, who came to save us from our sins. "Nice of you to offer yourself as a Savior, Lord. Thanks but no thanks. Others sure need you, but I don't." To claim to be without sin is to make Our Lord's death on the cross useless.

Some Catholics today ask why we have to confess our sins to a priest. Whereas the form of the Sacrament of Penance as we know it took centuries to develop, the principle of forgiveness of sins by an agent of Jesus dates from the first Easter night, when the Risen Lord gave His first priests, the Apostles, the authority to forgive sins in His name and by His power.

I once confided in some priests that we are partly to blame for people not flocking to the confessional, as we rarely preach it, encourage it, or teach about it.

Then along comes Pope Francis—the Pope of Mercy. He constantly speaks of the power and beauty of the Sacrament of Reconciliation. He is not shy about letting us watch him kneel in front of a confessor. He has softened the hardened heart of the world and preaches often of sin, Satan, hell, and the hypocrisy of those who judge others but not themselves.

He speaks about the power of reconciliation and the explosive, liberating medicine of mercy!

JULY 18

*Husbands, love your wives, even as Christ loved the church
and handed himself over for her.*

—EPHESIANS 5:25

"How was your marriage a success?" I asked couples celebrating their golden anniversary.

They all credited God. They had learned to count on His grace and mercy. As one of them mentioned, "Fifty years ago, we made solemn promises to God, one another, ourselves, and the Church. But we could not have kept them without God's grace."

Well said! That's what we mean by a sacrament. A half century ago, those jubilarians chose to enter the Sacrament of Marriage—not made-up vows before a justice of the peace on the beach, not a "trial arrangement" to see if it works. No! They asked God to seal and strengthen their love in a sacrament.

The couples talk about the presence of the cross in their marriage. They recall the tough times as pivotal. And they both tear up when they realize that what they're talking about is nothing less than the cross, which—as Jesus promised us—would always be part of genuine love.

They also credit their Catholic faith for the success of their marriages. Most of the time it goes like this: "We've had some tough times. There were even moments each of us thought about giving up and getting divorced. But that temptation didn't stay in our minds long, because we're Catholics! So we dug in and made it work. We're glad we did!"

These jubilarians are heroes. Their marriages are a perfect testimony to the true meaning of the sacrament.

*He is the one of whom I said, "A man is coming after me
who ranks ahead of me because he existed before me."*

—JOHN 1:30

The Lamb of God is a central figure in the Bible.

Christ is the Lamb of God—the spotless, innocent victim who takes away the sins of the world.

Isaac asked his father, "Where is the lamb of sacrifice?" And Abraham replied with tears in his eyes, "God will provide the lamb!"

"Where is this Lamb of God?" yearned the faithful people of Israel for centuries, until John the Baptist bellowed out, "Look, there is the Lamb of God," as he pointed to Jesus.

When I was rector at the Pontifical North American College in Rome, my vice rector had been diagnosed with multiple sclerosis. One day, as he was offering Mass, he slowly began his walk over to the pulpit to preach, but his weakened legs buckled, and he began to collapse. He caught himself on the edge of the altar and gradually straightened himself up.

"I'm okay," he assured us. "But I had better hold tight to this altar or I'm afraid I'll fall again." We could all say that!

So many seminarians told me that his example—a suffering priest uniting his agony with the sacrifice of the Lamb of God on the cross—bolstered their own vocation.

The Church teaches that the priest is configured to Christ the Shepherd in such an intimate way that he can actually act in His person. And I ask you: Where is Jesus most shepherd of His Church but on the cross? And from there He leads us to eternal life with Him.

A thief comes only to steal and slaughter and destroy;
I came so that they might have life and have it more abundantly.
—JOHN 10:10

Saint Paul VI said that "the most effective tool the Prince of Darkness has is to coax us into thinking he does not exist."

He most definitely exists. And Jesus would certainly tell us "I told you so," as He had to face the might of the evil one.

Saint Paul often warned us that our foe is the "realm of darkness"—the forces of evil, Satan himself, who continues to taunt us and ambush the Church. Saint Peter reminds us that Satan "prowls the earth seeking the ruin of souls."

We desperately need the weapons of prayer, reparation, and penance: three forms of ammunition that the devil dreads.

The only protection from Satan is Jesus. Satan is the *second* most powerful force in creation. We know the first.

Let us seek the help of Saint Michael the Archangel in fighting Lucifer's invasion of our world and our lives. Let us fight fire with fire. Beseech the good angel (Saint Michael) to attack and fight off the bad angel (Lucifer).

Jesus assured us that He will remain with us until the end of the world. He also was blunt in acknowledging that "the gates of hell will not prevail against the Church," although, as a wise confessor once whispered to me, that does not mean the devil will ever stop trying.

JULY 21

Simon Peter said in reply, "You are the Messiah, the Son of the living God."
Jesus said to him in reply, "Blessed are you, Simon son of Jonah."
—MATTHEW 16:16-17

We lifelong Catholics sometimes take the pope for granted. Or, even more worrisome, we sometimes consider unity with the Holy Father something of a shackle. It seems that we're a bit embarrassed at times that an essential part of our Catholic Creed is love for and loyalty to the pope.

That's rarely the case with people entering the Church. When I talk with our catechumens and candidates, they are eager for the bond with our Holy Father. This is part of the appeal of Roman Catholicism. Not for some lifelong Catholics. They may look at the pope as the English look at Queen Elizabeth: a great symbol of national unity but with no real authority or say in our lives.

Is that what we think about the pope? That he's just a symbol?

Walker Percy, a renowned Catholic writer, understood the papacy and wrote that the definitive voice in our Catholic faith is our Holy Father. Although we Catholics recognize that popes are sinners just like all of us, we also know that the foibles of the papacy only prove divine guidance over the Church, since God's grace can work in, through, and often in spite of sinful pontiffs.

JULY 22

For the sake of the joy that lay before him he endured the cross, despising its shame, and has taken his seat at the right of the throne of God.

—HEBREWS 12:2

When I was a parish priest, I used to bring Holy Communion to a man, Charlie, who had a neurological disease. He was confined to bed and couldn't move at all. He had a wife who tenderly cared for him.

He couldn't speak, but he could blink his eyes in response to the questions I would pose, and his wife would translate for me. She knew his thoughts and feelings just from the blinking of his eyes.

One day, she sensed by his blinking that he needed a drink of water, and so she went to the kitchen to get him some. I was standing there visiting with him, and I could see that he was getting agitated. This gentleman was always very serene, but something was wrong.

When his wife came back in, I said, "Charlie seems very upset. I think he's worried or bothered by something." She looked at me. Then she looked at the wall. She said, "Oh, you're standing in the wrong place." Wrong place? I thought to myself. "You're blocking his view of the crucifix," she continued.

When I turned around, I saw the crucifix on the wall. It dawned on me that from that bed of suffering, he would gaze constantly at the cross of Christ. And when I blocked his view of the Lord, Charlie became agitated.

There's not a one of us who does not have a worry or adversity or setback or problem or struggle. We sum them all up in one word: the cross. Not a one of us does not have the cross in his or her life. What power comes from keeping our constant gaze on Jesus. What power comes from the invitation from Jesus to be lifted up from the earth with Him on the cross.

JULY 23

The work of each will come to light, for the Day will disclose it.
—I CORINTHIANS 3:13

I remember being a kid in school, and when it would come time for final exams, we used to plead with the teacher: "Would you please tell us some of the questions you're going to ask us on the final exam?"

Well, with Jesus, we don't have to ask. He tells us in the Gospel exactly what He's going to ask us at the final exam, that is, at the end of the world: When I was hungry, did you feed me? When I was thirsty, did you give me drink? When I was naked, did you clothe me? When I was sick, did you visit me? When I was a stranger, did you welcome me? When I was in prison, did you come see me? When He comes as Christ the King at that cosmic final exam, our eternal salvation will depend on our answers.

One of the times the power of that Last Judgment most clearly dawned on me was during the conclave of 2013, when I had the honor of being a member of the College of Cardinals.

For most of the conclave, it was very prayerful and reflective, and so it gave me time to look around the Sistine Chapel. Michelangelo's dramatic representation of the Last Judgment caught my imagination, and I said to myself, "Timothy, this is very important what you're doing." My God, never did I think I'd be in a conclave to elect a pope. But as I looked at his depiction of the Last Judgment, I realized that when I appear before Jesus, the King, at the end of time, He's going to ask: What did you do for the least of these? And it is the answer to that question on which the salvation of my soul will depend.

The fervent prayer of a righteous person is very powerful.
—JAMES 5:16

Saint Charbel Makhlouf was a monk and priest from Lebanon whose profound spirituality touched hearts the world over with the gospel message that interior communion with God is not only possible but the privilege of all Christians. He didn't leave any writing behind, but he is known for his example of prayer. People go to him in times of need. And he's a miracle worker. Sometimes he's called the Padre Pio of Lebanon. On a visit to Lebanon, I was flabbergasted to find that he is so popular there. He has a magnetic attraction for the faithful even though we don't know that much about him.

Sometime after that trip, Father James Ferreira and I were caught in a vicious snowstorm. We were driving home from a priest's funeral, and we thought that we might soon be going to our own funerals. Our car was fishtailing; other cars were swerving and ending up on the side of the road. We really were scared. We decided to pray to Saint Charbel to get us through the snowstorm. At a certain point, we realized that we wouldn't be able to make it. We had to abandon the car and walk through the storm for a mile until we got to our destination. Saint Charbel didn't come through that time. Still, we were safe.

The next day, I called Bishop Greg Mansour, the bishop of the Eparchy of Saint Maron in Brooklyn, and told him I was disappointed by Charbel because he didn't help us in this snowstorm. To which Bishop Mansour replied, "Oh, I know the problem. Charbel is from Lebanon. He comes through in sandstorms."

Saints show us that though we don't always get the answer from God that we hoped for, God is always there with us. In snowstorms and sandstorms.

Mary, Undoer
of Knots

Remember the headlines in the sports pages that used to get chuckles? "Perpetual Help Trounces Immaculate Conception" or "Fatima Devastates Lourdes." It seems as if the many titles rendered to Mary, the Mother of Jesus, were in competition.

I'm always fascinated by her different titles in the Church. Our love for her and trust in her know no bounds.

Just when you thought you had heard them all, here's a new one: *Mary, Undoer of Knots.*

Think for a moment of a particular struggle in your life, a knot that seems impossible to undo. And now go to Our Lady and ask her intercession to help undo that knot.

As the prayer goes, "Remember, O Most gracious Virgin Mary, that never was it known, that anyone who fled to thy protection, implored thy help, or sought thine intercession was left unaided."

Mary, Undoer of Knots, pray for us!

JULY 26

The good leave an inheritance to their children's children,
but the wealth of the sinner is stored up for the just.
—PROVERBS 13:22

I often think about my grandmothers. Though I hardly have any recollection, sadly, of my grandfathers, I savor vivid, tender, and grateful memories of my two grandmothers. I fondly recall their laughter, their hugs, their visits, their baking, their hospitality, and their stories.

Grandmas and grandpas are among God's choicest gifts to us. They bring us love, joy, peace, and goodness.

We'd be in a big mess without our grandparents, because they often have a tremendous impact on the spiritual and moral development of their grandchildren. Faith is passed on to children by their grandparents. How often it is that grandparents teach their grandkids their prayers, Bible stories, the lives of the saints, and the rudiments of the faith. How often is it that grandparents take their grandchildren to Sunday Mass or sacrifice to see that they receive a Catholic education?

As we lovingly think of our grandparents, we lovingly and often think of Joachim and Anne, the parents of Our Lady, and Jacob, the father of Saint Joseph—all grandparents of Jesus. The annual reading of His genealogy reminds us that He had a family, He had relatives, He came from the line of David! And what a family He had.

Grandparents are a significant part of our lives. Grandma and Grandpa mirror the unconditional love of God to their grandkids. Thank you, grandmas and grandpas! Thank God for our families.

Why do you not understand what I am saying?
Because you cannot bear to hear my word.
—JOHN 8:43

It has been said that the best way to love someone is to tell that person the truth. Today, I'm afraid, we are reluctant to speak the truth for fear that it might sting, anger, or hurt. We seem only to want to affirm, condone, console, and approve.

The Church, though, is a true friend and always tells the truth, even if it hurts.

To a society that seeks security in weapons and war, the Church speaks the age-old truth that peace can come only with justice.

To a culture that believes it has the right to sex whenever and however we want, the Church teaches that sex is so sacred that it is intended only between a man and woman united in lifelong, life-giving, faithful marriage.

To those who would prefer to ignore the cries of the poor, the Church reminds us of the moral imperative of justice and compassion.

To a society that prizes wealth, possessions, and prestige, the Church dares to speak the truth that real treasure comes in giving, sharing, serving, and selflessness.

Many are stung, angry, and hurt over this truth, and so they search out other "friends" who will tell them what they want to hear.

But the Church teaches that love and truth must go together. Ask Jesus. He is the truth, and He teaches, "The truth will set you free."

JULY 28

I am the Lord; there is no savior but me.
—ISAIAH 43:11

Vatican II teaches that it's possible in certain conditions to be saved without hearing the gospel, but it also clearly teaches (*Lumen Gentium*) that those conditions are not met often and that "very often" human beings close their hearts to the grace of God, influenced by the culture, its lies, and our own sin.

However, the Church has exactly what we need: Jesus Christ, our Savior, who offers us eternal life.

We shrug and say, "No thanks. Who needs a Savior? I can save myself. I don't need the Church, the sacraments, or the mercy of Jesus, since I'm automatically assured of heaven. Leave me alone."

Understand that eternity is not a "sure thing." It is a sure thing only if we admit that we need Jesus as our Savior and live faithfully in His family.

We ignore the clear, cogent teaching of Jesus and His Church at our everlasting peril. At the moment of our death, we will stand before our eternal judge, knowing that heaven is not assured. This awesome experience will happen again when He comes in glory at the Last Judgment.

Like it or not, that's the message of the gospel.

How do I share in Jesus's gift of eternal life? In and through the Church!

That's the invitation of the gospel.

JULY 29

Venerable
Nelson Baker

They called him the American version of Saint Vincent de Paul because of his indefatigable charity for the neglected and marginalized of society.

Born in Buffalo in 1842, Nelson Baker served in the New York Militia during the Civil War. Afterward, he opened a feed and grain business, but he felt something was missing and gradually discerned his vocation as a priest. Selling his half of the business, he entered the seminary.

His first—and only—assignment was to St. Patrick's parish and orphanage for abandoned boys.

Using his own money and donations from people throughout the country, young Father Baker not only kept this boys' home open but opened a working home for teenagers and young adults. In addition, he established a hospital and an outreach program for single moms and women with difficult pregnancies.

When the Great Depression arrived in 1929, the hungry, sick, and homeless found a smile and a welcome embrace from Father Baker. Local officials estimate that his mission fed over a million people, clothed half a million, and cared for a quarter million sick in the 1930s.

Yet he gave all the glory to God, saying that his heroic charity flowed from and depended on a faith expressed in prayer. He unfailingly prayed to Jesus through Mary, especially under her title of Our Lady of Victory.

It seems to me we very much need the example and heavenly intercession right now of Venerable Nelson Baker, who had a heart like that of Christ Himself.

Jesus said to her, "Did I not tell you that if you believe
you will see the glory of God?"
—JOHN 11:40

Isn't it supposed to be the essence of the "good news" that we have a Savior who came to take away the sins of the world?

The heart of discipleship is our humble acknowledgment that we are sinners and the admission that we have committed specific sins. That occurs so tangibly in confession.

Many Catholics think they don't need to confess sins to a priest. This gets us right to the core of the sacramental nature of the Church. If we do not need the sacrament, where will that ultimately take us? Why would we need the water of baptism to wash us clean? Why do we need His body and blood to nourish our souls? Why do we need the Church? It's just between God and me, isn't it?

For some, it is. But not for Catholics. During Sunday Mass, as we hear the Gospels teaching how Jesus reached the Samaritan woman through the imagery of water; how He healed the blind man through the sign of mud, paste, and the anointing of his eyes; and how He raised Lazarus with His words, we profess our faith that the Lord still comes to us in tender signs such as water, words, anointing, bread, and wine.

The Sacrament of Penance is a gift, not a burden; a joy, not a drag.

To be a sinner is our great curse; to admit it is our great grace.

Nowhere is that more powerfully evident than in the Sacrament of Penance.

JULY 31

Feast of Saint Ignatius of Loyola

Saint Ignatius of Loyola, the founder of the Society of Jesus, was born in 1491 in Spain. As a young man, he fought as an officer in the Spanish army. When he was wounded and bedridden for several months, Ignatius began to read about the life of Christ. It was then that he experienced a conversion that eventually led to his founding of the Jesuits.

Ignatius taught that everything his spiritual sons and daughters would undertake should be driven by the need to form people to know, love, and serve God and His people in this life and then to live forever with the Lord in heaven.

Daily do I witness the evidence of the effectiveness of Jesuit universities. I meet their proud alumni in the classrooms of our Catholic schools, as nurses in emergency rooms, in the boardrooms of corporations eager to improve life in our community, on the front lines promoting the culture of life and battling injustice and poverty, raising families, engaged in scholarship and in the missions of Africa—all for the greater glory of God.

But with a nod to Saint Ignatius, the real evidence of the Jesuits' sterling effectiveness will be visible only when we reach heaven and there meet more alumni than ever, whose blessed years in those universities taught them to be a person for God—a man or woman for others—always mindful of our eternal destiny.

Ad majorem Dei gloriam—"to the greater glory of God!"

AUGUST I

For this is love, that we walk according to
his commandments.

—2 JOHN 1:6

A genuine problem exists in contemporary Catholic life. There is a gap between what the Church teaches and what many people in our culture, in our society, and even within our Church believe or do not believe.

There seem to be two different debates today: One argues that the Church is outmoded and needs to change its "old teaching" to conform with the needs of our modern generation, and the other argues that we need to change our behavior and values to conform with the teachings of Jesus and His Church.

I know I must stick with the latter. When I read the Bible, I ask how I can change my life to conform to the teaching of God's Word, not how I can revise the message to make me more comfortable. When I read the catechism, I try to refine my beliefs to make sure they are in obedience to the timeless truths of the Church, not critique the doctrine to see how it fails to soothe my modern ears. When I examine my conscience at night, I attempt to assess my conduct in light of the commandments, the Beatitudes, and the moral tradition, not to alter those expectations to justify my behavior.

Christ calls us to change our lives and our attitudes and to bring them into conformity with Church teaching. Instead of pushing the Church aside or walking away, we listen to Jesus, who always urges us to conversion of heart and interior reform.

AUGUST 2

But you are "a chosen race, a royal priesthood, a holy nation, a people
of his own, so that you may announce the praises" of him
who called you out of darkness into his wonderful light.
—I PETER 2:9

When I was studying Church history, I took a course titled "The Church in the French Revolution," and my professor lectured on how "secularism" began to be the new value system for the Western world. He defined secularism as our ability to get along just fine without God, our attempt to find all meaning and purpose in earthly life, and our drive to restrict faith and religion to the private, personal sphere. To the question "Is this all there is?" secularism replies, "Yes."

I am afraid many of us have become secularists.

A secular society celebrates Mardi Gras but not Lent, Christmas without Advent, and Halloween but not All Saints' Day and presumes salvation without conversion and repentance.

The syndicated columnist Cal Thomas once wrote that contemporary society is still worshipping a golden calf, just as the Israelites did at the foot of Mount Sinai. "Many prefer," he observed, "to worship things and are slaves to feelings, thus dulling their senses to the wisdom of the ages." He wrote that everywhere there is a "rejection of what previous generations called social norms, decency, virtue, values, propriety, modesty, integrity, and standards" and that "materialism has dulled our senses to anything that does not produce pleasure."

Secularism, idolatry, materialism—call it what you want. The fact is, we need Christ.

We need to be different in our values, our priorities, our behavior, and our speech. We Catholics don't want to be "just like everybody else."

AUGUST 3

I am the gate.
Whoever enters through me will be saved.
—JOHN 10:9

The liturgy of Baptism reminds us that parents are the first and best teachers of the faith. The Magisterium of the Church instructs us that parents are the primary catechists. And experience tells us that attempting to teach the doctrines, prayers, values, principles, virtues, and morals of our faith to children whose parents couldn't care less is nearly futile.

For example, a child who hears at school that weekly worship at Sunday Mass is a necessary part of Catholic life but whose parents prefer sleeping in on Sunday morning is confused, to say the least.

A child who is instructed in class that the Son of God teaches love, goodness, and mercy and then goes home to watch his folks yell and scream at each other is conflicted.

A child who hears at religion class that the Bible is the greatest book ever, that Jesus on the cross is the most wonderful act of love ever, and that Mary is our mother, but who cannot find the Scriptures, a crucifix, or an image of our Blessed Mother in his home wonders just who is telling the truth.

Children unfortunately can pick up from the family the message, "Well, religion is nice, and yes, we are Catholics, but it's hardly the most important thing in life, and we cannot let it inconvenience us or get in the way."

Jesus doesn't get in the way. He *is* the way.

AUGUST 4

Feast of
Saint John Vianney

For forty-one years, the French village of Ars had a legendary pastor, or curé, by the name of John Vianney.

Have you ever heard about Father Vianney's arrival in Ars? He got lost in the hills getting there, only to come across a little fellow on the path.

"Little boy," asked the curé, "do you know how to get to Ars?"

"Sure," the child replied. "I live there."

"Well," remarked the curé, "I tell you what: You show me how to get to Ars, and I'll show you how to get to heaven."

John Vianney preached with intensity and directness. Soon after arriving in Ars, he noticed that Sunday observance was not what it should have been in that village. He told the villagers: "You keep on working, but what you earn ruins your soul and your body. If we ask those who work on Sunday, 'What have you been doing?' they might answer: 'I have been selling my soul to the devil, crucifying Our Lord, and renouncing my baptism.'"

Hearing that, we may immediately protest: Life is more complicated now, and our culture makes it necessary for some to work. Fair enough, but Saint John Vianney's words remind us that we should at least feel a sense of urgency about Sunday observance. The words *Sunday obligation* may have disappeared from our vocabulary, but they have not disappeared from the Ten Commandments or from the *Catechism of the Catholic Church*!

If we do not spare an hour or so to worship God, does He really occupy the proper place in our lives? If the Lord's Day is apparently no different from any other day, can we say that He is truly Lord of our life?

We all need to rededicate ourselves to Sunday! For if we let our Sunday observance slide, how can we hope to follow the Lord's will in more difficult things?

AUGUST 5

Such, you must know, is wisdom to your soul. If you find it, you will have a future, and your hope will not be cut off.
—PROVERBS 24:14

The belief in the dignity of the human person is certainly not unique to us Catholics. It characterizes the values of many. It's a bedrock principle of this great republic founded on certain self-evident, inalienable rights.

Yet daily, we see a tension or tug-of-war between the within and the without, between the substance and the superficial.

Inside is the mind, the heart, the soul. In our interior life, we locate reason, thought, and love. We find character, value, and virtue. And we nurture, strengthen, and develop this interior life by studying, reasoning, questioning, wondering, and praying, for the Lord has told us that He dwells within the heart and soul of the believer.

The outside is not as substantial, for "out there" tends to emphasize the superficial over the substantial; urges rather than values; impulsive decisions rather than thoughtful, rational discernment; the immediate over the lasting; and the passing rather than the eternal.

Choosing the interior and acknowledging the dignity of the human person over the exterior ensures that we have gained not only knowledge but wisdom.

AUGUST 6

Feast of the Transfiguration

Summer, like the other seasons, lasts about ninety days, beginning June 21 and concluding September 21. If you count, you will find that the midpoint of summer is today, August 6.

It's no wonder we celebrate the Transfiguration at summer's halftime.

At the Transfiguration, Jesus goes up Mount Tabor, taking with Him three of His Apostles—Peter, James, and John—and there He is made so bright and dazzling that the three men can hardly look at Him.

The Gospels use the Transfiguration to teach us that Jesus is the light of a world that is often dark and gloomy. In His splendor, His divinity is dramatically apparent. In fact, the Apostles even hear the voice of God the Father thunder, "This is my beloved Son." It's easy to believe that Jesus is divine and the Light of the World at the Transfiguration!

But Jesus was also a wise rabbi who wanted to remind His three students that times would come when it would not be easy to have faith in Him. One of those times would come on another hilltop, this one called Calvary.

These radiant days of summer can be a carefree, enjoyable time of vacation, family, friends, and relaxation. They can be a Mount Tabor experience—a time of unity and grand experiences! Save these memories to draw upon when Calvary comes in the slush and dreariness of the midwinters of our lives.

AUGUST 7

Put on then, as God's chosen ones, holy and beloved, heartfelt compassion, kindness, humility, gentleness, and patience.
—COLOSSIANS 3:12

Every time we stumble and fall and then pick ourselves up again, we find ourselves with an admirable sense of zeal, eager to do more things for God: I will pray more, I will read the Bible more, I will stop skipping Mass, I will go to confession more frequently, and so on.

However, we have to be careful. Life is not so much about us doing a lot of things to impress Jesus or to earn His grace. Life is about opening ourselves in humility so that He can do a lot more for us.

It's simply a matter of motive. Praying more or doing more penance to win salvation or to court favor from God is impossible! God's love and His salvation are pure gifts, and there's not a thing we can do to earn or merit them.

But if our motive is to accept the Lord's gracious invitation to "come back to me with all your heart" and to open ourselves humbly to His saving grace, bring on the acts of prayer, penance, and charity!

Why? Because they then become means of opening ourselves and our hearts to the Lord's grace, mercy, and salvation.

So go ahead: Do more prayer and penance! Just make sure your motive is pure. We're not doing it for Jesus; we're doing it with Him. We're not boasting of all we can do for Him; we're letting Him know that without Him we can do nothing.

AUGUST 8

And we have this confidence in him, that if we ask anything
according to his will, he hears us.
—1 JOHN 5:14

Prayer is the ultimate source of our strength. The Church was
founded by Jesus as a reply to the trusting prayer of His disciples.

What did the bewildered, scared, confused Apostles do upon
Our Lord's Ascension into heaven? They took our Blessed
Mother Mary, locked themselves in a room, and prayed! Their
prayers required perseverance, for it took nine days for Jesus to
reply. The response He gave to that patient prayer of His mother
and best friends was beyond their most exalted hopes: the Holy
Spirit!

That's what prayer can accomplish.

On a beach vacation with my fellow priests one year, I saw
an older priest sitting alone outside. He was looking at the couples and families walking by, and I felt sorry for him, thinking
he was lonely. I went to him, but as I approached, I saw his lips
moving as if he were in conversation with a friend. His eyes
were closed even though he was not asleep. He hardly looked
lonely at all, because a smile showed on his face.

Then I saw the rosary in his hand and the breviary (a priest's
book of daily readings and prayers) open on his lap, and I realized he was enjoying the best company of all.

AUGUST 9

And Mary kept all these things,
reflecting on them in her heart.

—LUKE 2:19

Haunting. That's the only word I can find to describe it.

Many years ago, the archbishop of Nagasaki pleaded at the United Nations for an end to all nuclear weapons. He was pastor of the tiny Catholic flock of a Japanese city where 75,000 people were reduced to ash by a single atomic blast on August 9, 1945. On that day the archbishop was still a baby in his mother's womb and survived because she was far enough away from ground zero.

He brought with him to the UN something else from Nagasaki that survived: the head of the statue of Mary Immaculate.

She is scarred and singed badly, and her crystal eyes were melted by the hellish blast. All that remains are two empty, blackened sockets.

I've knelt before many images of Mary before: Our Mother of Perpetual Help, the Pietà, the Virgin of Guadalupe, and Our Lady of Lourdes, to name a few. But I've never experienced the dread and revulsion I did when the archbishop showed us the head of Our Lady of Nagasaki.

We traditionally crown the Blessed Mother's head with flowers and sing songs of veneration. At Nagasaki, she *absorbed* the radiation, the incinerating heat, and the suffering of her children.

Like any good mother, Mary absorbs our sorrows, our worries, our sickness, and our fears. She takes them—and us—to the only one who can do anything about them: her Son.

AUGUST 10

Come, children, listen to me; I will teach you fear of the Lord.
—PSALM 34:12

Today I want to consider the most effective and potent religious formation anywhere, anytime, anyplace.

I see it at our parishes as I stand at the entrance to the Church ready to begin Sunday Mass, as Dad dips his little boy's fingers into the holy water font and helps him trace the Sign of the Cross, or as Mom walks with her little girl up to Holy Communion.

I watch it with admiration as I have supper with a family, and Mom and Dad say grace before meals and a little later lead their children in prayer before they get into bed.

There it is again when Dad brings his teenage son with him to serve food at a soup kitchen and Mom takes her seventh-grade daughter with her as she takes Holy Communion to the homebound.

I see it as parents help their kids with homework, not just assisting with math and spelling but asking about religion class.

The greatest classroom for teaching the faith is the home; the primary and most important catechists of all are parents.

No Catholic school and no religious education program can match the example and instruction of parents in the home. They are partners with our parents, not replacements. When they work in partnership with the parents and when the lessons of the Bible and the catechism are reinforced, supported, and lived out at home, miracles will happen.

AUGUST 11

Strive to enter through the narrow door, for many, I tell you,
will attempt to enter but will not be strong enough.
—LUKE 13:24

In Luke's Gospel, the people ask Jesus a very significant question: "Will only a few people be saved?"

In other words, is it easy to get to heaven? Is salvation assured? Can I relax and take eternal life for granted?

Today we seem to give a thundering yes to those questions.

Jesus tells us that "many will attempt to enter but will not get through." He speaks of the door to heaven being locked, with a lot of folks still clamoring outside.

We know that God our Father wants us all to spend eternity with Him in heaven (theologians call this the "universal salvific will of the Lord"). He invites us to eternal life. He tells us how to get there. He sent His Son to bring us with Him to heaven because we can't get there on our own.

But God respects our freedom to turn down His invitation. Sadly, many do.

Thus the existence of both hell and purgatory.

The Church is the community of those longing for heaven. Its mission is to unite its members with Jesus and make the journey of life in, with, and through Him back to God.

We fail that mission if we ignore the words of Jesus, believe instead that getting to heaven is a snap, and presume that we can get there easily and all by ourselves.

AUGUST 12

*For the Son of Man has come to seek
and to save what was lost.*

—LUKE 19:10

"I just can't see it," the young man confided in me. We've had a lot of conversations about the fact that he's struggling with his faith.

"Why in the world," he went on, "would I put absolute trust and confidence in a man who lived two thousand years ago? I can admire Him, learn about Him, and even want to imitate Him, but why would I give Him my life and believe that He's my Lord and Savior? He's not around anymore!"

Sounds logical, doesn't it? A lot of people say that. They readily admit that Christ is worthy of study and emulation, a wonderful teacher, but He's gone, He left us.

What do we say to that claim?

We say, "He's with us everywhere!"

The good news is not that Jesus left us and went to heaven but that He is still powerfully with us!

How? He lives through the Holy Spirit, in our prayers, as we speak to Jesus, at the Mass, in the seven sacraments of the Church, and in a special way in the Holy Eucharist.

Simply put, Jesus is as alive, as active, and as accessible to us now as He was when He walked the shores of the Sea of Galilee. We do not worship one who was but one who is and ever will be.

The wonder of Christ is not that He left us but that He always remains with us. Space and time have no control over Him.

May the Lord direct your hearts to the love of God
and to the endurance of Christ.
—2 THESSALONIANS 3:5

Several years ago, I had one of those rare but dramatic moments of divine illumination. I had just finished celebrating the Sacrament of Confirmation for about two dozen special needs children. The president of Ireland had attended that Mass and was very moved by the ceremony. She graciously asked to meet each of the children and their families.

As I began the introductions, I took her to our first child. "Madam President," I began, "this is a wonderful Down syndrome young man."

The proud parents, with all the courtesy and respect possible, wisely and properly corrected me. "Oh, no. . . . This is Mark, who happens to have Down syndrome."

I was given a great reminder that day: Mark's identity is a child of God, made in God's own image and likeness, redeemed by the precious blood of God's only Son. Mark happens to have a condition called Down syndrome, but he is hardly identified by the condition that he has.

This is so for all of us. We are not special because of what we do or what we have. We are special because we are God's children. We belong to Him. He loves us simply because we are.

And behold, I am with you always,
until the end of the age.
—MATTHEW 28:20

In recent memory, all the occupants of the Chair of Saint Peter have been virtuous, good, even saintly men.

Only the naïve will consider that statement a no-brainer. Why? Because this has not always been the case. We have had more than one bad pope! We have had philanderers, tyrants, and bloodthirsty rogues.

Come to think about it, the first one, Saint Peter, was no gem, as he denied even knowing Jesus, three times, at the very moment the Lord could most have used a loyal friend.

What's remarkable, of course, is not that there have been knavish, scandalous popes—there sure have been—but that the Church keeps going in spite of them.

No surprise there if you trust the promise Jesus made that "I am with you always, until the end of the age."

In our time, though, the Successors of Saint Peter have been men of sanctity and honor, real luminaries for the Church and the world.

I'm just thinking of the pontiffs in my lifetime: Pius XII, Saint John XXIII, Saint Paul VI, John Paul I, Saint John Paul II, Benedict XVI, and Francis, all wonderful pastors. But face it: We've had quite a few popes throughout our 2,000-year run who have been real lemons, hardly worthy of the high dignity of the office. Thank God Jesus is in charge!

But in our time, we've had great, holy, and good popes. These are the good old days for us as Catholics.

AUGUST 15

Feast of the Assumption
of Our Blessed Mother

As a kid, I used to know summer had reached its peak on about August 15: the cantaloupe, watermelon, corn on the cob, and tomatoes were at their best, the pennant race was heating up, the sun was hottest, and, alas, school was not far off.

Good cooks tell me that August is their favorite time of year because of the fullness of the harvest, when the life-giving purpose of the earth is so evident. As Pope Francis eloquently pointed out in *Laudato Si,* his encyclical on the environment, when we treat the earth with tenderness, care, and respect, she returns the favor, for God made the earth to bring and sustain life.

No wonder Mother Church has us turn to Mary's Assumption at this height of summer. She is, after all, the "peak" of God's creation. She is the culmination of the Father's intended harvest, giving birth to "the fruit of your womb," Our Lord and Savior Jesus Christ. As August shows us God's creation at its best, with sun, flowers, lavish vegetation, the fullness of fruits and vegetables, the summer harvest in, and light and life in abundance, so Mary is the Lord's creation at its best.

In bringing her, body and soul, to be with Him forever in heaven, the Lord not only rewards her but powerfully reminds us of the harvest that awaits us. She shared in the full fruits of her Son's triumph over sin and death. Where she has gone, we hope to go. As she escaped eternal death, so will we. As she is united, body and soul, with Jesus forever in heaven, so will we be. What God has done for her, He intends to do for us.

A blessed height of summer! Enjoy the watermelon, tomatoes, and corn on the cob.

AUGUST 16

The husband is head of his wife just as Christ is head
of the church, he himself the savior of the body.
—EPHESIANS 5:23

I once met with a group of young people years ago and posited the question: "Who do you think has a more exalted, uplifting, noble view of sex: *Playboy* founder Hugh Hefner or the Catholic Church?"

Everybody had a different viewpoint. But after about an hour, a consensus seemed to have developed: Hugh Hefner's promiscuous "anything goes" mentality about sex had led to disastrous consequences, such as the objectification of women, the reduction of sex to a contact sport instead of an act of love, abortion, venereal disease, AIDS, divorce, and the disappearance of reverence, mystery, and romance from sex.

In the Bible, God compared His love for us to the passionate attraction of a young man courting a beautiful young woman, and He told us that His relationship with us is as strong, romantic, and tender as that between a husband and a wife. Saint Paul tells us that Christ loves His Church (us) just as a groom loves his bride.

The group ended up agreeing: If you want a freeing, exciting, respectful, uplifting approach to sex, look to the Church, not Hugh Hefner!

Sexual love between a man and a woman in marriage is an actual hint of the love God has for us and as such is a tremendous gift. This gift is freeing, not enslaving; selfless, not selfish; giving life, not just satisfying an urge. As with any gift, it requires care, reverence, and proper use.

His fame spread to all of Syria, and they brought to him all who were sick with various diseases and racked with pain, those who were possessed, lunatics, and paralytics, and he cured them.
—MATTHEW 4:24

The sick were the favorites of Jesus, and so they are the favorites of His Church. Our priests, deacons, extraordinary Eucharistic ministers, parish nurses, and pastoral ministers continue the mission of Christ to care for the sick. Our Catholic hospitals and healthcare systems continue the solicitude Jesus showed for the sick, aged, and suffering. So many of our dedicated physicians, nurses, pharmacists, social workers, and healthcare professionals are Catholic and look to their faith to provide meaning and motive to their work. How grateful we are to them.

Our beloved sick, we hope, realize that they are at the heart of the Church. You may be confined at home, in a wheelchair, in a sickbed, in a hospital, or in a nursing home, but you are strong in faith, persevering in prayer, and a tremendous reservoir of inspiration and love for the Church. Jesus and Mary love you, and so do we.

We honor ourselves as children of God, made in His image, endowed with inalienable rights and duties, destined for eternity. Thus do we treat ourselves with immense reverence and allow only words and actions to flow from us that are worthy of our birthright.

What I believe about myself, I believe of others, and I will treat others only as the reflection of the divine they truly are. Every one of us matters. No person is defined by someone else's choices. No life exists only as a means to someone else's ends.

AUGUST 18

And the prayer of faith will save the sick person,
and the Lord will raise him up.

—JAMES 5:15

I once went to visit an "old married couple." We had chatted often on the telephone as I would inquire about the wife's health. She had been in and out of the hospital battling cancer. The husband's arthritis was nearly crippling, and I could not imagine how he could give her the daily care she needed. But he would have it no other way, as they'd been at it "for better or worse, in sickness and in health," for sixty-two years.

He had just finished bathing her and medicating some awful bedsores that had developed, and he asked if I could wait just ten minutes or so.

I could hear her struggle as he got her clothes on; I could hear him coax her to lift her arms, then her feet, so he could finish dressing her.

Finally, he called for me to come in. She had declined so much since I had last seen her, and I could sense her agony and frailty.

Nevertheless, we had a grand visit, laughed a lot, prayed, and chatted. No words of complaint, no regrets. They spoke of faith, the cross, and how they appreciated visits from the Eucharistic minister and the parish priest.

I saw in his care for her Veronica soothing the face of Christ. I saw in him the love that Christ has for us.

For you were once darkness, but now you are light in the Lord.
Live as children of light.
—EPHESIANS 5:8

In the Gospel of Matthew, Jesus said, "You are the light of the world."

In the good old days, we called that giving a good example. Today we gussy it up a bit and call it giving witness.

It comes down to the same thing: We act on the basis of our belief. Our faith is not compartmentalized. It profoundly affects everything we say, think, and do.

When I was growing up, we always dressed special for Sunday Mass. Dad would wear a coat and tie. One Sunday, he told my sister and me: "Your religion is not like my coat and tie. I put this coat and tie on for Sunday Mass, then put it away the rest of the week in the closet. Our faith is something we wear every second, every day. We never take it off!"

Dad was talking about Catholic values in action.

At the core of our very being is the conviction that our faith has an impact on everything we do, that the values, principles, and beliefs we cherish are not limited to an hour on Sunday morning but affect a person's entire life.

Saint Paul VI said that people learn more from witness than from words. Remember when Saint John Paul II visited his would-be assassin in prison? He embraced, forgave, and blessed the man who had shot him. That action taught more about mercy than any sermon or book.

That's what being a "light of the world" means. That's putting your Catholic faith into action.

AUGUST 20

Do not fear nor be dismayed, for the Lord, your God,
is with you wherever you go.
—JOSHUA 1:9

Jesus knows that there are times in our lives when we are confused, pained, or hopeless, but what He did on the road to Emmaus and in the Upper Room, He does with us every day.

We can learn so much from that first Easter day. In the glory of His risen body, He first revealed Himself to the faithful women who came to the tomb and to Peter, the first of the Apostles. Then He opened the eyes of the men on the road to Emmaus.

In the evening, He was with the disciples who didn't go into the night, who didn't leave the Upper Room. They weren't perfect, they did not understand everything, they weren't without doubts and failings, but they were where they were supposed to be—together, awaiting confirmation of the astonishing news brought by Saint Mary Magdalene that the Lord was indeed risen!

We all have a little bit of these first Church members within us. Fear, anxiety, sin, and uncertainty can grip even the most faithful Catholic. There are those trying heroically to remain with the Church, even if behind locked doors for fear of what it might mean to be known as a follower of Christ. Others, despite many difficulties, strive to remain in the open, in the company of the saints, as the first Christians called one another.

Jesus wants us to know that through all of our difficulties and fears and even despite our sins, He has never left our side.

AUGUST 21

Our Lady of Knock

My love for Ireland results in large part from the Irish Sisters of Mercy who taught me when I was in school. They spoke about the Marian shrines of Lourdes, Fatima, and Guadalupe. But they didn't speak much about Knock, Ireland, perhaps because they felt they shouldn't be pushing Ireland's devotion.

Yet I was accompanied by the sisters on my first visit there in 1973. And that was where I got my devotion to Our Lady of Knock.

It is said that a good mom shows up in tough situations, and in 1879 the people of Ireland needed a visit. It was a troubled time there, and people felt hopeless. Yet what moved me is the fact that she showed up with her husband, Saint Joseph. And she was there with the Beloved Disciple, John, whom Jesus entrusted to her. And they were in adoration of the Lamb of God. The vision is heavily Eucharistic.

One distinguishing thing about this apparition is that the Blessed Virgin didn't say anything to the fifteen people who witnessed it. Instead, it was pure silence. Of course, as the joke goes, perhaps Our Lady didn't say anything because with the Irish there, she couldn't get a word in edgewise!

Yet her maternal presence was so consoling. It was the consolation of being in their mother's presence. Simply her presence. It teaches us of family. Of silence. Of Eucharist. Of marriage. Of discipleship. Our Lady of Knock is a powerful catechesis.

AUGUST 22

*Be self-possessed in all circumstances; put up with hardship;
perform the work of an evangelist; fulfill your ministry.*
—2 TIMOTHY 4:5

My grandma used to say, "When you feel helpless over your own problems, help somebody else with theirs." Not bad!

Saint Paul wrote that we are compelled by the charity of Christ. Charity and love certainly have compelled people of faith.

I recently heard of a hardened convict who was condemned to life in prison without parole for a particularly hideous crime. He could spend his days in anger, hatred, and violence in jail. Instead, believe it or not, he makes teddy bears, which are distributed to police departments to be given to children in traumatic situations.

We can become absorbed, overwhelmed, or crushed by our worries and problems, or we can go to help somebody else in need.

At the Visitation, our Blessed Mother did just that, and by doing so, she became the first missionary. Saint Paul VI called her "the star of evangelization," as she literally brought the glad tidings of our salvation to Elizabeth. She was eager to share the news that the Savior is here.

That missionary enterprise is explosive; it's contagious! Elizabeth hears it, and even the baby in her womb senses it. This good news cannot be stopped: Gabriel, Mary, Elizabeth, John the Baptist, the man in prison, you, and I all continue it.

Nobody can keep Christ to himself. As soon as we accept Him, we must share Him.

My grace is sufficient for you, for power
is made perfect in weakness.
—2 CORINTHIANS 12:9

Our faith is *internal*. Jesus taught that "the Kingdom of God is within you." The essence of our faith is an interior and sincere acceptance of Christ as Our Lord and Savior and of all the truths He and His Church have revealed. The soul is nourished by this faith.

Yet our faith is also *external*, because our internal acceptance of Christ has profound exterior effects. Thus, as we internally profess our faith in the Eucharist, we are moved to manifest that faith externally, especially in the sacraments, in which God freely gives us a share in His new life.

We call this share we have in His life *grace*.

Forget about earning, achieving, or meriting this grace. It's a pure gift!

God gives us this grace in Baptism.

God nourishes this grace in the Holy Eucharist. As earthly food nourishes the body, heavenly food—Holy Communion— feeds the soul.

God strengthens this life in Confirmation. Again, look at the word: Through the outpouring of the Holy Spirit, God confirms the grace He lavished upon us at Baptism.

And don't forget, God restores His grace in the Sacrament of Penance when we profess sadness for our sins.

God desperately wants us to share in this life of grace. His Son told us, "I came so that they might have life and have it more abundantly."

And He invites us to share in this fullness with Him forever in heaven.

And when I am lifted up from the earth,
I will draw everyone to myself.
—JOHN 12:32

As I've mentioned before, I enjoy my regular visits doing prison ministry. During one visit to a men's prison, something happened that I'd like to share with you.

Before Mass that day, I noticed a little disturbance in the sanctuary. I could see that one of the prisoners was kneeling under the cross. He was whispering something to Jesus. He had his face near Christ's feet and was kissing them. When I asked the guard what was going on, he said, "Well, we don't know, but we can't have him up there while you're saying Mass. I'll ask him to move."

Upon further reflection, though, I asked the guard to allow the man to stay where he was. That guy, who might not have had much hope, was literally clinging to the cross of Christ. That prisoner, I would propose to you, knew the meaning of what Jesus said: "When I am lifted up from the earth, I will draw everyone to myself."

What did Jesus mean when He said He must be lifted up? Well, He was talking about being lifted up on the cross. He also was talking about being lifted up during His Resurrection as well as being lifted up for His Ascension.

But Jesus lifts us up as well. He lifts us up out of discouragement and out of sin.

Finally, He has been lifted up so that He will raise us up to eternal life.

Once you were "no people" but now you are God's people;
you "had not received mercy" but now you have received mercy.
—I PETER 2:10

After leaving the Church for nearly three decades, a woman I know returned. What brought her back after a quarter century of searching, doubt, study, prayer, and membership in other churches is that for the Catholic Church, certain matters are nonnegotiable. In matters of faith, she knows that the Creed we pray at every Sunday Mass expertly sums up the nonnegotiables in what we believe. In morals and the way we behave, she has concluded that the nonnegotiable is the innate, inherent, inviolable value and dignity of every single human life.

She attributes this discovery to Saint John Paul II. At the time of his death, she began reading his teachings and distilled all of his moral legacy to one nonnegotiable: that every human life is an unrepeatable miracle, created in the very image and likeness of God, and thus deserves dignity, protection, and respect from the moment of conception until the advent of natural death.

Thus, she claimed that the Church is "batting a thousand" on life issues: The baby in the womb, the hungry child, the expectant mother with no insurance, the undocumented refugee family, the death-row inmate, the little girl killed on the playground by a stray bullet, and the brave man near the end with Lou Gehrig's disease all deserve dignity, protection, and respect.

Think of how differently we would treat ourselves and one another if we all truly believed that.

AUGUST 26

Pope Francis proposes that discipleship united for mission will be characterized by and effective only with joy.

Joy is not pleasure or giddiness; joy is not some syrupy, superficial feel-goodness, is it?

Joy, as Saint Paul teaches, is a fruit of the Holy Spirit, a gift of God. Saint Thomas Aquinas says that joy flows from hope: If we trust that all is in God's hands, that all works for the good of those who believe, no trial, adversity, or setback can crush us.

I believe that a renewal of joy is essential for a deepening of Catholic vitality and confidence today. We are tempted to concentrate on problems, worries, bad news, scandals, and darkness in our lives. Lord knows we can't ignore them, but neither can we be dominated by them.

People may claim that they do not want faith, hope, or love, but rare is the person who does not crave joy.

The Lord does not delay his promise, as some regard "delay,"
but he is patient with you, not wishing that any should perish
but that all should come to repentance.

—2 PETER 3:9

God tells us: "A humble, contrite heart I will not spurn."

We must never forget the importance of the Sacrament of Penance. Through a good confession, our souls are restored to the innocence, beauty, order, and radiance of the day of our baptism.

Indeed, Jesus made repentance the core of His invitation to His followers.

What does that mean? Simply put, it means turning away from sin and turning to the Person, message, salvation, and call to discipleship of Jesus.

We Catholics used to be constantly aware of repentance. In years past, we performed many acts that showed God the sorrow we felt for our sins. We would complete an examination of conscience and say an Act of Contrition before falling asleep at night. We would go frequently to confession and fast on the vigil of holy days and on Fridays. If we had not gone to confession and were conscious of having committed a grave sin, we would refrain from receiving the Eucharist.

Now we have become lax. We don't give the same import to some of these things. Many of us are even afraid to go to confession.

I admit that customs, traditions, and practices change. Often it's good when they do.

What can't change is the call to repentance and conversion of heart at the very core of the Scriptures and of our traditions. How we respond may change; that we do penance must never change.

AUGUST 28

Feast of
Saint Augustine of Hippo

His is the story of an odyssey. Of a search. Augustine was looking for truth. For God. For happiness. In fact, it reminds me of the old country-and-western song: He was looking for love in all the wrong places.

Finally he discovered the one true God who was revealed to us in God's only begotten Son, Our Lord and Savior, Jesus Christ.

He became one of the greatest saints we've got. One of the more towering intellects of Western civilization, in fact. Keep in mind a couple of lessons:

First, let's look at the Divine Initiative. Augustine would say it wasn't so much that he was looking hard for God. Instead, it was God looking for him, as He searches for all of us.

Second, think of the power of our mothers. It was due to his mom, Saint Monica, that he received God's grace and mercy. Her years of prayer paid off. God promises us that our prayers will as well.

AUGUST 29

The community of believers was of one heart and mind.
—ACTS 4:32

Our readings from the Bible often describe a *paradox:* something seemingly contradictory yet still true.

One paradox I have in mind is found dramatically in the Acts of the Apostles. It is the story of the first generation of followers of Jesus. In this book, we hear often about two seemingly contradictory facts: that the Church was flourishing, growing, and spreading, filled with joy, and that the first followers of Jesus were constantly persecuted. How can the Church be persecuted yet still grow and be filled with joy?

I witnessed a contemporary version of this paradox during a trip I once took to visit the "internally displaced persons" of Iraq: 110,000 Christians who had fled the extremist cutthroat fanatics of ISIS to the relative security of Kurdistan. There I saw and embraced so many who, though tearful and downcast over the brutality that had expelled them from their homes, were still able to smile at the warm and loving reception they received from their fellow Christians in Kurdistan.

Here's the paradox: In situations in which the Church is comfortable, with ample resources, and people are free to practice their faith—as in America—we hear glum news of inertia, lack of participation, and people leaving or not practicing their faith.

In a shattered, violent country where Christians were being killed, threatened, and thrown out of their ancient homes by fanatical bullies, the Church remained dynamic and growing.

If you call the sabbath a delight . . . If you glorify it by not following your ways, seeking your own interests, or pursuing your own affairs— then you shall delight in the Lord.
—ISAIAH 58:13-14

Are we Catholics living for Sunday? I am afraid that if you asked someone today whether he lives for Sunday, he might think you want to know if he's a football fan.

Don't get me wrong. When I grew up, as soon as we got home from Mass on Sunday, my father would put beer in the cooler and sports on TV. But that was *after* we got home from Sunday Mass.

Do we Catholics think that Sunday is the "climax of living"? Do we look forward to Sunday as a day dedicated to the Lord— a day that gives meaning and purpose to our whole week? Or have we become accustomed to a weekend mentality in which we sleep late, catch up on chores, run errands, drive the kids to sports, and then fit Sunday Mass in between everything else, if at all?

Saint John Paul II wrote about the difference between the weekend mentality and a proper Christian Sunday observance: "Unfortunately, when Sunday loses its fundamental meaning and becomes merely part of a 'weekend,' it can happen that people stay locked within a horizon so limited that they can no longer see the heavens. . . . The disciples of Christ, however, are asked to avoid any confusion between the celebration of Sunday, which should truly be a way of keeping the Lord's Day holy, and the 'weekend,' understood as a time of simple rest and relaxation."

We must ask ourselves: Are we living for Sunday?

AUGUST 31

The word of God continued to spread, and the number of
the disciples in Jerusalem increased greatly.
—ACTS 6:7

The Acts of the Apostles—the inspired book of the New Testament written by Saint Luke and often called the "Fifth Gospel" or the "Gospel of the Holy Spirit"—carries a bracing message to Christ's followers. Its main point is that Christ, crucified and risen, is alive and active here and now in His Church.

In Acts, Saint Luke describes some characteristics of the early Church: Although they were in the world, the first followers of Jesus also realized that they were not of it, and they knew they had to nurture their communal togetherness if they were to fulfill Our Lord's will. They looked to the Apostles and their delegates as authentic teachers of the primitive faith revealed by Jesus. They gathered together often to listen to the Scriptures, to praise God, and to do what Jesus did the night before He died—celebrate the Eucharist. Finally, they evangelized, telling others about Jesus by word and example, inviting them to a conversion of heart, repentance for sin, and initiation into His Church through baptism.

Reflecting upon the Acts of the Apostles is an examination of conscience to determine how we can imitate the characteristics of our first-generation Christian ancestors.

If we're lucky, we have attractive models today who base their daily lives on the gospel and lead us in the way of the Apostles. They show us that the Church of the Acts of the Apostles is still very much alive!

SEPTEMBER 1

In all labor there is profit,
but mere talk tends only to loss.
—PROVERBS 14:23

Back in the 1880s, the labor force in our nation was made up mostly of Catholic immigrants. Many of those hard workers were active in the earliest attempts by laborers to organize and promote their basic human rights to a living wage, safe and humane working conditions, and protection for their families in case of their own death or injury.

One of the earliest "unions" in our country, the Knights of Labor, was almost two-thirds Catholic. There was trouble, though: To protect themselves, the Knights of Labor had to be a "secret society," since membership could lead to the loss of a job. But the Catholic Church taught that membership in a secret society was immoral.

Cardinal Gibbons wrote a letter to the Holy See pleading the case of those men. He observed how the working class in America looked to the Church as a friend and that laborers took their faith very seriously.

The appeal was successful: Rome did not condemn the Knights of Labor.

I am proud that the workers of our county look to the Church as an ally and realize that she has been in the lead from the earliest days in protecting and promoting the legitimate rights of the laborer.

I thank God that Catholics in America are among the best-educated, most prosperous people in the country. And we are still grateful to number among our people those brave workers struggling for a decent wage and elementary justice.

Peter said, "I have neither silver nor gold,
but what I do have I give you."
—ACTS 3:6

Eight days after the cataclysmic 2010 earthquake in Haiti, I visited leveled Port-au-Prince in my role as chair of the board of Catholic Relief Services. The misery and devastation were beyond belief. We spent Saturday evening with our 300 CRS workers who resided in Haiti, who had all been there that dreadful day, and who were physically, emotionally, and spiritually exhausted after nine days of intense relief and rescue. They cried, worried, described their obstacles, dreamed of rebuilding. As I left, I asked them, "Is there anything I personally can do for you?"

One young woman raised her hand. I expected her request to be for more supplies, medicine, tents, or food or for me to go home and shout from the skyscrapers of New York the towering needs of Port-au-Prince.

Instead, she simply said to me, "Father, tomorrow is Sunday. Will you say Mass for us?"

What she wanted from me was not money, supplies, or earthly goods. She wanted the Lord, and she assumed I had that treasure to share with her in the Eucharist.

Sometimes I wonder if we are today being invited back to the Church of the Acts of the Apostles. Sometimes I wonder if we priests and bishops—indeed the entire Church—have been reduced to the utterly basic reply of Peter and John to the crippled beggar in Temple Square in Jerusalem, as recorded in Acts 3: "I have neither silver nor gold, but what I do have I give you: In the name of Jesus Christ . . . walk."

Pizzazz, glitter, gold, clout, prestige, power, property, wealth—we ain't got! All we got is Jesus—and that's the greatest treasure of all.

SEPTEMBER 3

In the world you will have trouble, but take courage,
I have conquered the world.

—JOHN 16:33

Something is missing in our world today. The culture, our country, and even our families are not whole. We need some help from outside.

Our lives can be a mess, out of whack, lacking purpose and meaning. We might futilely seek that meaning by working harder, investing better, buying more toys, getting a trainer. Or, sadly, we might rely on drugs, alcohol, or sexual promiscuity, but we learn the hard way that these things only make our lives more of a mess.

Christ wants us to acknowledge our brokenness and to tell Him that we need Him.

That can be hard because we are part of a culture that wants us to feel comfortable with anything that makes us feel good. But the Church invites us to a different way of life and to acknowledge that we need someone to intervene. In the vocabulary of believers, that means "I need a Savior."

Acknowledging this is easy. Through prayer, we tell God that we need Him. Even a simple prayer such as "Dear God, my life and this world are a mess; I am not whole. I need a Savior!" will work to bring us closer to God.

He knows that we are not happy without Him. Our mistakes come when we try to find replacements for Him. So we humbly tell Him that we cannot go through life alone. And when we open our hearts and listen, we can hear His voice tell us, "I am with you always, until the end of time."

SEPTEMBER 4

I fed you in the wilderness, in the parched land.
—HOSEA 13:5

Many of us are not very familiar with the desert and can only picture it: the scorching, unrelenting sun; no water; and the dry air draining every drop of hydration from you.

That's why the desert often becomes a metaphor for our spiritual life. We see this image in the Bible frequently. In Psalm 63, for instance, we pray: "O God, you are my God—it is you I seek! For you my body yearns; for you my soul thirsts, in a land parched, lifeless, and without water."

That's the spiritual desert.

Our souls can be as scorched, dry, lifeless, and desolate as the desert.

Yet surprisingly, the desert can also be an oasis—an arena of the divine.

Think of Moses as the drama of the Exodus begins, standing before the burning bush to meet "I am who am" and to receive his divine mandate to set Israel free. Consider the Exodus itself: forty years in a desert filled with sin and setback but also with signs and wonders of the Lord's mighty presence.

A lot of people are in a spiritual desert these days, wondering if life has purpose. But God tells us that He is as much with us in the desert as He is at the oasis.

When we are not sure where to turn, these times give us an opportunity for terror or trust, to damn the Lord or turn to Him in prayer.

SEPTEMBER 5

Saint Teresa of Calcutta

There's a story told by a former governor of Colorado. He had occasion to visit with Mother Teresa when she was in Denver to open one of her houses for the poor and dying. In her characteristically disarming way, she asked, "Governor, what do you do?" He was caught off guard by such a direct, simple question but finally replied, "Well, Mother, I try to help people live." Then he quizzed her, "And Mother, what do you do?" to which she responded with no hesitation, "Oh, I help people die."

She of course meant that she and her sisters not only tenderly cared for those left in the gutter to die but wanted to help usher them into eternal life.

A case could be made that this is the mission statement of our Holy Mother Church: The Church helps people die.

That's not morbid at all. No one enjoys life more than a believer, who relishes all of life's exquisite gifts and wonders but who also knows that they will not last. Indeed, these gifts are but hints of the eternal happiness that God has in store for us.

The towering temptation of this world is to conclude that the eternal is now and that this life on earth is all there is.

The Church helps people die precisely so that they can live—live with dignity now and live forever with the Lord.

SEPTEMBER 6

*In every way I have shown you that by hard work of that sort we must help
the weak, and keep in mind the words of the Lord Jesus who himself said,
"It is more blessed to give than to receive."*

—ACTS 20:35

No matter what our job or profession is, we all work hard. Sometimes work makes us weary. But God wants us to know that He understands our weariness. In fact, He respects the worker so much that He wanted His only Son to be raised in a workshop: that of Saint Joseph.

The Church teaches that human work is sacred, an arena of God's grace, as we are invited to collaborate in God's continual "re-creation" of His universe. Our labor—whether in the factory, field, classroom, office, hospital, kitchen, workshop, boardroom, or marketplace—gives us an opportunity to share in the constant care God exercises over His creation. As Saint John Paul II taught, the worker deserves dignity, respect, protection, and certain rights. He or she is not an object to be drained, used, or taken advantage of but a collaborator in God's plan of continual provision for His creation.

Work is not mere drudgery. Work should not feel useless and mundane. Our faith has implications in the way we work, in the pride, care, sense of duty, and practice of charity and justice we bring to our jobs.

The Church constantly reminds us that work is not an end in itself but a means to an end, with the end always being care for the person and for the laborer's family, stewardship of creation, attention to the needs of a just society, and the achievement of life's real purpose: union with God.

Pray without ceasing. In all circumstances give thanks,
for this is the will of God for you in Christ Jesus.
—I THESSALONIANS 5:17-18

Christ reveals to us that His Father, with the Son and the Holy Spirit, desires to live in the soul of the believer. We have the life of God, the indwelling of the Blessed Trinity, within us. We call that sanctifying grace, and it's very good news!

This should inspire us to make sure that the life of God, the indwelling of the Trinity, is steady, strong, and secure in our own souls.

But understand this: No one gives what he or she does not have! If we do not have God's life steady, strong, and secure in our souls, we can't offer it to others. Therefore, the number one priority of every Catholic is to foster an interior life in which the life, light, and love of God dwells.

One of the most important things we can do for ourselves is to pray daily and faithfully. The gift of God's life in our souls is ours for the asking. We can't earn it, but we can ask for it.

Prayer is asking God to increase, steady, strengthen, and secure His life within us. Prayer is humbly and gratefully acknowledging that Father, Son, and Spirit are there within us so that we can whisper: "I love you, I welcome you, I thank you, and I sure need you."

The omnipotent Lord of creation is indeed within us as our Savior and best friend.

SEPTEMBER 8

He said to them, "Go into the whole world
and proclaim the gospel to every creature."
—MARK 16:15

At the end of a liturgy many years ago, we processed outside with the Blessed Sacrament and walked around the block in a beautiful public expression of our faith that Christ really and truly remains with us in the Holy Eucharist.

As I carried the Blessed Sacrament through the cathedral doors, it hit me that we believers also were giving public expression to another aspect of our Creed: that we are indeed to carry the effects of the Eucharist outside, to the world, to our culture, and to society.

There is a missionary dimension to every Eucharist. One of the final words of the celebrant is, literally, *go*. In fact, our common word for the celebration of the Eucharist—Mass—comes from the Latin close of the liturgy, *"Ite, missa est"*: "Go, you are sent." As I carried the body and blood of Christ outside the cathedral, so are we all summoned to bring Christ to the world. We are missionaries, evangelists, apostles.

The missions need us very much, yet it is also true that we need the missions very much! We are Catholics. That means that our faith is never some cozy, tidy, private, local possession. By its nature it calls us beyond ourselves, it expands our horizons, and it stretches our hearts.

There is not just one solitary mark of the Church. The Church has four marks: one, holy, Catholic, and apostolic. And we are all called to be missionaries of this Church.

SEPTEMBER 9

Feast of
Saint Peter Claver

Today we celebrate the feast of a citizen of heaven who can give us confidence by his example. Saint Peter Claver was ordained a priest of the Society of Jesus—the Jesuits—in Colombia in 1616. There he labored ceaselessly to care for the "poorest of the poor," those whose dignity was denied and whose lives were considered chattel: the African slaves. His vow was to be "the slave of the blacks."

From his own bare, austere room in the seaport of Cartagena, Colombia, he kept watch for the "coffin ships" carrying innocent black men, women, and children to be sold as animals in the New World.

Off he'd go to meet those boats, sneaking on with friends carrying bundles and baskets of fresh water, food, clean clothes, and medicine. He would labor nonstop to soothe and comfort the slaves. In addition to his first aid were words of hope. He whispered assurances that God was with them, that His Son Jesus had suffered like them, and that they were treasures, not trash.

The Church has always looked to the example of the saints for hope and encouragement, especially in times of trial. Jesus is, of course, our best model and a uniquely potent helper, but His mother and His friends—the saints—are up there with Him begging the world to recover our conviction that every human person deserves dignity and that each human life must be respected.

SEPTEMBER 10

Welcome one another, then, as Christ welcomed you,
for the glory of God.
—ROMANS 15:7

When I was seven or eight, my buddy Freddie from across the street and I were playing outside. Mom called me for supper. "Can Freddie stay and eat supper with us?" I asked.

"He'd sure be welcome if it's okay with his mom and dad," she replied. I was so proud and happy. Freddie was welcome in our house, at our table. We both rushed in and sat down. "Freddie, glad you're here," Dad remarked, "but ... looks like you and Tim better go wash your hands before you eat."

Simple enough—common sense, in fact. You are a most welcome and respected member now of our table, our household, Dad was saying, but there are a few very natural expectations this family has. Like washing your hands! So it is with the supernatural family we call the Church: *All are welcome!*

But welcome to what? To a community that will love and respect you but that has rather clear expectations defining it, revealed by God in the Bible through His Son, Jesus; instilled in the human heart; and taught by His Church. This balance can cause some tensions. But as Saint John Paul II used to say, the best way to love someone is to tell him or her the truth: *To teach the truth with love.*

Jesus did it best. Remember the woman caught in adultery? The elders were going to stone her. At the words of Jesus, they walked away. "Is there no one left to condemn you?" the Lord tenderly asked the accused woman.

"No one, sir," she whispered. "Neither do I condemn you," Jesus concluded. "Now go, but sin no more."

SEPTEMBER 11

God is our refuge and our strength,
an ever-present help in distress.
—PSALM 46:2

A remark made by one of my brother priests about the fateful events of September 11 remains imprinted in my heart: "We New Yorkers don't just remember the horrors and sorrows of September 11th; we also celebrate September 12th."

It took me a while to get the insight of his statement: New Yorkers were shocked, scared, angry, saddened, and shaken by the unforgettable death and destruction of 9/11, true, but they were not paralyzed or defeated! They immediately rallied, becoming people of intense faith, prayer, hope, and love as the rescue, renewal, rebuilding, and outreach began.

We could have let 9/11 turn us into petrified, paranoid, vicious animals, and our demented attackers would have won, but instead we allowed it to bring out what is most noble in the human soul, such as heroic sacrifice, solidarity, nonstop rescue efforts, the bonding of communities, and countless prayers. 9/11 did not have the last word; 9/12 did.

Thank you, New York and America, for that amazing example.

This same lesson is taught in the Bible. Sadness and adversity will come to all of us sometime in life.

When they come, we can react in one of two ways: We can be frozen into self-pity, curl up in a ball, give up, and let the crisis defeat us, or we can rely on God, dig in, rally, count on family and friends, and keep going.

God's Word strongly encourages option number two.

SEPTEMBER 12

While they were eating, he took bread, said the blessing, broke it,
and gave it to them, and said, "Take it; this is my body."
—MARK 14:22

Are we getting a bit sloppy in our approach to the sacred mystery of the Mass?

Here are the facts: Jesus Christ is really and truly present in the Holy Eucharist. Every time we go to Mass, we renew His Last Supper with His Apostles—a sacred meal—and His offering of Himself for us on the cross—a Holy Sacrifice. When we receive Him in Holy Communion, we are as close to Him as we can get this side of heaven. And when we gaze upon Him in the monstrance or in the tabernacle, we believe that He's really there.

To show our love for this mystery of our faith, we Catholics foster traditional practices of piety, which also keep us from taking the Holy Eucharist for granted or losing the sense of awe and reverence that this Blessed Sacrament deserves.

In other words, we have certain safeguards against getting sloppy about the Holy Eucharist.

For instance, Church discipline asks that we abstain from all food and drink except water an hour before Mass. Since we are receiving Communion, if we are aware of any serious sin that would rupture Communion with Jesus and His Church, we should make a good confession before receiving the Eucharist. We take a time of quiet thanksgiving right after receiving Our Lord. We participate actively at Mass by reciting the prayers, singing, and listening attentively to God's Word.

When we partake in all these safeguards, we can truly say we are faithful to the Sunday Mass.

His master said to him, "Well done, my good and faithful servant. . . .
Come, share your master's joy."
—MATTHEW 25:21

"Praised be Jesus Christ" were the first words Saint John Paul II uttered when he was elected pope.

Those are my words now as I thank God for a pastor who taught us how to live and how to die.

I've written quite a lot about Saint John Paul II in this book, and I'd like to share three more words that come to mind when I think of him.

The first is *serenity*. They say he was serene until the very end. Sure he was: He was a man of unshakable faith and hope who had as his motto *totus tuus*, "all yours," as he surrendered his whole life to the Lord.

The second is *solidarity*, which he made a household word. It seems as if the whole world, certainly the entire Church, stood in solidarity around not only his papacy but his canonization. We Catholics are deeply touched by the solidarity he fostered, and now we can ask for his intercession on our behalf.

The third is *savior*. Yes, Karol Wojtyla was a poet, a Polish patriot, a philosopher, a diplomat, a linguist, a priest, and a pontiff, but first and foremost he was a believer—a disciple of Jesus Christ our Savior.

And when he met his Savior face-to-face, we feel sure that he heard the words we all long to hear from Jesus: "Well done, my good and faithful servant!"

SEPTEMBER 14

As he who called you is holy, be holy yourselves
in every aspect of your conduct.
—1 PETER 1:15

Dear families, you can be holy! The Church does not lack confidence in you. God calls all married couples and children to holiness in family life. And, when God calls, He never fails to provide the necessary grace.

The capacity for heroic holiness is not just for the saints; it's also possible for us today.

At the conclusion of *Veritatis Splendor,* Saint John Paul II's encyclical letter on the moral law, he teaches that the moral, or holy, life and the experience of mercy are connected because they both come freely from God. It is by His mercy that sins are forgiven in baptism and reconciliation.

It states: "At times, in the discussions about new and complex moral problems, it can seem that Christian morality is in itself too demanding, difficult to understand and almost impossible to practice. This is untrue, since Christian morality consists, in the simplicity of the gospel, in following Jesus Christ, in abandoning oneself to Him, in letting oneself be transformed by His grace and renewed by His mercy, gifts which come to us in the living communion of His Church."

We need only accept those gifts.

Jesus our Savior is always in your family's midst. He joins you at your dinner table; He comes through the doors of your homes; and He is with you today so that you might one day be with Him forever.

SEPTEMBER 15

Proclaim the word; be persistent whether it is convenient or inconvenient;
convince, reprimand, encourage through all patience and teaching.
—2 TIMOTHY 4:2

As Jesus brought us God in His Person—in His humanity—so are we called upon to bring Him to others in our person, our humanity. By our kindness, our goodness, our virtue, our talent, our love, and our courtesy, we are called to attract others to God.

Saint Paul describes this when he encourages charity, selflessness, gentleness, and patience—all at the service of the Body of Christ.

Saint Thomas Aquinas speaks of it when he gives us the principle that "grace builds on nature," reminding us how God's power, mercy, and invitation work through one's character and personality.

Saint John Paul II drives it home when he reminds us that we are all to be a bridge that leads others to good, never an obstacle that keeps people from Christ.

Rare is the person whose very humanity and very person, by his goodness, decency, charity, and just plain courtesy, can bring people to the Father, who does it with selflessness and gentleness, who puts his human talents totally at the disposition of God's grace, who attracts souls by the honey of his temperament, and who serves as a bridge to the divine.

We have all encountered that selfless person who exudes the love and light of Christ and draws us closer to Him. Such people, along with the saints before them, serve as our models of love, charity, and compassion. Can we emulate their words and actions so that one day we, too, may become saints?

Therefore, he is always able to save those who approach God through him,
since he lives forever to make intercession for them.
—HEBREWS 7:25

The Church must remain alive, present, and strong.

The church—our parish—is not just a building where we go for Mass, to baptize our babies, or to bury our beloved, as essential as all this is. The church is where we go to spread the faith, serve those in need, and bring others into the Church—with a capital C.

We have challenges that demand energy, love, and compassion. We must care for our elders, the sick, the homeless, families, children, the immigrant, and the expectant mother. Christ calls us to reach out to others in the community. He calls us to provide a welcome home to those who have lost their faith. He calls us to speak for Him and to show His love and compassion to those who need it.

This is our sacred mission. We cannot just go to church without being a part of the Church. Yet we know that we are not doing this work alone. We see the benefits of our labors everywhere we turn—in our parishes, in Catholic hospitals, in our charities, and in many more places. We see this everywhere because the Church is universal!

We are all children of God—Catholic members of the household of the faith. The Church will be alive, present, and effective when we are alive, present, and effective.

Trusting in Jesus, trusting in one another, and guided by the Spirit, we will make His Church come alive.

Therefore, since we are surrounded by so great a cloud of witnesses,
let us rid ourselves of every burden and sin that clings to us
and persevere in running the race that lies before us.
—HEBREWS 12:1

When you look into the lives of the saints, you see that there are basically two kinds: saints who are esteemed because of their example and saints who are renowned for their intercessory powers. Of course, all saints are both kinds. The reason we have saints is for their example and for the help they give with their prayers from heaven.

We don't usually think of Saint Francis as a miracle worker. His is more of an example.

Yet, when I was a seminarian in Rome in 1972, I was desperately homesick. The farthest I'd ever been from my home state of Missouri was Kentucky. And there I was in Italy. This was a difficult time; my family couldn't come see me because my folks didn't have the money. I missed them every day.

Cardinal John Carberry, who was the archbishop who sent me to Rome, knew I was nervous and scared. Before leaving, I asked him, "Your Eminence, if I don't like it, can I still be a priest?" He said, "Maybe. But not a priest for the Archdiocese of St. Louis. For me, if a man doesn't like Rome, he shouldn't be a priest." That was pretty daunting.

About three weeks after our arrival in Rome, I went to Assisi with a group of seminarians. The welcome and warmth of the city were so evident. The natural beauty. The churches. The aura of Saint Francis. In Assisi, I felt at home.

I said to myself, "You know what? The Church is my home. The Church is my family. I miss my family and home in Ballwin, Missouri, but I am home."

I've often attributed that miracle to Saint Francis.

SEPTEMBER 18

My sheep hear my voice; I know them,
and they follow me.
—JOHN 10:27

Saint Augustine tries to make clear both for himself and for his faithful the nature of priestly service. It came to him from meditation on the figure of John the Baptist, in whom he finds a prefiguring of the role of the priest.

He points out that in the New Testament, John is described as a "voice," whereas Christ appears in the Gospel of John as "the Word." The relation of "voice" (*vox*) to "word" (*verbum*) helps make clear the mutual relationship between Christ and the priest.

The Word exists in someone's heart before it is ever perceptible to the senses through the voice. Through the mediation of the voice, it enters into the perception of the other person and is then present in his or her heart, without the speaker having in any sense lost the Word. While the voice that carries the Word from one person to the other passes away, the Word remains.

On this basis, the stature and the humbleness of priestly service are both equally clear: The priest is, like John the Baptist, purely a forerunner, a servant of the Word. It is not he who matters but the other. Yet he is, with his entire existence, *vox*. It is his mission to be a voice for the Word, and thus, precisely because he is radically dependent on someone else, he takes a share in the stature of the mission of John the Baptist and in the mission of the Logos Himself.

*My foot has always walked in his steps; I have kept his way
and not turned aside.*

—JOB 23:11

The Bible teaches us that there are two roads we can choose to take in our life's journey.

Road number one claims that what is most important in life is what satisfies us and what we can get. The most essential thing on this path is me: my wants, my cravings, my needs, my urges, and my convenience. Life is rather selfish on this road. This road is wide, smooth, and well taken.

Then, according to the Bible, there's road number two. This path—admittedly less traveled, narrow, rocky, harder to walk—emphasizes selflessness, not selfishness; virtue, not vice; service over being waited upon; duty over rights; and giving rather than receiving.

The most radiant example of the second way is Christ. He walked the second path up to a hill called Calvary to sacrifice His life on a cross so that we who believe in Him might have eternal life.

People who walk path number two radiate the light of Christ. These people make a difference in the world and change lives.

God calls us to choose that road less traveled; the way of Jesus and His saints; the road of goodness, truth, and love; and the road that leads to life, for "it is in dying that we are born to eternal life." And when that path is concluded, we pray that we will see God's beatific face and hear His voice welcome us to eternity with Him.

He will wipe every tear from their eyes, and there shall be no more death
or mourning, wailing or pain, [for] the old order has passed away.
—REVELATION 21:4

Did Jesus have any favorites?

I think He did. We know that Our Lord's favorites were not the stuffy learned ones, the smug leaders, the complacent rich, or the proud, powerful, prestigious, or popular.

But I know who did have a place deep in His Sacred Heart: the sick.

Think of the many stories in which He healed illnesses or diseases: Peter's mother-in-law, the paralyzed man, the woman with the hemorrhage, the blind beggar, the ten lepers, the boy with convulsions, and countless more.

Whether they were sick in body, soul, or mind, these people were prized by the greatest doctor of them all—the Divine Physician.

Is it any wonder, then, that His mystical body, the Church, would continue to reach out in His healing name to the sick?

We know that the Church has ministries to help those dying in hospices and to offer solace to those dealing with sick family members. We take the Eucharist to the sick when they cannot come to church. We're gratefully aware of our hospitals, health-care facilities, nursing homes, clinics, parish nurses, and devoted physicians, nurses, and volunteers whose faith drives them. In all of their patients, they see the face of Christ.

Just as Christ carried the cross for us, so are we called to carry the cross for our sick brothers and sisters who cannot carry it on their own. We are called to unburden them, lift the weight a bit, and comfort them when they feel forgotten, lonely, and scared.

We know that all creation is groaning in labor pains even until now; and not only that, but we ourselves, who have the firstfruits of the Spirit, we also groan within ourselves as we wait for adoption, the redemption of our bodies.

—ROMANS 8:22-23

Prayer is easy. And prayer is tough. And sometimes prayer is groaning. Saint Paul says, "We do not know how to pray as we ought, but the Spirit intercedes with inexpressible groanings."

I remember the first time I had the honor of going to Saint John Paul II's private Mass. It was a tiny chapel. Maybe fifteen people could fit into it. He was at his *prie-dieu* (his kneeler) in prayer. As we came in, we were very quiet. We could see how intensely he was praying. And we heard him go "ohhh," like a groan.

The skeptics may say he was groaning in the sense of "Ohhhh, I've gotta turn around now and greet these people." But of course we know that he was so deeply in union with his God in prayer that he was just groaning. Think about how natural that is.

We've all had moments in life that make us groan. I remember that when I was a kid my dad lost his job. When he told us all what happened, some of us groaned. But my grandma said, "Oh, Bobby, we've been through all this before. In fact, we've been through worse than this. Things will get better tomorrow. Just sleep on it." That's an act of trust. Almost like the people of Israel recalling their past yet remembering how God came through.

That's why Saint Paul says that as you get more advanced in prayer, you usually end up grunting or groaning.

SEPTEMBER 22

There are friends who bring ruin, but there are true friends
more loyal than a brother.
—PROVERBS 18:24

If you could meet your best friend for thirty minutes every morning before beginning your workday or taking care of all of life's chores, would you jump at the chance? Most of us would. The good news is that we can. Jesus—our best friend—invites us to break bread with Him each and every day. What a great way to foster God's life within our soul.

As the old saying goes, "Daily Mass is not just part of our day but the heart of our day."

Just as we can foster God's life within us through daily prayer and in the Eucharist, He comes to us in the Sacrament of Penance. God is very much at home in our souls. He enjoys living there. He wants to move in permanently so that we can share His life forever. We're the ones who tell Him to leave; we're the ones who extinguish His light within us. We do that by our sins. Confession is the way to make things right with Him—to take ownership of our sins and apologize for the pain we have caused.

When we foster Christ's presence within us through Mass, the Eucharist, prayer, and confession, we come to understand that life is not just about "me." It's all about the One who lives within me.

The more we shrink the shadow of the self and let in our best friend, the more the light of the Divine within radiates.

SEPTEMBER 23

Feast of Saint Padre Pio

Padre Pio is an example of an extraordinarily popular saint whom people go to for help. He was a faithful Capuchin, he had the stigmata, and he worked lots of miracles. He was a powerful man of God, and the stories of his intercessory power are innumerable.

As with the wounds of Saint Francis of Assisi, he experienced stigmata. We are all summoned to bear the cross, and Padre Pio did it literally. When people questioned why he had the stigmata he would reply, "Don't ask me. I don't particularly like these four wounds, I didn't ask for them, I wish they'd go away, but I've got them." And he'd say to people, "You can see physically the share that I have of the cross. But you have one, too."

At Padre Pio's beatification in 1999, a gentleman told me a story about how when World War II was over, he was waiting in Rome to go home. Two of his Catholic buddies said, "Let's go down to San Giovanni Rotondo, and maybe we could see Padre Pio." This man hadn't heard of him before and said he didn't believe all this superstitious stuff like stigmata and such but he'd go anyway.

They went and indeed were able to meet Padre Pio. The man scoffed at him and said, "I hear you've got these wounds. Let me see them." Padre Pio had had them covered, but he said, "I'll show you my wounds if you show me your wounds." The man said, "What are you talking about? I don't have any wounds." Padre Pio took him by the arm and walked him into the confessional. And this gentleman said that, almost in spite of himself, he had a life-changing conversion of heart in there. Sure enough, afterward, as they came out of the confessional, Padre Pio took his gloves off and showed the man his wounds. Then he said, "Yours are as deep as mine."

See how a person is justified by works and not by faith alone.
—JAMES 2:24

Jesus told us, "Not everyone who says to me, 'Lord, Lord,' will enter the kingdom of heaven, but only the one who does the will of my Father."

In other words, actions speak louder than words.

That's living our faith.

We can pray, talk religion, and never miss Sunday Mass, but if all that does not affect the way we act, if it does not result in lives of virtue, love, service, and selflessness, then as Saint Paul warns, it's all just a cymbal clanging.

They'll know we are Christians by our love, right?

One of the many things I've appreciated about our great community of Catholics is how we live our faith.

I don't think we fully appreciate the blessing of religious freedom and ecumenical friendship we have in the United States. Thanks be to God, we are mostly free from the strife, violence, and persecution that we see in other countries and we can live our faith openly.

The Gospel tells of how Simon of Cyrene lived his faith when he helped Jesus carry His cross. A man caring for his very sick wife once told me, "Oh, it's nothing, Father. I'm just trying to be Simon of Cyrene helping her carry her cross." That's not a bad description of our call to living our faith.

God calls us, too, to live our faith by our actions.

*He is the head of the body, the church. He is the beginning, the firstborn
from the dead, that in all things he himself might be preeminent.*
—COLOSSIANS 1:18

Remember the book *The Da Vinci Code*? Though it is fiction,
the vision of the Church in this book did a lot to make people
question the Church. This view held that the Church is
founded on a lie that has been perpetuated for nearly two
millennia by power-hungry men who want to keep the rest of
the world, especially women, oppressed. In this view, Jesus
was an all right guy but certainly was neither divine nor a Savior. The Church, as presented in the novel, is rotten, wicked,
and corrupt.

Then there is the other vision of the Church, which has sustained believers since Pentecost Sunday. This Church is beautiful, forever young, always promising and clinging to Christ.
This Church is actually the body of Christ.

You bet she has her flaws, her sins, and her moments of corruption, but she also has her saints, her faithful people, her
beauty, her teaching, her worship, her charity, and the promise
given her by her founder, Jesus, that He would always be with
her.

Therefore, we cling to her, love her to death, and cherish
belonging to her. People have been harassing her, mocking her,
and persecuting her since the days of the Acts of the Apostles,
and so it hardly surprises us that they're still at it today. But we
smile, shrug, and recall that Jesus assured us that "the gates of
hell shall not prevail."

Feast of
Saint Paul VI

Saint Paul VI's encyclical *On Priestly Celibacy* eloquently speaks of the Christological reason for celibacy: Priests accept the invitation to follow Jesus with an intimacy so deep that it is not shared with another human person.

You remember the Gospel passage in which the first disciples left everything to follow Jesus. Priestly celibacy is also an abandonment of something, namely, leaving behind one of life's most appealing, sacred, and beautiful joys—intimacy with a woman and fathering children. Yet, also like those first priests on the shore of the Sea of Galilee (who were not, granted, all celibate), not only do we give something up, we embrace something more—an intimate union with Jesus so fruitful that we share in the nuptial love He bears for His bride, the Church.

Paul VI goes on to describe the ecclesial value of celibacy, as the priest is so united to Jesus in His love for the Church that he actually is betrothed to her in an exclusive bond.

The legendary president of the University of Notre Dame, Father Ted Hesburgh, considered his celibacy of great value for his priesthood. On one occasion, he invited some young men he was talking with to walk around campus with him. Listen, he urged them. Hundreds will greet me, and they won't call me "Reverend" or "Doctor" or "Pastor." They'll call me "Father," because they know I belong to all of them.

SEPTEMBER 27

Feast of
Saint Vincent de Paul

Saint Vincent de Paul is considered by many to be the star saint of Christian charity and concern for the poor. Many people, including those who don't know much about this great saint from the seventeenth century, know of the work of the Saint Vincent de Paul Society, which is active in so many parishes and dioceses around the world, offering direct help to people in need.

Just as Saint Vincent was a champion of the poor in his time, we must be champions of the poor today. Christ calls us to provide for those who are struggling. The basic human needs for good jobs, food, and housing continue to challenge tens of millions throughout our country.

As we celebrate the Feast of Saint Vincent de Paul, we affirm that the poor must receive our special attention to ensure that they have the basic necessities of life. Although Saint Vincent may be the star saint, the directive to help the poor comes directly from Jesus and was first formally recognized by the appointment of deacons to care for Greek-speaking widows. Throughout Church history, there has always been a preferential option for the poor.

This generous work continues and grows today throughout Catholic hospitals, charities, and educational institutions. All these make service to the poor the hallmark of their labor in building the common good to ensure the dignity of all.

And how can people preach unless they are sent? As it is written,
"How beautiful are the feet of those who bring [the] good news!"
—ROMANS 10:15

If we believe God is the supreme governor of the universe, the definitive lawgiver—as indeed we do—and if we believe that, to borrow the words of Saint Paul, "here we have no lasting city" but, rather, "have our citizenship in heaven," how does a person of faith approach what we might call our worldly, our temporal, our political, and our civic duties?

We can learn an important lesson from Christ's meeting of the men on the road to Emmaus. He did not leave them until they understood who He was. So, too, are we called to help others understand the true nature of Christ.

If we only accompany but do not convert, we simply walk beside people farther into the night, away from the community of faith. If we only question and listen, we withhold from people the saving news of salvation. If we only rebuke, we afflict those already suffering. If we only teach the objective truth of the Scriptures, we fail to show how it is good news for each particular soul.

Our mission as disciples of Christ is to accompany, to question, to listen, to rebuke the lack of faith, to teach the truth of the gospel, to reveal Christ, to restore hope, to convert, and to return to the Church.

Mary said, "Behold, I am the handmaid of the Lord.
May it be done to me according to your word."
—LUKE 1:38

Notre Dame—Our Lady—Mary, the Mother of Jesus, is perhaps the most important human person who ever lived.

Even history itself is divided into "before" and "after" her giving birth to her Son.

Might I propose to you that she's not just our queen but our model? It all comes down to this: Mary humbly, selflessly, generously, and with trust placed her life in God's hands, allowing her life to unfold according to His plan. She gave God's Son a human nature. She gave flesh to the Eternal Word—God the Son, the Second Person of the Blessed Trinity. We call that the Incarnation. Because of Mary's *fiat*—her yes—to Gabriel's question, God became one of us.

As you grow in faith and love for God, you are asked the same pivotal question the Archangel Gabriel once posed to her: Will you let God take flesh in you? Will you give God a human nature? Will He be reborn in you? Will the Incarnation continue in and through you?

It's your turn to give God your *fiat* and let Him take flesh in your life—to let Him live in your words and in your actions. You can turn your back on Christ and live only for the earthly things, or you can answer the way Mary did: "May it be done to me according to your word."

SEPTEMBER 30

A clean heart create for me, God; renew within me
a steadfast spirit.
—PSALM 51:12

It seems that no one can talk about virtue anymore without at the very least being labeled out of touch with reality. God tells us that a pure heart is a chaste heart, a heart that loves others for who they are and not simply for how they can satisfy us.

Is this not the way each of us wishes to be appreciated and desired by another? At the same time, however, we know that our hearts can feel restless and unfulfilled even in the best love stories. Some of that restlessness is good; it attracts us to God and to heaven. But some of it is dangerous and can make us self-centered, promiscuous, irresponsible, and inconsiderate of others.

A pure heart leads to generosity, peace, and fulfillment. We are all called to chastity—to keep God's gift of sexual love within marriage. And married couples are called to live in faithful fidelity to each other in keeping with God's plan. Yes, sex is a beautiful gift from God, but we see the effects of the misuse of this gift all around us.

The epidemic of pornography, adultery, divorce, and treating others as objects and not as people made in the image and likeness of God can be traced back to the lack of virtue and purity in our lives.

This is why we must remember Jesus's promise: "Blessed are the pure of heart, for they shall see God."

OCTOBER 1

Feast of
Saint Thérèse of Lisieux

Saint Thérèse of Lisieux, or as she's also known, the Little
Flower, was a cloistered nun who lived in the 1800s. When I
was a kid, I learned a prayer: "Little flower, little flower, use
your power in this hour." I also learned that she was a potent
miracle worker. She said, "I will spend my heaven doing good
on earth." She didn't let us down.

But we often make the mistake of thinking: Now, that's the
ideal of a saint. Living in a cloister with daily Mass and a constant life of prayer. She didn't have to deal with the busyness
and all the ups and downs of day-to-day living.

In fact, she showed us that sanctity comes in doing the ordinary things of life extraordinarily well, all for the glory of
God. Whether it was baking altar bread, cleaning and ironing
altar linens, or speaking to one of the older nuns who had de-
mentia and keeping company with those sisters, she said that
doing these ordinary things is where sanctity comes from.
That's one of the great insights she gives us.

Years ago, I remember stopping by my sister Deb's house as
I was on my way to a retreat. At the time, she had five kids, all
under the age of seven. As we spent time together, she shared
with me that she'd give anything to be able to go on a retreat
but just didn't have the time. Instead, she told me, she said a
Hail Mary every time she changed a baby's diaper. I replied,
"Well, with all the ones you've got, that's probably a rosary a
day!"

I don't know if my sister would attribute that marvelous
insight to the Little Flower, but it's certainly what Saint Thérèse
meant: We grow in holiness through the ordinary moments of
life.

OCTOBER 2

Feast of the Holy Guardian Angels

Some of us can remember a time when the Church celebrated angels, invoked their help, cherished their protection, and spoke of them often. Some years back, we began to forget them, to ignore them, and we were even embarrassed about them.

Well, guess what? Society has become fascinated by what the Church cast aside, as songs, poetry, TV shows, novels, and statues have all made *angels* a household word and a national pastime.

I propose that we renew our belief in and devotion to the angels. First, angels are ubiquitous in the Bible. They're all over the place as agents of God's messages and protection, and as voices ceaselessly praising Him in heaven.

Second, not all angels, tragically, are good! Lucifer, an angel of darkness, uses his considerable talents to lead us away from God and straight to hell.

Third, angels have been a prominent part of Catholic theology, the liturgy, art, and Christian piety for two millennia. The *Catechism of the Catholic Church* devotes a good chunk of its pages to angels. We may have ignored them recently, but angels are very much still with us in our belief and teaching.

The angels have been there since the Garden of Eden. They were there at Christmas, there during the Agony in the Garden, there Easter Sunday morning, and there at the Ascension, and they will be there, obviously, when "Gabriel blows his horn."

Our guardian angels are with us now, and I for one am sure glad they are.

OCTOBER 3

For so the Lord has commanded us, "I have made you a light to the Gentiles,
that you may be an instrument of salvation to the ends of the earth."
—ACTS 13:47

We especially recall missions this month. This is a special time to understand that as members of a universal Church, we have a unique missionary duty to the entire world. The mission that Christ gave His disciples continues to be our own. We are invited to carry out Christ's mission in the context of the times and situations in which we live.

The mission of the Church is a continuity of the mission of Christ and draws special energy from the Eucharist. In the Gospels, Jesus urges the disciples to give the crowd something to eat. He takes bread and blesses, breaks, and gives it to the disciples to distribute. When they share the little that they have, everyone is nourished.

It's that spirit of Eucharistic sharing of oneself that fosters the spirit of mission in our country. In every instance of mission, people have set a high priority on establishing caring relationships with their sisters and brothers at home as well as in other countries, especially in those areas of the world where the Church is fragile, young, and lacking in resources.

A local church cannot live in isolation, unconcerned for other peoples. We are united with the entire human family. That's what makes us "Catholic": concern for *all.*

OCTOBER 4

Feast of Saint Francis of Assisi

Among the things that make Saint Francis appealing is his story: a dashing, cocky, wealthy playboy, uninterested in anything but his own desires, suddenly converted to a life of primitive simplicity, service to the poor, and passionate commitment to Jesus and His Church. Those of us who wonder if God's grace and mercy can triumph over our sin and selfishness have a radiant success story in Saint Francis.

Another appealing feature of Francis is his attachment to the humanity of Christ. For Francis, the divinity of Jesus shone in and through His humanity! This, of course, is the awesome mystery of the Incarnation. God knows what we're going through, shouts Francis. He's one of us. Yes, He's true God, but He's also true man.

This flows into the third reason for his magnetism: Everything in creation is a reflection of the divine! God's artistry is detected in the beauty of creation; God's work is evident in nature; God's face is seen in the sick; and God's presence is brewing deep within us.

Jesus is always calling new "Franciscans" to "rebuild His Church," not to mock, leave, or ignore the Church but to love her and help renew her. And not some "ideal" Church of our own making but the one Christ gave us, because it is His Church, not ours.

OCTOBER 5

See, upon the palms of my hands I have engraved you;
your walls are ever before me.
—ISAIAH 49:16

In the Catholic tradition, October has become synonymous with promoting respect for human life. During this special month, we focus on those among us who are seen as persons of no value by certain segments of society: preborn children, older people, and those with terminal illnesses or disabilities. Not only are their lives devalued, even our laws fail to adequately protect these most vulnerable people.

Why has it become necessary to devote great attention to those who are so precious in God's eyes? We have witnessed a slow, steady erosion of respect for life over the last four decades. Life has become "relative" instead of sacred. Individuals are valued for what they produce or how burdensome and costly they are rather than for their innate goodness and individual personhood. Isn't loving unconditionally one of the most important lessons taught by Jesus? How can we believe that we are following this important truth if we ignore the basic sanctity of human life or the human person?

All are familiar with the infamous 1973 *Roe v. Wade* decision that led to abortion on demand in the United States. Tragically, over 60 million preborn children have died at the hands of abortionists.

Respect Life Month raises valuable awareness of the needs of those victimized by the culture of death. We prayerfully and joyously renew our commitment to the sanctity of all human life.

OCTOBER 6

God blessed the seventh day and made it holy, because on it he rested
from all the work he had done in creation.
—GENESIS 2:3

Keep holy the Lord's Day!

That's not just a nice idea and suggestion from me; it happens to be the third of the Ten Commandments.

For us as Catholics, the most effective way to keep holy the Lord's Day is by Sunday Mass!

I deal with "problems" in the Church daily, and you know them as well as I do: not enough priests and sisters, breakups in marriages and families, a culture that treats human life cheaply, money shortages threatening our beloved Catholic parishes and schools, ignorance of our faith, a secular culture that ridicules and sidelines religion, people leaving the Church, scandals in the Church, and so much more.

Let me propose that all these problems can be healed and helped if people will make Sunday Mass the center of their week.

This is not just a hunch on my part: Research shows that when folks are faithful to Sunday Mass, their lives are more in order, marriages and families are more stable and happy, vocations rise, stewardship and generosity go up, people's knowledge of and allegiance to the faith is enhanced, and God's flock is energized to bring His message and invitation to a hurting world.

Jesus teaches us, "Seek first the Kingdom [of God] . . . and all these things will be given you." Seek first His Kingdom that first day of the week by attending Sunday Mass and let Him keep His promise!

OCTOBER 7

*And Mary said: "My soul proclaims the greatness of the Lord;
my spirit rejoices in God my savior."*
—LUKE 1:46-47

Today I want to bring to light two courageous women of deep, heroic faith who have inspired the world.

The first is Immaculée Ilibagiza, who survived the vicious genocide in Rwanda in which most of her family was slain. She was one of eight women hidden by her pastor in a cramped latrine for ninety-one days. Those women turned that bathroom into a catacomb, and for three months they prayed, encouraged one another, and kept hope alive.

The second woman is Ingrid Betancourt. A senator and presidential candidate in Colombia, she spoke out against corruption and the drug trade. Tragically, she was kidnapped by rebels and held for six years.

Both of these courageous women tenderly speak of their reliance on another woman who knew trial, sorrow, and exile: Mary, the Mother of Jesus.

Both describe their devotion to the rosary and how it kept them focused, hopeful, and connected.

We also have our trials. Though they are nowhere near the tragedy of Immaculée's or Ingrid's, we do worry about many things. Sometimes we're even tempted to wonder if God has left us, but of course we know better. He never lets us down.

Think of the value of the rosary: It is biblical; it is Jesus-centered; it is communal, in that at any given time thousands somewhere in the world are praying it; and best of all, it is prayed in union with Mary.

The rosary never fails to bring us closer to Jesus and His mother. It is indeed a source of life, sweetness, and hope.

OCTOBER 8

*For God is not unjust so as to overlook your work and the love you have
demonstrated for his name by having served and
continuing to serve the holy ones.*

—HEBREWS 6:10

The Catholic Church sees itself as a community partner, with participation in the building up of the community as a virtue and as a moral imperative.

From its very beginning, the Church has promoted enterprises such as healthcare, education, strengthening of family life, and care for those on the margins of society. The Catholic Church elected not to remain in the catacombs but to be on the front lines.

When the Church remains on the front lines, we find that virtue and religion are tonics for society. For example, couples that share faith and pray together have happier, more permanent marriages. Children who attend a faith-based school usually graduate at higher rates, are more involved in community endeavors, and have happier relationships than those who do not. And prisoners who take the Bible, worship, prayer, and interior conversion seriously usually get out more quickly and return less often.

All this helps explain why religion is an important, essential partner in our community. America can never and should never become a theocracy, as we are blessed with the First Amendment providing separate spheres for religion and government— a guarantee intended to protect the Church from the government more than vice versa.

But America is at her best when virtue, morality, and faith have a place in the public square.

The legacy and continued goal of the Catholic Church is to be a partner, not a proselytizer, and a neighbor, not an ivory tower, serving people because we are people of faith, not because they are.

May the God of peace himself make you perfectly holy and may you entirely, spirit, soul, and body, be preserved blameless for the coming of our Lord Jesus Christ.

—I THESSALONIANS 5:23

God gives us the gift of sanctifying grace—this life, His very life, that dwells in the heart and soul of the believer—through the sacraments. If we really and truly are convinced that we have within us this sanctifying grace, that's extraordinarily good news, is it not?

It affects how we think and it affects how we treat ourselves. If we really believe that we are the house of God and that we are the temple of God's life, we will never treat ourselves with anything less than the reverence and dignity we deserve.

Never would we compromise ourselves, never would we harm ourselves, and never would we cheapen ourselves because we know God thinks so much of us that He has His dwelling place within us.

Think of how we would treat one another. If we look at other people and understand that they have the life of God within them, too, never would we want to hurt them.

Do you see how extraordinarily fruitful this good news is? It affects our faith—what we believe. And it affects how we act—our morality. They are connected. Because this grace shines through us in the way we treat ourselves, it has implications in the way we treat one another.

The gift of sanctifying grace, the life of God in our soul, is not something we earn. God gives it to us freely. Our gratitude to Him lies in using it well.

Yet when you seek the Lord, your God, from there, you shall indeed
find him if you search after him with all your heart and soul.
—DEUTERONOMY 4:29

Christopher Columbus is perhaps the greatest explorer the planet has ever known. This deeply committed Catholic radiated a sense of dream, daring, excitement, and energy that is part of the Italian genius.

Keep in mind that, for Columbus, his voyage of discovery was a work of evangelization. On board were missionaries, and his first act upon landing in the New World was to plant the cross, claim the new lands for Christ and His Church, and ask the missionaries to offer Mass.

As the Roman roads provided Peter and Paul with a way to spread the faith, the seas gave Columbus the chance to serve his first sovereign, Jesus Christ.

As an Italian, Christopher Columbus was raised to discover God in everything: God was there in His Son Jesus Christ and His Church, in the liturgy and sacraments, in the awe of a cathedral, in a fresco by Giotto, in a canticle by Francis of Assisi, and in a crucifix by Cimabue.

Life revealed God everywhere, and no part of His creation—even though uncharted—was beyond the pale of His loving providence.

Columbus realized that this discovery was not just some navigational feat with geographical, economic, and political implications but an act of faith—an act flowing from the very purpose of life: to find God everywhere, in everything, in everybody, for God is radiant, alive, and brimming over with love and excitement, just waiting for us to discover Him and claim Him.

OCTOBER 11

But now you have had yourselves washed, you were sanctified, you were justified in the name of the Lord Jesus Christ and in the Spirit of our God.
—I CORINTHIANS 6:11

The triple mission of the Church is to sanctify, to serve, and to teach. How can we follow the teaching of Jesus and the Church and incorporate this mission into our daily lives?

SANCTIFY: Receive the Eucharist frequently, attend daily Mass, and sit with Jesus in Eucharistic Adoration. Experience a "conversion of heart" through the Sacrament of Penance, missions, and retreats. Employ a rich devotional life with novenas, feast day observances, Stations of the Cross, and the recitation of the rosary.

SERVE: Welcome the poor, the hungry, and those who are struggling. Protect and care for the sick, the physically and mentally challenged, and the preborn. Establish community outreach in cooperation with other parishioners. Welcome our young people (teenagers and young adults) and help them feel a part of the parish.

TEACH: Teach your children about our faith. Volunteer to teach at your parish's religious education program. Renew your faith and learn more with ongoing faith formation. Read religious literature, the Bible, and the catechism. Invite non-Catholics or Catholics who have drifted away to learn about the faith.

Therefore I tell you, all that you ask for in prayer,
believe that you will receive it and it shall be yours.
—MARK 11:24

Even the Son of God, true man as well, wanted friends around Him as He prayerfully began that hour of severe trial and suffering in the Garden of Gethsemane.

"Keep watch with me!"

"Keep me company!"

This touching plea from Our Lord is also addressed to us. He wants our presence. He wants us near Him!

Stay near Him by praying daily. The gift of God's life in your soul is yours for the asking. We can't earn it, but we can ask for it.

Prayer is asking God to increase, steady, strengthen, and secure His life within us. Prayer is humbly and gratefully acknowledging that Father, Son, and Spirit are there, within us, and so we can whisper to Him, "I believe you are within me, I love you, I welcome you, I thank you, and I sure need you."

The omnipotent Lord of creation is within us as our Savior and our best friend. Holiness, as Pope Benedict XVI taught, is friendship with God.

Thus, we pray in silence and we pray with words; we pray alone and we pray with the Church. We pray in the Mass, we pray with Our Lady, and we pray with the saints. We pray before His Real Presence and we pray outside when we are walking.

Prayer is our daily communion with our best friend who lives within us.

OCTOBER 13

*[Joseph] came from the Jewish town of Arimathea
and was awaiting the kingdom of God.*
—LUKE 23:51

One of the unsung heroes of the Gospels is Joseph of Arimathea. He was the "virtuous and righteous man" who asked Pontius Pilate for permission to remove Jesus's lifeless body from the cross late on Good Friday afternoon. Joseph carefully wrapped Jesus in a linen shroud, according to Jewish tradition, and laid him gently in the new rock-hewn tomb he had planned to use for his own family.

We don't know a lot about Joseph of Arimathea. The Gospels suggest that he was a secret disciple of Christ and a "member of the council [who] had not consented to their plan." He was probably grief-stricken, exhausted, and confused after the arrest and execution of Jesus. Yet he understood the importance of adhering to tradition, and his love for Christ propelled him to care for His body.

We have a lot in common with Joseph of Arimathea, don't we? When a loved one dies, we are sad, somewhat numb, and always at a loss. At that sad moment, we may not be thinking of the Resurrection of Jesus on that first Easter Sunday and all of the faithful on the Last Day, but we know from our Catholic faith that with our hope and with the mercy of the cross, we will be with Jesus and our loved ones in heaven.

Through His death and Resurrection, Christ gives us that hope. Just as Joseph of Arimathea took care of Him, so He will take care of us and those we love.

OCTOBER 14

Jesus said to Simon Peter, "Simon, son of John, do you love me more
than these?" He said to him, "Yes, Lord, you know that I love you."
He said to him, "Feed my lambs."
—JOHN 21:15

It's usually one of the very first things I do on my first full day back in Rome.

Early in the morning, I walk down the Janiculum Hill—where I stay at the Pontifical North American College—to Saint Peter's Basilica, there to go to confession and then to celebrate Mass.

Two powerful sacraments, Reconciliation and Eucharist, constants of our spiritual life, at the heart of the Church, near the tomb of Saint Peter.

I don't want you to think that I approach confession only when I'm in Rome. At home in New York I try to go every two weeks, because I need it. But it does have a special urgency and meaning here in Rome.

Near the tomb of Saint Peter, I can hear Jesus ask Him three times: "Simon, do you love me?" and then examine my conscience to see how I have failed to love the Lord and take care of his sheep.

Near his tomb, I picture myself, like Saint Peter, doubting Jesus and sinking in the waters of the storm.

Adjacent to his burial place, I even admit that, like Peter, I have, in my thoughts, words, and actions, denied Jesus.

Thus, my contrition is strong, my purpose of amendment is firm, and I approach one of the Franciscans for confession in the corner of the massive basilica.

Then I say my penance before the tomb of Peter, under the high altar, and go to vest for the greatest prayer of all, the Holy Sacrifice of the Mass.

And then I go for pasta. . . .

Then Jesus said to her in reply, "O woman, great is your faith! Let it be done
for you as you wish." And her daughter was healed from that hour.
—MATTHEW 15:28

I don't know about you, but sometimes when I pray hard for something, I get discouraged when my prayer is not answered. I'm tempted to give up and say, "God, you're not listening." At those times I remember the story of the Canaanite woman and her patience and persistence and perseverance.

The story from the Gospel goes that a Canaanite woman approaches Jesus with a need. The woman calls out: "Have pity on me, Lord, my daughter is tormented by a demon." The Gospel says that Jesus did not say a word in answer to her. Turndown number one.

What does she do then? Jesus's disciples come and say, "Master, this woman is driving us nuts. Won't you please answer her?" Jesus still does not answer her prayer. Turndown number two.

The woman comes back and does him homage. "Lord, help me." Jesus dismisses her. Turndown number three. Three strikes, folks. But she's not out.

What does the Canaanite woman do? She says, "Please, Lord, even the dogs eat the scraps that fall from the master's table." And Jesus says, "Woman, great is your faith. Let it be done as you ask." And the Gospels say that the woman's daughter was healed at that moment.

You get the lesson here, right? Jesus is trying to teach us something about the nature of our prayer. She wouldn't give up. She wouldn't take no for an answer. What a great lesson for our humble prayers.

OCTOBER 16

In praying, do not babble like the pagans, who think that they will be heard because of their many words.
—MATTHEW 6:7

I love to eat. I enjoy going out to restaurants, too. When I give my name to the person taking reservations, I don't go too far. I live in fear that when the table is ready, I won't hear my name called over the noise or because I'm chatting with the friends I'm with. I listen hard and attentively so that I don't miss my name being called and therefore not get the table.

That makes me think of what sometimes happens with God. God calls us, but do we hear Him?

The Latin word for "call" is *vocatio,* from which we get our word *vocation.* A vocation is a call from God to serve Him with our lives in a special way.

This may be as a priest, sister, deacon, brother, or spouse who serves Him as a layperson. He never ceases calling, but problems arise when we aren't listening or when we allow worldly things to get in the way of hearing His voice. When we talk with God in prayer, we can hear Him calling our names and revealing His will.

We can speak as Samuel did to God in the Bible when he said, "Speak, for your servant is listening."

Rejoice in hope, endure in affliction, persevere in prayer.
—ROMANS 12:12

I notice these days that when people come into our beloved St. Patrick's Cathedral, right in the heart of New York City, the first move for many is to snap a picture. Usually a selfie.

But then I watch as they often get a little more comfortable and settle in. It's my prayer that they find something of what they're looking for in the relative silence. You see, the cathedral may be a landmark on any tourist's must-see list in Manhattan, but what it really is, is a house of prayer. It's an open door into all that your heart desires.

When I chat with folks in the cathedral, I meet people with burdens and questions. With fears and memories. With pain.

It is in these times that we try to fight the sometimes over-whelming temptation to discouragement. So what do we do? We pray! We turn to Jesus.

And I try to share my joy. It may never be easy to believe in God's plan when times are tough, but it can become more plausible when we see joy, when we see joyful people who draw us into their treasure, which is their gift of faith.

I invite them to discover for themselves the source of my joy so that their joy may be complete. I hope that they meet God in that beautiful church. And I hope they see that He is truly living and present in our world today.

OCTOBER 18

Feast of
Saint Luke

Saint Luke is the patron saint of doctors and, we believe, the first Christian physician. The Gospel of Luke is filled with episodes of Jesus showing compassion for those who are suffering, sick, and in need of help. What better time, then, to give thanks to those in the healthcare ministry?

You may be tempted to think that Catholic healthcare is in retreat. We've seen the closing of many of our hospitals. These losses are deeply felt in the communities in which they occur and are very troubling to those who responded so generously to Jesus's call to care for the sick.

But those closings do not eclipse the wonderful things the Church does to help the sick, the elderly, children, mothers, and the poor each and every day. I am always encouraged by the many devoted Catholic faithful who have dedicated their lives to caring for others as doctors, nurses, therapists, emergency medical technicians, and volunteers. Their faith inspires their healing ministry.

I once met a doctor who told me, "Cardinal, I'm not a Catholic—I really don't practice any faith at all. However, I am always glad when I can hire a person of faith, because along with their medical skills, they bring with them joy and hope to the people whom they serve." What a wonderful testimony to those in the healthcare field!

This service mentality is exactly what Christ asks of all of us.

OCTOBER 19

Feast of
Saint Isaac Jogues

Saint Isaac Jogues was one of the North American martyrs, who labored in the northern part of New York.

The early missionaries were not having much success in their efforts at evangelization among the Native Americans. Understandably, the Native Americans were suspicious of them and seemingly uninterested in the faith.

Nevertheless, those early Jesuits kept at it, mostly hoping to win the trust of the Native peoples through their attention to the sick, care for the children, interest in and respect for Native customs and traditions, and hospitality in their primitive dwellings—in other words, by their charity.

One day, Saint Isaac Jogues recalled, some members of the tribe were harassing the Jesuit missionaries. Suddenly, the chief himself came to their defense! He reminded the unruly men that the "blackrobes" had been good to them and deserved to be treated with respect.

Father Isaac was ecstatic because this was a sign of gratitude! And he knew from the Bible that gratitude is the beginning of faith. Now their strategy was to lead those people to be grateful not only to the missionaries but to the one true God!

We, too, must learn to be grateful. When we're grateful to God and acknowledge that without Him we can do nothing, and that everything we have is an unmerited gift from a good God who loves us passionately, we become a people of faith, trust, humility, and generosity!

*For we are his handiwork, created in Christ Jesus for
the good works that God has prepared in advance.*
—EPHESIANS 2:10

We are different! We are unique! We are charged to stand out!

In a world that says our value depends on what we have, we say our value depends on who we are.

In a culture that claims that sexual pleasure is a right and a fling is okay, we embrace chastity, reverencing sexuality so much that we believe it is intended only for a man and woman in lifelong, life-giving marriage.

In a world that treats human life frivolously and experimentally, we proclaim, "Life is sacred from womb to tomb," and must be protected and cherished.

In a culture that measures a person's worth by his prestige, power, or property, we say a person is a child of God regardless of his possessions or profession.

In a society that is mired in dodging truth and putting oneself first, we claim that honesty, values, integrity, and principle are nonnegotiable.

In a world that acts as if God does not exist or, at best, does not care, we claim a Lord who responds to prayer, who feeds us, and who remains with us in the body and blood of His only Son.

In a culture that teaches that anything goes and that morals and commandments are obsolete, we know that we are sinners, that we are daily summoned to interior renewal and contrition, and that the Lord has given us a way to live.

Yes, we are indeed different.

OCTOBER 21

The Lord is close to the brokenhearted,
saves those whose spirit is crushed.

—PSALM 34:19

When something is broken, we usually consult the one who made it to find out what's wrong and how we can fix it.

God is our creator. When His creatures are broken, we best listen to His instructions for repair.

God's Word does not let us down. The people of Israel were, like us, worried, wayward, and weary. Moses spoke to them, imploring them to keep the commandments and return to the Lord with all their hearts.

What are these lessons we should learn from the Lord? We know them deep down. We were raised in families and faiths that taught them and modeled them.

"Thou shalt not kill." "Thou shalt not bear false witness against thy neighbor." "Blessed are the peacemakers, for they shall be called children of God."

"Do unto others as you would have them do unto you."

"Love one another."

Sound familiar? These exhortations come from God.

God made us in His own image and likeness. He loves us, treats us with dignity and respect, and asks us to do the same thing.

Do we seek solutions to problems from discredited peddlers of anger, division, and more violence? Or do we go to the Creator and consult the users' manual to fix what seems broken?

OCTOBER 22

Feast of
Saint John Paul II

On this glorious feast day, we remember this extraordinary pontiff who taught us so much about Christ's love.

We first saw him in Saint Peter's Square on October 16, 1978, when he was introduced to the world. He spoke so beautifully, so assuredly when he said: "Be not afraid."

"Be not afraid." Not his own words but those of God to Abraham, to Moses, to Ezekiel, to Jeremiah, to Mary, to Joseph. And to us.

"Be not afraid." The frequent words of Jesus to His Apostles.

In John Paul II, the Lord found a disciple who obeyed that exhortation.

He was not afraid to profess faith in a climate of doubt, to offer hope in a world ravaged and often discouraged, to proclaim life in a culture of death, and to forgive in a society that often preferred revenge.

We still recall the images of "John Paul the strong," the vigorous world pilgrim, the indefatigable apostle. But we also recall with tenderness "John Paul the weak," crippled, trembling, dying. On Easter Sunday, just days before his death, he valiantly went to the window to bless the pilgrims gathered in Saint Peter's Square. He desperately tried to speak, but the words just wouldn't come.

Yet we know that God was whispering to him: "Be not afraid."

And we know that Saint John Paul II now basks in the radiance of Christ, no longer in pain. If we listen quietly, we can hear them both exhorting, "Be not afraid."

*Therefore, we who are receiving the unshakable kingdom should have
gratitude, with which we should offer worship
pleasing to God in reverence and awe.*
—HEBREWS 12:28

Saint Augustine taught that gratitude is the beginning of wisdom, sanctity, virtue, and happiness. The English poet George Herbert says, "Thou that has given so much to me, give one thing more: a grateful heart."

A spirit of thanksgiving is an antidote to one of today's most debilitating attitudes: entitlement. An attitude of entitlement is when someone believes, "I've got rights; I've got things coming to me; I am owed certain things."

Those who feel entitled think: "My family, my faith, my friends, my country, my job, all owe me. They exist to serve me and meet my needs; the world revolves around me. People exist to satisfy my needs, so they are to be respected only when they are useful to me. Convenience becomes my creed, while sacrifice, service, selflessness become dirty words."

Christ teaches the exact opposite. We are put here on earth to know, love, and serve Him. While we're here, it is our task to be our brother's keeper—to look out for others and treat them with dignity and respect.

When we do that, we're expressing our gratitude to God for all that He has given us. That's Christianity. That's decent, civil, thoughtful, responsible living.

Historians say that modernity began when Copernicus discovered that the earth was not the center of the universe.

Well, maturity begins when I admit that neither am I. In the end, it's all about "thank you," not "give me."

In my name they will drive out demons,
they will speak new languages.
—MARK 16:17

All the baptized faithful are called to act in the person of Christ—as beloved of the Father, as chosen child, as lover of humanity, as healer of wounds, as sent to bring the good news, as reconciler, and so on.

The priest, however, is called to act *in persona Christi*—"in the person of Christ"—as head, shepherd, and spouse of the Church, uniquely, sacramentally, and personally. By the Sacrament of Holy Orders, his identity is so configured to the Person of Christ that he is united with Him in shepherding His flock. Thus, we call a parish priest a pastor, a shepherd.

Thus, when a priest celebrates the sacraments, he *is* Christ. When we in Holy Orders preach at the Eucharist, our persona is transformed. We assume a new, elevated identity: We preach not in our name but in the name of Jesus. At the consecration of the Eucharist, for instance, the priest does not say, "This is His body; this is His blood." No! He says, *"in persona Christi,"* "This is my body; this is my blood." What a beautiful image!

Through ordination, the priest is invited by Christ to share in His love for His spouse. The Church is the bride of Christ. So, too, is she the bride of the priest. It's a lovely image of our spiritual family, isn't it?

Keep my sabbaths, and reverence my sanctuary.
I am the Lord.
—LEVITICUS 19:30

Should it shock us, Pope Francis asks, that a culture that violently intrudes on the life of a baby in the sanctuary of his mother's womb would lose reverence for all places intended by God as safe and secure? Should it shock us that a society that finds the poor bothersome instead of brothers would lock the doors to a nation celebrated as a sanctuary? Should it shock us that people would burden the dying with guilt for peacefully and patiently savoring each day until God takes them?

Can any of us claim sanctuary anywhere when the first and most significant sanctuary of them all—the mother's womb—can be raided and ravaged?

I think of another sanctuary, Saint Peter's Basilica in Rome, and the massive square leading into it, brilliantly designed by Bernini. When asked about the massive colonnades surrounding the square, he explained that they were the arms of God, the outreach of Jesus gathering us in, the embrace of our Mother Mary and the Church tenderly protecting her children.

Behold our model—a sanctuary that beckons us, where we are safe and secure in our mother's tender yet strong embrace, where the Creator assures us of protection and life itself.

Now behold the baby in the sanctuary of the womb. Once that's violated, once a society deems it legal to invade it, the integrity of the natural and the supernatural is ruptured, and we have no place safe and secure left to go.

OCTOBER 26

And how does this happen to me,
that the mother of my Lord should come to me?
—LUKE 1:43

A visit to Mom's house is something that fills us with unfailing joy. It's something we always look forward to.

With Mom, there is no need to impress anybody. The place is familiar, the conversation is natural, the food tastes better, and someone loves us unconditionally. We always leave refreshed and renewed. A visit to Mom's house is a blessing indeed—a gift, a renewal.

This is also how we feel when we visit our Mother Mary. She has many homes: Fatima, Czestochowa, Knock, Guadalupe, Pompei, Loreto, our parish shrines, our own backyard grottos, and under her image in our homes.

Our Blessed Mother never lets us down. She has gotten us out of jams, helped the people we love and send to her, and at times gotten us back on the right path.

Our spiritual mother loves us unconditionally. She listens while we pour out our guts. She is not bored when we tell her what we're worried about. She promises she'll help. The conversation is always great.

When she catches us crying, she asks what's wrong. She listens as we tell her the ways we're afraid we've hurt her Son and her other children. She'll encourage us to tell her Son "I'm sorry."

We go to our Blessed Mother because we need her. We need to tell her that we love her and we need her. In Mary's presence, just as in our own mother's, we will always feel at home.

*When God created human beings, he made them
in the likeness of God.*
—GENESIS 5:1

Ideas have consequences, don't they? Convictions have corollaries. And God's Word enchants us with one of the most profound ideas of all—that we are made in His image and likeness, that God actually abides in us and we in Him, and that deep in our being is the very breath of the divine.

This noble tenet—that human nature reflects God's own nature, that God looks at us and smiles with delight—has particularly cogent consequences for the republic we call home.

John Adams wrote: "Let us see delineated before us, the true map of man. Let us hear the dignity of his nature, and the noble rank he holds among the works of God!"

Yes, our second president expressed it well: This "true map of man" is a map engraved in human reason and natural law, a map whose paths can be walked only with a reverence for life, a respect for others, a grasp of virtue, and a responsible civility.

This soaring idea has consequences now, as it has throughout our history, in the quest for independence, in abolition and civil rights, in the waging of war and the promotion of peace, in care for others, in the strengthening of marriage and family, and in the promotion of a culture of life.

Ideas do have consequences, and I pray that we all have the wisdom to recognize that we are indeed made in God's image and that deep in our being is the life of God.

OCTOBER 28

May the God of hope fill you with all joy and peace in believing,
so that you may abound in hope by the power of the holy Spirit.
—ROMANS 15:13

Faith means we believe in God; hope means we believe in a God who makes and keeps His promises.

How, where, and when? We don't know. But we do know that God's love has been sealed in our hearts through the Holy Spirit. We know that He is always there and will never leave us.

That's good news.

That's what we call sanctifying grace.

We have hope because we belong to Jesus Christ. He has claimed us as His own; He has purchased us with His precious blood.

The woman at the well said to Jesus, "I know that the Messiah is coming, the one called the Anointed; when he comes, he will tell us everything." And Jesus said to her, "I am He."

Yes! He is the One. He is "God from God, light from light, true God from true God, begotten, not made, consubstantial with the Father."

That's why we have hope. We belong to Him.

If we place our hope in anyone or anything else, we're going to be disappointed.

We can look futilely for hope or faith elsewhere, but any results will be fleeting. Only in Christ will we hear the same words that He spoke at the well: "I am He!"

OCTOBER 29

Who [indeed] is the victor over the world but the one
who believes that Jesus is the Son of God?
—1 JOHN 5:5

It is becoming more and more clear that our society is looking down on religion. Recent scholarly studies report that fewer people belong to a religion, identify themselves as a member of a particular church, or attend Sabbath worship. We Catholics in the United States, for instance, attract only about 28 percent of our people to Sunday Mass, the heart of our faith.

Although many Americans feel that religion is losing its influence, they regret this fact, believing that one's faith should have public expression and that faith is good for us individually and as a nation.

Even so, we cannot deny that these are difficult days for those who both believe and belong. A society that pushes "tolerance on steroids" seems to have little tolerance for those who practice their faith. We are branded as superstitious, as backward, or even as narrow-minded bigots. And any church that believes that its deepest convictions have an impact on the way we work, marry, love, teach, serve, die, and have and raise children is considered intolerant.

Jesus warned us that the world would hate us as they hated Him. As the teachings of our faith become more and more scorned, we can expect to be dismissed and derided and have our freedoms questioned and intruded on.

This is our cross to bear. And perhaps this is where we can best be a light to the world.

OCTOBER 30

*Whoever has two tunics should share with the person who has none.
And whoever has food should do likewise.*
—LUKE 3:11

People in our communities are hungry. And when they hunger, one of the first places they come for help is the Church. We cannot let them down, especially as the weather grows colder. It is now that the need grows.

Our great communities do a rather good job of feeding the hungry. Our municipal, county, state, and federal agencies; our volunteer programs; and our neighbors of all faiths daily provide meals in a generously effective way. But when feeding the hungry, the Church must be on the front lines. And thanks to the inspiration of Jesus and the care of our great people, we are. So many of our parishes, schools, programs, and organizations do this splendidly already. Those that are doing it are asked to do more; those that are not are asked to start now.

Christ commands us to feed the hungry. How can we approach the altar for the bread to nourish our souls if we refuse to share our daily bread with people who need to nourish their bodies? We're hypocrites if we distribute and receive the food of heaven but do not share the food of earth with our hungry neighbors.

In the early Church, bringing food to every Sunday Mass was an ordinary practice. It would be distributed to those in need. Let us get back to that and share what we have.

For whatever we do for others, we also do for Christ.

OCTOBER 31

But our citizenship is in heaven, and from it we also await a savior,
the Lord Jesus Christ.

—PHILIPPIANS 3:20

On a few occasions when I was a child, I dressed up as a "hobo" for Halloween. The word *hobo* isn't a very courteous one to use, but a friend of mine recently reminded me of what the word means.

It was a term used in the Depression. During that time, when thousands and thousands of men lost their jobs and livelihood, they simply said, "We should go back home." A man like that was "homeward bound": a "hobo."

In that sense, we are all hobos. We are all homeward bound, that is, on our way to heaven. Because this world is fleeting. We know it's transitory and fading.

That might be a bit of a depressing thought because we love our lives. Yes, life is good. Life is beautiful. Life is filled with so many joys. But it's just an antipasto—that is, an appetizer—to what almighty God has prepared for us for all eternity. We have our true citizenship in heaven. We're just passing through, are we not?

That's why the believer is not afraid of death. Eternal life is God's pure gift to us. We cannot merit it or earn it. It is a gift of God's mercy. The one who merited it for us was Jesus. By dying, he destroyed our death. By rising, he restored our life.

NOVEMBER 1

All Saints' Day

We are all called to be saints.

A rather startling reality, isn't it? Yet there is a universal call to holiness.

In Rome, one of my favorite shrines is Il Santuario del Divino Amore. It's right outside of Rome, in the suburbs. A beautiful prayer is there: *"La Madonna Del Divino Amore, fatti santi."* "Our Lady of Divine Love, make us saints."

We're called to be saints.

When I became the archbishop of New York, some journalists asked me if I wanted to become a cardinal. "Well," I responded, "what I really want is to become a saint. And I want to help people be saints." I've got a long way to go, of course.

Here are a few bullet points for today as we grow in holiness:

- It's not about you. It's about God and other people.
- It's not about our strength. It's about our trust in God.
- It's not about going after things exotic and extraordinary. It's doing the ordinary things extraordinarily well for the glory of God.

That's sanctity!

NOVEMBER 2

All Souls' Day

On this day we remember and pray for the faithful departed, our loved ones.

It's November and nature is dying, and so Mother Church invites us to consider death! We will all one day die; this life is but a preparation for eternity. By dying, Jesus destroyed our death, and by rising, He restored our life.

Perhaps with both a lump in our throat and a smile of love and gratitude, we reverently recall those who have gone before us, thanking God for them and asking Him to bring them mercifully to their true and eternal home of heaven, where we hope to see them again one day.

At a funeral Mass, we realize that it is not as much about the celebration of the life of the deceased as it is about the celebration of the life, death, and Resurrection of Christ. True, we gratefully remember the person who has died, praising God for his or her life, but the center of everything is the life, death, and Resurrection of Jesus—and the deceased's incorporation into that mystery.

The Bible instructs us to pray for the dead. Meaningful Catholic tradition such as Masses and prayers offered for the faithful departed, Mass cards sent to the family, visits to the cemetery, and prayers for the souls in purgatory are all most commendable.

The Church is our home, our family. We especially appreciate her at the hour of death. We're part of a communion that not even death can shatter!

NOVEMBER 3

The Lord shall reign forever, your God, Zion,
through all generations!
—PSALM 146:10

After elections, many people inquire about how I think "the Church did" on election day.

This question usually triggers a mini-catechism lesson from me as I reply that actually "the Church" wasn't on the ballot and the election was not a referendum on her. The Church was founded by the one who stated that "my kingdom is not of this world." The Bible's caution "Put not your trust in princes" would today probably be rendered "Put not your trust in politicians."

This attitude gives us a benign indifference to politics and elections. We "seek first the Kingdom of God," not the power and platforms of worldly politics.

But this indifference is tempered by faithful citizenship. We are, as a matter of fact, very concerned about matters in this world, precisely because God has revealed truths about the human person that have serious implications for people of faith. So yes, although we are much more passionate about heaven than about earth, about the teachings of Jesus and His Church than about the promises of any candidate, we do have a duty to bring the values of faith to the political process.

Though we have grave concerns, we plod along, knowing that this side of Gabriel's trumpet we'll never have a perfect setup, that Christ is our king, and that faith—and the freedom to live it out—is the greatest protection of all for the dignity of the human person and the sanctity of life.

NOVEMBER 4

But whatever gains I had, these I have come to consider
a loss because of Christ.
—PHILIPPIANS 3:7

He was out of jail and came to chat. I was very happy to see this gentleman, as he was one of the men I'd met years earlier while doing prison ministry in the archdiocese.

I was also sad to see that he was on hard times, as you might imagine. Just released from jail, looking for a place to stay and a job, that kind of thing. I did my best to help him out.

I was happier yet when, a couple of months later, he came back to visit me and I could see the change. He was now well dressed and said he had an efficiency apartment and a good job and was able to pay his bills. Good news, I said. When I asked what his job was, he was vague in telling me about it and I didn't pry.

Well, the cycle went on. Another couple of months later, he came back and was in trouble again. I asked what had happened and got a fuller version of the story. Turned out that having the job was good, but it wasn't a good job.

"I was working as a bouncer at a strip club," he shared with me. "The money was good, but wow, it wasn't the best place for me. You know, when I was in prison, I tried to get my life together and returned to my Catholic faith. I figured that's what's most important in life. And so, good as it was, that job had to go if I was going to remain a man of faith."

His was an example of how, as we try to follow Christ, we lose things in our lives. It may be family. Or friends. Or jobs. The gains can be losses. And losses can be gains.

A person should examine himself, and so
eat the bread and drink the cup.
—I CORINTHIANS 11:28

If you want your faith to wither and die, quit going to Sunday Mass. As the body will die without food, the soul will expire without nourishment. That sustenance comes at the Sunday Eucharist.

The Eucharist is the most beautiful, powerful prayer we have. To miss it is to miss Jesus—His Word, His presence, and His body and blood.

As Catholics, we must look forward to Sunday as a day dedicated to the Lord, a day that gives meaning and purpose to the whole week. The heart of Sunday must be the Mass!

We need Sunday to enter into the respite of God, to worship Him, and to realize that our salvation comes not from the many good things we do but from what God has done for us.

Sunday expresses what most unites us as disciples of Christ. On Sunday, we proclaim the Risen Christ. It is the first day of a new creation, the day of a new covenant. In the Mass—the one sacrifice of Calvary—this new covenant ratified in the blood of the Lord Jesus is made present.

No matter how much we accomplish during the week, nothing can compare to what God does at Mass. He draws together His people, fashions them into the communion of the Church, sanctifies them by the outpouring of the Holy Spirit, and nourishes them with the body and blood of the Lord Jesus offered on the cross for the redemption of the world!

NOVEMBER 6

Trust in the Lord with all your heart, on your own intelligence do not rely;
In all your ways be mindful of him, and he will make straight your paths.
—PROVERBS 3:5-6

Life is a journey that comes from God and goes back to Him at death.

In the Gospels, we often hear Jesus speak of his journey to Jerusalem to suffer and die for us on the cross.

The early Church in Rome relived these biblical pilgrimages as believers walked to a different church each day for a procession and Mass—a custom still alive in those churches.

Every day, we see powerful reminders that life itself is a journey that begins with God at conception and goes all the way to our death. We trust, by the mercy of God, that it will culminate in eternal union with Him in heaven.

The tour director of this remarkable travel is God, who is in charge, has an itinerary, knows what He's doing, and walks with us. Our history, and the world's, is His-story.

We accompany one another on this pilgrimage of life. The Church is that group of folks who realize they are on a sacred trip together and who offer help during the difficult stages.

Of course, we know the hard way that there will be unfortunate detours and potholes on our journey. We call them sins. One hopes these wrong turns last just a short time. God asks us to admit them, confess them, and do penance for those detours in order to get back on the right track so that when our journey ends, it ends with Him.

Therefore whoever eats the bread or drinks the cup of the Lord unworthily will have to answer for the body and blood of the Lord.
—I CORINTHIANS 11:27

John the Baptist calls us to "make straight the path of the Lord."

Let us ask ourselves if we are worthy to receive Christ in the Eucharist. The answer is no, we're not.

The Eucharist is not a right, an entitlement, or a reward but a pure gift, and the best way to prepare to receive it is by admitting that we do not deserve such a sacred gift.

When we are conscious of being seriously at odds with God, that is, in a state of mortal sin, we must be reconciled with Him through the Sacrament of Penance before we approach Holy Communion. That teaching is as ancient as Saint Paul, who reminds us never to eat the bread or drink the cup "unworthily."

The most effective way to become worthy is to admit that we are not. This means approaching the Sacrament of Reconciliation when we know our friendship with the Lord has been broken by serious sin.

When we've been away from the family of the Church for a while, it is a wonderful grace to return. But we can't act as if everything is just fine. It's not. We need to apologize for our sins and ask forgiveness. The beauty of this is that forgiveness is ours for the asking.

I am the living bread that came down from heaven;
whoever eats this bread will live forever.
—JOHN 6:51

The *Catechism of the Catholic Church* reminds us of the different aspects of the mystery of the Eucharist. It is a memorial, as we reverently obey the command Jesus gave us at His Last Supper to "do this in memory of me." It is a sacrifice, as the eternal oblation Christ made on the cross is renewed. The Eucharist is a meal, as God's family comes together in community to be fed with the body and blood of Christ. Finally, it is a presence, as Jesus remains really and truly with us in the Blessed Sacrament.

Saint John Paul II taught that the Risen Jesus answered the prayer of the two disciples on the road to Emmaus—"Stay with us"—by celebrating the Eucharist. Jesus remains with His Church in the Eucharist.

That's why the tabernacle in our churches must be prominent, readily seen, beautifully decorated, and highlighted. The Church's guidelines stipulate that the tabernacle must always be part of the main body of the Church, never in a separate structure, visible to the congregation, inviting reverence and prayer, and suitably adorned.

Many years ago, after the dedication of a wonderful new church, I chatted with the pastor about the power of the liturgy. He told me that what moved him most was lighting the sanctuary lamp for the first time, concluding: "Then I knew Jesus was in His new home."

And He remains always in our home, waiting for us to come visit.

NOVEMBER 9

Blessed are those who have not seen and have believed.
—JOHN 20:29

Our lives seem to be ruled by numbers.

We can grasp, understand, and tackle numbers. They are clean and clear. Numbers can cheer us up; numbers can depress us. The human intellect relies on what can be measured, charted, graphed, or scientifically or medically examined.

However, the Lord is infinitely wiser than we are. Our measurements do not apply to Him. For Him, a thousand years is but a day. No earthly metrics define or constrain Him.

As people of faith, we place our confidence in what we cannot see, analyze, measure, count, or quantify. We trust what is invisible—the power, mercy, promises, and revelation of the God who cannot be programmed into a computer.

We trust:

That the bread and wine become His body and blood
That He is alive in a stumbling and sinful Church
That our whispered prayers are heard and answered
That He is still with us even when our hearts break
That sins can be forgiven and progress in holiness is
   possible
That eternal life awaits and that the joys of this life are
   but hints of what is to come
That nothing can separate us from the love of God
That the man on the cross rose from the dead

None of these things is measurable, but all are worth counting on!

NOVEMBER 10

For if we live, we live for the Lord, and if we die, we die for the Lord; so then,
whether we live or die, we are the Lord's.
—ROMANS 14:8

A California funeral home once boasted of a bestselling casket that had the words RETURN TO SENDER stamped boldly on it. Not a bad anecdote for November, the month in which the Church reverently recalls the faithful departed.

We can count on nature to set the atmosphere: The days are shorter, the dark comes earlier, the sun is shy, the trees are stark, the flowers shrivel, and the grass subsides.

Nature is dying as winter approaches. No wonder Holy Mother Church advises us to contemplate death. Is that morbid? Not for the believer. Death is as natural as birth.

Some trepidation is understandable. After all, preservation of life is our most potent instinct. Thus, in a human way, we shudder at the prospect of death, and we fight it. God wants us to savor and hold on to life until He calls us back to Him.

Way back on the day of our birth, we fought leaving the safety, security, and comfort of the womb, didn't we? "It's nice and cozy in here, and who knows what's out there, anyway?" is the question the baby in the womb unconsciously asks.

Likewise, we shudder at the birth to eternal life to which we all are invited.

But the believer embraces death as a friend. Saint Francis calls it "Sister Death."

We come from God, and we are destined to return to Him for all eternity. We are all marked—from the moment of conception—RETURN TO SENDER.

NOVEMBER 11

You are the light of the world.
—MATTHEW 5:14

Some years ago after Mass, a young man named Les introduced himself to me.

"Hey, Cardinal Dolan," he said enthusiastically. "I'm going to become a Catholic at the Easter Vigil." I was intrigued and asked what attracted him to the faith.

"About six months ago," he said, "I was diagnosed with cancer and I had to do chemo. I went in three days a week and met a woman named Margaret." Turns out Margaret was there getting chemotherapy as well. She was in her sixties and Les was in his late twenties, but they sat next to each other three days a week and got to know each other. Les said it was a really tough time for him. He was physically sick and nauseated, feeling discouraged and depressed, but Margaret always managed to cheer him up. She always seemed to have a smile and seemed serene. He came to love and appreciate her and one day decided to ask about her secret. "What makes you tick?" he asked. To which she responded, "I guess it's my faith. I'm Catholic. Which means I pray, I go to Mass. I got the Sacrament of the Anointing of the Sick, and my faith gives me a lot of hope and trust."

Les asked if he could have some of that, and she said sure. So Les joined the RCIA, that is, the Rite of Christian Initiation for Adults. And he would soon become Catholic.

"Les, let me give you a hug," I said. "And let me meet Margaret, too. I want to give her a hug. She should get a commission or something for this one!" Well, Les got a little somber and said Margaret had died a couple months ago. Her cancer took her. But there's no doubt that she obeyed the exhortation of Jesus to be a light to the world. Les today is glorifying his Heavenly Father in the family of the Church because Margaret allowed her light to shine before him.

NOVEMBER 12

Know this, my dear brothers: everyone should be quick to hear.
—JAMES 1:19

In 1992, I was on a study tour/pilgrimage in the Holy Land. In the middle of a long hike, we came across two shepherds chatting in a patch of shade. Their flocks were all mixed together. Through our guide, we asked how the sheep would know their rightful shepherd when the time came to move on. They demonstrated by each going to opposite sides of the path, shouting a command, and walking away. Immediately, the sheep ran behind their proper shepherd. It was clear: The sheep knew their shepherd; the shepherd knew his sheep.

Once more, the two leaders allowed their flocks to mingle. In an obvious attempt to trick the sheep, they exchanged their outer apparel. Once again, each went to an opposite side of the path, gave his familiar call, and began to walk away. Without a second's pause, the sheep followed their proper shepherd! The sheep knew their shepherd so well that they could not be deceived by a disguise.

So, too, must we learn to follow our Shepherd. Jesus, the Good Shepherd, tends to His flock in a variety of effective and tender ways. The problem, of course, is not that Jesus isn't calling; the problem is that we are not listening.

I believe that we best hear Christ's voice in silence. The Bible tells us that the language He prefers is silence and the atmosphere He best works in is silence.

"Be still and know that I am God," He whispers. To hear His voice, we must be quiet. To let Him talk, we must shut up.

NOVEMBER 13

Sing to the Lord, praise the Lord.
—JEREMIAH 20:13

Saint John Paul II began World Youth Days in 1984 with a hunch that young people from all over the world were hungry for the chance to come together in the solidarity of faith, prayer, witness, and celebration.

And come they have. The nearly weeklong festival of World Youth Days has become a constant of Catholic life. The "fireworks" usually don't begin until later in the week, with the arrival of the Holy Father, but other events serve to educate, stimulate discussion, discern vocations, and rejoice in prayer and song.

What's the appeal? First, young people who feel alone in their faith appreciate the solidarity. As they look around at millions of other youth from all over the world, they are exhilarated by the reality that they belong to a family—the Church—and are not all by themselves.

Second, they are energized by the Holy Father's call to greatness, to heroic virtue, and to sanctity.

Third, the pilgrims are unfailingly moved by the universality of the Church. To meet, pray with, and listen to other youth from all over—including from countries where to practice the faith means to risk one's life—is a real boost for everyone. Our own problems shrink when we hear others describe their challenges and crosses.

This solidarity in faith becomes life-changing for many. Their heroic embrace of their faith, their zeal, and their passion serve as an inspiration to us all who may need a rejuvenation of faith.

NOVEMBER 14

Let us come before him with a song of praise,
joyfully sing out our psalms.
—PSALM 95:2

Gratitude is a virtue that is appropriate for every moment of our lives.

Gratitude keeps us humble people, never snobs, as we realize that every talent, every break, every breath, every success, is a gift from God.

Gratitude keeps us selfless, never selfish, as we realize that as Jesus teaches, "Without cost you have received; without cost you are to give."

Gratitude keeps us prayerful as we express our thanks to God, the giver of all good things.

Gratitude keeps us faithful when adversity comes as we remember the good to get through the bad.

Gratitude keeps us open-minded and accepting as we realize that we're no better than anybody else and that we can hardly brag or look down on anyone else, since all we have was given to us.

God has been so good to us. Among His many gifts are life, health, family, talents, friends, and faith. Thank Him for those gifts. Use them to the very best of your ability and share them with others.

That's gratitude; that's Christianity. For in the end, it's all about giving, not getting; sharing, not hoarding; loving, not hating; forgiving, not taking revenge; helping, not harming. In the end, it's not all about "me." It's all about God and His people.

*Rather, living the truth in love, we should grow in every way
into him who is the head, Christ.*
—EPHESIANS 4:15

In my senior year of college, I led a delegation to the rector to argue that it was time to drop the "outmoded" expectation that we seminarians had to major in philosophy. Those "revolutionary" days—this was 1971—required, we insisted, that we future priests be specialists in more "relevant" areas such as psychology and sociology.

The rector, a wise man, listened carefully and patiently. He thanked us and asked for some time to think and consult about our demand.

A week later he called us back in and told us that the philosophy requirement would remain. (I'm now sure glad he did!) One of the more fiery students piped up, "See, you never listen to us! You do not respect us."

The rector calmly explained: "Just because I do not agree with you or do not accept your proposal does not mean that I did not listen, nor that I do not love and respect you."

Not a bad philosophy lesson, by the way.

To listen to every person. To love every person. To respect every person.

We are part of a Church in which, yes, all are listened to, loved, and respected, but no, not a Church of anything goes.

An effective pastor cherishes, protects, feeds, and leads his flock while welcoming his sheep into the fold. But he will not let them wander off and do whatever or go wherever the sheep might want. His duty is to bring them back and rescue them from danger.

This shepherd is still trying to learn how to be like that, to *love* all without ever compromising the *truth*.

NOVEMBER 16

*It is my wish, then, that in every place the men should pray,
lifting up holy hands, without anger or argument.*
—1 TIMOTHY 2:8

Glory to God in the highest!

In the Gospel of Matthew, Jesus promised: "For where two or three are gathered together in my name, there am I in the midst of them."

Do we understand the power of the promise He made? I sure do. I have seen Him where 2 or 3, 200 or 300, and 2,000 or 3,000 gather in His name.

In dynamic parishes all over our amazing country; in prayer groups and youth groups; in soup kitchens and classrooms; in faithful priests, deacons, and religious women and men; in committed parish directors and pastoral ministers; in seminarians and novices; in sickrooms and nursing homes; in choirs and catechists; and in our homes and families, Jesus is with us whenever we gather.

I have met Him as two or three gather, everywhere I've been. Jesus is alive, active, teaching, serving, sanctifying, and forgiving. He is with us. Don't you ever doubt it.

I have seen Him in your faces, heard Him in your expressions of hope, and felt Him in your energy. My sacred task is to remind you of His presence with us.

He keeps His promise. He is in our midst. That's why we are not afraid. That's why we can "cast out to the deep." That's how we become saints. That's why we are filled with joy. That's why we can be heralds of hope. That's why we say: "Glory to God in the highest!"

You shall treat the alien who resides with you no differently than the natives born among you; you shall love the alien as yourself; for you too were once aliens in the land of Egypt.

—LEVITICUS 19:34

Throughout American history, whenever there is tension and turmoil in society—economic distress, political rifts, war, distrust and confusion in culture—the immigrant unfailingly becomes the scapegoat.

It's a supreme paradox in our American culture—where every person, unless a Native American, is a descendant of immigrants—that we seem to harbor an ingrained fear of "the other."

We can chart periodic spasms of anti-immigrant fever in our nation's history: the nativists of the 1840s, who led mobs to torch Irish homes and Catholic churches; the anti-Catholic Know-Nothings of the 1850s, who wanted to deny the vote to everyone except native-born, "pure" Americans; the Ku Klux Klan of the 1920s, which spewed hate against blacks, Jews, Catholics, and foreigners; and the proponents of the eugenics movement of the 1920s and 1930s, who worried that racial purity was being compromised by the immigrant and non-Anglo-Saxon bloodlines.

The anti-immigrant strain in our American heritage, however strong, is not dominant. Thank God, there's another sentiment in our national soul—one that welcomes and embraces the immigrant. That's the ethos that is most especially a part of our Catholic culture, which has been a spiritual mother to immigrants to America.

To welcome immigrants, to work hard for their legalization and citizenship, to help them feel at home, to treat them as neighbors and allies in the greatest project of human rights and ethnic and religious harmony in history, flows from the bright, noble side of our American and Catholic character.

NOVEMBER 18

The chief priests and the entire Sanhedrin kept trying to obtain testimony against Jesus in order to put him to death, but they found none.
—MARK 14:55

We do not think about it that often. Perhaps we are embarrassed about it; more likely, we have sanitized it over the centuries and it does not dawn on us anymore.

I am speaking of the fact that we belong to a Church whose founder was executed as a criminal! Yes, our God was arrested, imprisoned, tortured, judged, convicted, and put to death in the most brutal way. Our God was a prisoner.

He was judged by the Romans, by the mob, and by the religious leaders of His day to be a threat to public safety. To heck with justice; forget about the apparent innocence of Jesus. Charges were trumped up. His arrest was arranged for late at night as the city prepared for a big holiday, and so few could come to His defense. And in less than twelve hours He was prosecuted, condemned, tortured, and executed.

The only ones there to console Him, to stick by Him, were His mother, sobbing with grief; His best friend; and a fellow criminal on His right, whom legend calls Dismas, who defended Him and acknowledged His innocence right before he himself died.

Is it any wonder that the earth quaked at this injustice?

The Church, ever conscious of the violence done to her founder, calls us—through the Corporal Works of Mercy—to care for those accused and those imprisoned. For as Christ taught, what we do for others, we do for Him.

*For you will be his witness before all
to what you have seen and heard.*

—ACTS 22:15

How do we renew, restore, repair, and reenergize our faith in the Person, message, and invitation of Jesus, Our Lord and Savior? That's the challenge posed by the New Evangelization.

One of the most prominent and influential converts to Catholicism in the history of the Catholic community in the United States was Dorothy Day. Day herself related a number of features that drew her to Jesus and His Church.

One especially powerful one was when she shared a meager room in Greenwich Village with two other young women who were struggling, like her, to make it in New York City.

The two roommates were Catholic. Day at the time was a socialist, probably an agnostic, living a rather hedonistic life.

She watched the two other girls. She admired them. What moved her? What inspired her?

For one thing, they went to Mass every Sunday morning (their only morning to sleep in, by the way). For another, they prayed silently every night before bed. For a third, they were deeply in love with two men and had set their wedding dates but wanted "to wait" until marriage, something they admitted was tough to do. That virtue impressed Day. For a fourth, they were from poor, struggling families and thus had a heart for others in need.

Not bad: Sunday Mass; daily prayer; virtue, even when it's tough; and a humble charity. Their example evangelized a future saint, Dorothy Day.

Maybe the *New* Evangelization requires the recovery of some *old* stuff!

NOVEMBER 20

Whatever you do, do from the heart,
as for the Lord and not for others.
—COLOSSIANS 3:23

During my happy years in Washington, D.C., I used to try to take a long walk as often as possible (as I still do). One of my routes would bring me by the National Cathedral, where I came to know one of the workmen rather well. He was a stonecutter, and I would often meet him as I passed his workshop. At first I'd just wave at him and he'd yell out a greeting, but after a while we "shook" and introduced ourselves; soon I'd be stopping for a chat.

"Your work is hard," I observed one day, "and it must get tedious. Yet you seem to enjoy it." Never will I forget his reply: "How could I not? I'm helping to build the Lord's temple!"

You realize that 90 percent of Our Lord's time on earth was spent without notice in Nazareth. In other words, 90 percent of His life was in the company of a carpenter, in a workshop. Later on, in amazement, His townspeople, stunned by His message and miracles, would ask, "Isn't this the carpenter's son?" The Church proudly proclaims, "You bet it is!"

Thus can all workers say, as did my stonecutter friend in Washington, "I'm helping to build the Lord's temple."

For the Son of Man will come with his angels in his Father's glory,
and then he will repay everyone according to his conduct.
—MATTHEW 16:27

If there was not some sacrifice, hardship, and challenge to living our Catholic faith, we might end up taking it for granted and setting it aside.

In the Gospels, Jesus said, "Whoever wishes to come after me must deny himself, take up his cross, and follow me."

Dr. Philip Jenkins, a scholar of religion at Penn State University, once observed that the Church grows rapidly and the faith of her believers is deep and vibrant in countries where there is persecution. Conversely, it languishes and gradually loses its luster in countries that prosper.

Convenience, ease, no demands, no sacrifice, blending in, drifting along—that's a poisonous recipe for faith.

Hardship, sacrifice, harassment, ridicule, standing for gospel values, loyalty to our faith—that's the recipe for a deep, sincere, dynamic faith.

We see it in the Old Testament: When the people of Israel are at peace, prosperous, free, and unfettered in their faith, they turn to false gods. When they are under attack, persecuted, and vilified for their faith, their religion is pure and strong.

Seems like "easy religion" languishes and "hard discipleship" flourishes.

So what do we do?

We voluntarily take on sacrifices to remind us of the cross Jesus asks us to carry with Him. We offer penance. We fast. And we pray.

When it's easy to be a Catholic, look out because it's tougher to be a good Catholic; when it's hard to be a Catholic, it's easier to be a good one!

NOVEMBER 22

Feast of Saint Cecilia

Saint Cecilia is the patron of church musicians, cantors, and choirs.

One of the great gifts to the Church flowing from the liturgical renewal of the Second Vatican Council has been that we Catholics now sing and that music and song are looked upon as very significant for communal worship.

If there were a Catholic Rip Van Winkle who had been asleep for a hundred years and finally woke up, what would certainly astonish him the next Sunday when he went to Mass would be the music.

I'm not saying that we do not have a long way to go. We do! I still am surprised at the number of people in the congregation whose faces look like those on Mount Rushmore and who do not sing. Progress we need, but progress we have certainly made, and this is due in large part to the musicians, cantors, and choir members who lead us reverently and joyfully. Thank you!

Make a joyful noise to the Lord. I find a wonderful "catholic" approach to music: contemporary, traditional, Gregorian chant. And to quote another great saint, Saint Augustine once said, "He who sings prays twice."

*The headwaiter called the bridegroom and said to him, "Everyone serves
good wine first, and then when people have drunk freely, an inferior one;
but you have kept the good wine until now."*
—JOHN 2:9-10

Jesus is the greatest and most effective teacher ever. Every action, word, gesture, and miracle of His is meant to convey a deeper lesson.

In the Gospel of John, we read about His first miracle: He changes water into wine at Cana. And He chose to work this miracle—His first—at a wedding reception.

By working His first miracle for a newly married couple, Christ teaches that He is present at every marriage and that every marriage is yet another occasion for Him to work a miracle by changing the water of selfishness, loneliness, and willfulness into the wine of sharing, family, and love. He could have performed His first miracle anywhere; He chose a wedding.

We as Catholics believe that marriage is a sacrament. That means that it reveals to us the divine. When we watch a husband and wife, we see a hint, a reminder, a metaphor of how God loves us.

Marriage is a sacred, noble, and miraculous calling, but I fear it has become cheapened, tarnished, abused, and weakened. We need Jesus again to transform it from the shallowness and sadness of empty wine jars to the exciting, intoxicating fullness of new wine. We need the miracle at Cana again!

Jesus is telling us something today: Husbands and wives, your marriage is a miracle! It is a sacrament! Your married love speaks of My love! You are living, breathing mirrors of My love.

He has a name written on his cloak and on his thigh,
"King of kings and Lord of lords."
—REVELATION 19:16

The Bible drives home the point: Christ is our king: the king of our hearts, the king of the nations, the king of history. The Old Testament foretells the coming of a son of David who will rule over the House of David forever. We believe that's Jesus. In the Gospel, He speaks of the Son of Man sitting upon His glorious throne. The Book of Revelation gives us an image of the heavenly court. Thus, the acknowledgment that Christ is our king is as old as the Bible. But the Feast of Christ the King is rather new, established by Pope Pius XI only in 1925.

What does it mean to be a subject of Christ the King in America? Part of the answer is given in the great biblical charter for the Corporal Works of Mercy: Feed the hungry, give drink to the thirsty, welcome the stranger, clothe the naked, care for the sick, visit the imprisoned. This has been a hallmark of the Catholic Church.

Every day and every night, out of love for the least of these and out of obedience to Christ the King, Catholics do all these things through our vast network dedicated to the Corporal Works of Mercy. We do it all precisely because of our Catholic faith.

The last Sunday of the Church year allows us to profess: Jesus Christ is our king. Him we love. Him we serve. Him we obey.

There is no salvation through anyone else, nor is there any other name under heaven given to the human race by which we are to be saved.

—ACTS 4:12

Advent begins soon. It is the holy season of spiritual preparation for Christmas, in which we prepare for the coming of our Savior, whose birth the world celebrates at Christmas.

But it's all a sham or a winter cultural celebration if we figure we really don't need a Savior.

Many people lament these days that Christmas has lost its primary religious meaning.

That's not surprising. God the Father sent His Son to save us from sin. If we have concluded that we have no sin, if we are convinced that we do not need mercy, we're really telling God that He's wasted His time. It's like saying, "What a nice idea to send a Savior to bring us mercy, Lord, but that's not really on my gift list. Haven't you heard? I don't need it."

I'm no Scrooge, but a splendid Advent practice is to examine our consciences and discover our sins. In our Christian worldview, as Pope Francis reminds us, this leads not to gloom and sadness but to a humble prayer for mercy, which is ours for the asking. Then comes real joy and peace.

Then every day is Thanksgiving as we whisper, "Give thanks to the Lord for He is good, for His mercy endures forever!"

Then every day is Advent as we long for a Messiah to bring us mercy.

Then every day is Christmas as we welcome the birth of the Savior in our lives.

When he broke open the fifth seal, I saw underneath the altar
the souls of those who had been slaughtered because of
the witness they bore to the word of God.

—REVELATION 6:9

Are you prepared to shed your blood for Christ? Every Christian disciple should aspire to be brave enough to do so. Please God, the day of shedding one's blood for the faith will not come to America, but that very thought should invite us all to ask some questions and examine our consciences.

As Saint John Paul II observed, "A faith not worth dying for is not worth living for." God, family, faith, freedom, one's country, friends, honor, virtue, life itself, the Church—all worth dying for. And all worth living for!

For my part, I have to ask myself: If I can't be courageous now in small things, how might I be ready to answer the summons to shed my blood in grave matters? Do I defend the Church when she is maligned or attacked or when her liberties are threatened? Do I stand fast with those around the world who are persecuted and even martyred for their faith? Do I do my utmost, with the help of God's grace, to live the virtues, especially those of humility and charity?

Might I invite you to ask the same questions?

We are grateful to be Catholic, to be heirs to the promises of Christ and the blood of the martyrs. We renew our love for Christ, His Church, His vicar on earth. We strengthen our courage to be witnesses of that love for the entire Church—and for the world that so urgently needs her witness.

NOVEMBER 27

When did we see you a stranger and welcome you?
—MATTHEW 25:38

Saint Benedict said: *"Hospes venit, Christus venit."* "When a guest comes, Christ comes."

God taught us a lot about the virtue of hospitality. Think about the reading from Genesis in which the three visitors went to see Abraham and Sarah. Abraham actually bowed before them as if they were divine, so much did he honor them. He bathed their feet and prepared a meal.

As a matter of fact, Abraham's three visitors *were* divine, and his welcome to them—his hospitality—was rewarded when the trinity of visitors told him that Sarah, his wife, would soon be pregnant.

The Hebrew Scriptures extol hospitality. Moses, in his law, orders the people of Israel to treat the alien fairly and justly, reminding them that their ancestors, too, were once strangers in a foreign land.

In the Gospel of Luke, Jesus was a guest in the home of Martha and Mary. He enjoyed their hospitality. He would even go so far as to tell us that on Judgment Day we will be examined as to how we treated strangers.

Throughout history, we in America have had glorious moments of hospitality. There have been years when the verse on the Statue of Liberty has been accurate. America has been at her best when she has welcomed the immigrant, the refugee, the alien. Our beloved country becomes stronger and more robust when we open our doors to the immigrant.

Learn to give all people the hospitality we would offer Christ.

For if he were not expecting the fallen to rise again, it would have been superfluous and foolish to pray for the dead.

—2 MACCABEES 12:44

I remember once visiting a rather prominent man in the hospital who had been diagnosed with terminal cancer. He knew the end was near, and he was pretty down about it.

"Cardinal Dolan," he said, "I really thought I'd live forever." I replied to him, "I think you'll live forever, too." That's our destiny: immortality. God wants us to live with Him forever.

We know that life here on earth is fleeting. It's transitory and fading. That's one reason our wise and Holy Mother Church invites us to think of the dead and dying, especially in November. Nature is dying. The trees are bare. The grass has turned brown. The sun shines less. We think of the fleeting nature of our lives as well.

At the moment of our personal death, what does the Church tell us will happen? Our immortal soul will go to stand before the judgment seat of God. We call that the particular judgment. And at that moment, there are three places where each of us may go: heaven, hell, or purgatory.

Purgatory is the beautifully consoling thought that for many of us, we'll need some final touch-up and cleansing. Purgatory is a final gift of God's lavish mercy before we're quite ready for eternal citizenship in heaven.

That is why it's good for us to pray for the dead. We hope they're in heaven. We trust by God's mercy that they are. But we don't take it for granted.

The Irish people have a custom that I love: Whenever they mention the name of someone who died, they say, "Oh, Tom Murphy, Lord have mercy on him." Or "Sally O'Connell, God be good to her." It's a natural part of their speech pattern. It is so beautiful to pray for the souls of the faithful departed, for the souls in purgatory.

Whoever eats my flesh and drinks my blood has eternal life, and I will raise him on the last day. For my flesh is true food, and my blood is true drink.
—JOHN 6:54-55

We joke in our family about how we enjoy the days after Thanksgiving almost as much as Thanksgiving itself. The "great meal," so long prepared, so impeccably served, so savored, and so enhanced with good conversation, is still dominant in our minds. It's as if the life of that Thanksgiving dinner is so strong that it lingers. It stays with us literally as we extend the meal through days of turkey sandwiches and cold pumpkin pie.

Can I elevate this "Thanksgiving cycle" and apply it to the greatest Thanksgiving meal of all—the Eucharist? The word itself means "thanksgiving." For us as Catholics, we come together as a Church family for a great meal every Sunday. It has been well prepared, it is carefully served, everyone has a part, and it is savored and enjoyed with words, song, and stories from the Bible. Furthermore, the food is heavenly, as we are nourished with the very body and blood of Christ.

This solemn meal is so powerful that the presence of Christ remains with us in the Holy Eucharist. Before Our Lord in the Blessed Sacrament we can extend the graces and benefits of the Mass, savor its message, and look forward to our next Thanksgiving meal.

As the joy, the solemnity, the company, the reminiscing, and the wonderful food of the great Thanksgiving meal are extended over the next few days, so is the sacred banquet of the Sunday Eucharist continued in the Real Presence of Christ in the Blessed Sacrament.

Now you are Christ's body,
and individually parts of it.
—I CORINTHIANS 12:27

The Church is our family. But here's an intriguing corollary to that image: The Church is not just our family; it is also a dysfunctional family.

Everybody talks today about dysfunctional families, to which I respond, Have you ever met a functional one? To own up to the flaws, the sins, the failings, the mistakes, the dysfunction in our spiritual family, the Church, is a productive venture.

During the Great Jubilee Year 2000, Saint John Paul II apologized publicly for specific sins of the Church on fifty-four occasions. I don't know about you, but I have no problem at all admitting that at times it can be tough to love the Church because of her imperfections. The great novelist Flannery O'Connor, a radiantly sincere Catholic, wrote, "It seems to be a fact that you have to suffer as much from the Church as for it."

Yet the Church remains our Holy Mother. Our family. Just as our earthly family can irritate, hurt, and frustrate us, so can our heavenly family. Yet we love her and cling to her all the more.

As the priest and theologian Henri de Lubac said, "What would I know of him without her?"

DECEMBER I

They are to make a sanctuary for me,
that I may dwell in their midst.
—EXODUS 25:8

A few years ago, around Christmastime, a young woman gave birth to a baby boy. Feeling alone and scared, she remembered the parish she loved, and so she went there and placed her baby in the empty crib in the manger scene. She hid and watched to make sure he stayed safe and would be found, and shortly afterward some parishioners did find him.

God bless the culture of life that led this scared woman to trust the Church to take care of her baby. God bless the parish for radiating such a spirit of welcome, joy, warmth, love, and outreach that she felt comfortable taking her baby there.

It is not far-fetched to imagine what *might* have happened. The mother's apprehension and isolation could have led her to seek an abortion. She could have been going to a parish that she found unwelcoming, cold, and impersonal. Or she might have run to a church to find it locked, with a sign telling her to come back during office hours. Thank God these were all only scenarios that might have been.

Let every parish in our nation be one that promotes the culture of life! Let all our people be like those parishioners whose smiles, greetings, and welcomes assured this young mother that her baby would be safe there.

In a world that often says there's no room at the inn to those in need, this young woman found sanctuary—a manger—in the Church!

DECEMBER 2

And this will be a sign for you: you will find an infant
wrapped in swaddling clothes and lying in a manger.
—LUKE 2:12

This radiant season of the year showcases the three ways the Lord shows up in the world and in our lives.

Simply put, He did show up, He does show up, and He will show up.

On Christmas Day, we will recall with joy that God did show up, born in a crib at Bethlehem, announced by the angels as Our Lord, Savior, and Messiah.

Advent prods our trust that He will come again, as judge of the living and the dead, at the end of time.

So that's the past and the present. Those two comings of Jesus are clear and evident. Where we get fuzzy is when it concerns His coming now. But He comes right now in the Eucharist!

Thus do Advent and Christmas summon us to faith.

The Lord gave us a hint of His preferred manner of coming to us now in the very way He arrived over 2,000 years ago.

Think of the birth of Jesus. He could have arrived with trumpets and drums, but He came in an extraordinarily simple, humble way.

He was born not in a palace but in a barn, not to an earthly queen but to a meek virgin of Nazareth. He was worshipped not by the elite but by shepherds and was surrounded not by splendor but by cows, sheep, and donkeys.

God came in a way so humble, simple, and routine, so gentle and quiet, that most missed Him. That's the way He shows up now!

DECEMBER 3

Be eager to present yourself as acceptable to God, a workman who causes
no disgrace, imparting the word of truth without deviation.
—2 TIMOTHY 2:15

Are people constantly asking you what you want for Christmas? That seems logical: We have to speak up and let people know what we need.

But our greatest needs are spiritual; our real wants are inside.

And one of the best places we make a list and let the Lord know what we really need and want is in the Sacrament of Penance.

We need mercy, we want forgiveness, and we're looking for reconciliation with God and others and within ourselves. We express all this to the Lord—the only one who can grant our request—in a sincere confession.

We're full of pride and need humility. We're worried about money, family, work, and health, and we want to trust in God. We're craving to get and really want to give. We're acting like it all depends on us when we should be praying as if it all depends on Him. We waste time instead of spending it with the sick, the poor, the lonely. We're sinners and need healing.

There's our spiritual Christmas list. And we do not take it to Santa but to the Savior.

We do that in the Sacrament of Penance.

That first Christmas, the angels at Bethlehem announced the birth of a Savior.

From what did Jesus come to save us? The Romans? High taxes? High cholesterol? No. He came to save us from our sins.

There's no better time than Advent to talk to God in confession and give Him your list.

See, days are coming . . . when I will raise up a righteous branch for David;
As king he shall reign and govern wisely.
—JEREMIAH 23:5

Advent is a special time of the year when we await the coming of Christ. The temptation is to jump right into Christmas, but we know that we first must prepare ourselves so that we properly receive Him. How can we salvage Advent from a society so intent on rushing Christmas?

Enjoy the Advent feasts: Saint Nicholas, December 6; the Immaculate Conception, December 8; Our Lady of Guadalupe, December 12; and of course the four Sundays of Advent.

Hang an Advent wreath, open a daily calendar, or create a Jesse Tree.

If you worry that Christmas has become too commercial, shop for others. Participate in one of the many Christmas charity events and endeavors in which you can help the poor.

Enhanced prayer is a tried-and-true Advent practice. Daily Mass or increased reading from the Bible is a great place to start. I cheat and say the joyful mysteries of the rosary every day in Advent, since they prepare me for Christmas.

Identify one person you've had a falling-out or a fight with or one you have not heard from in a long time, and reach out to him or her in the spirit of Advent peace and reconciliation.

Let's keep Christ in Christmas by keeping Advent alive!

DECEMBER 5

Whoever receives one child such as this
in my name, receives me.
—MARK 9:37

Christianity began with the birth of a baby in Bethlehem.

Civilization began when we started placing babies and children first: focusing on them, loving them, protecting them.

Young couples tell me at the baptism of their new babies how their lives have been transformed, no longer self-centered but baby-centered.

No wonder God sent His Son as a baby—the literal center of history—hoping that we finally would pay attention and want to make Him the focus of our lives.

Yes, we love babies and children, and that is why we worry. We are concerned when their life in the womb is unprotected and in jeopardy through abortion on demand.

We cringe when babies are raised in shelters or lack proper nourishment, water, and medicine.

Civilization halts when a baby is looked at as a threat, a problem, or a commodity. But at the middle of all this history is the birth of a baby whose name means "God saves." God still saves us through our babies.

Finally, all of you, be of one mind, sympathetic,
loving toward one another, compassionate, humble.
—I PETER 3:8

I must have been only seven or eight when my dad took me Christmas shopping. I had managed to save up the huge sum of $1.71 to buy Christmas gifts for Dad, Mom, and Deb, my sister. I found a measuring cup for Mom and a bow for Deb's hair, but that left me with 3 cents for Dad's present. He could see my consternation and asked what was troubling me, and so I told him. Dad replied, "Tim, don't worry. You got gifts for Mom and Deb. That's gift enough for me, too."

That is Saint Joseph, isn't it? The quiet man who steps aside and points to Jesus and Mary, his foster child and virgin spouse.

Saint Joseph wants them, not him, to get the attention and the glory.

That is a splendid paradigm for the work of the priesthood. We priests are in it not for ourselves but for Christ and His Church. Like Saint Joseph, we often are most effective when we simply and humbly get out of the way, stand in the background, and lead others to Jesus and Mary.

Saint Joseph, that strong man of silence, faithfully fulfilled the demands of his vocation, allowing his wife and foster son to have center stage.

Like Saint Joseph, we do this more by actions than by words. Silence, a quiet presence, is often our most valuable tool as a priest.

As God holds us in His loving arms, so does Saint Joseph, that wonderful father figure, ever quiet, ever present.

DECEMBER 7

Prepare and get ready, you and the company mobilized for you,
but in my service.
—EZEKIEL 38:7

I was spending time with family in St. Louis when "Silent Night" by Perry Como came on the radio.

"Nobody sings a Christmas song like Perry Como," I observed.

"Who's he?" replied my niece's boyfriend.

Yep, things have changed; I'm out of it. Today people don't even recognize Perry.

I get critical this time every year because we start celebrating Christmas way too early. My preference is to go back to the Perry Como days, when the tree didn't go up until Christmas Eve, the cookies could not be enjoyed until Christmas Day, no carol could be heard until at least mid-December, and no "holiday parties" took place until Christmas.

Then, once Christmas arrived, look out! We celebrated until Epiphany on January 6.

No more. The decorations have been up for a while, the songs are heard all over, the trees are up, and the season will end—not start—on December 26.

We need Advent!

Mother Church is shrewd: She knows that all good things demand preparation. Christmas is surely a good thing. Advent invites us to prepare.

I love Advent, and I know that Christmas is more meaningful if we use this rich season to prepare our hearts.

I only wish Perry Como had sung an Advent hymn!

Feast of the
Immaculate Conception

In a few days, on December 12, we will celebrate the feast day of a pregnant woman: Our Lady of Guadalupe. That same woman has a feast day today: We call her the Immaculate Conception.

People at times get this one confused. They think we're celebrating Jesus's Immaculate Conception, which would be strange since we will celebrate His birth in just a few weeks. Instead, here we're talking about the conception of Mary in her mother's womb.

God's plan started in the Garden of Eden. Once our first parents, Adam and Eve, sinned, God could have said, literally, "to hell with them," but He didn't. Already He thought of a way to restore His original design. He had to pick a new Adam and a new Eve, because the first ones blew it.

Jesus is the Second Adam. Who's the New Eve? Mary. Our Blessed Mother. Thus, from the beginning, in the Garden of Eden, God was thinking about the future. She's without sin. We call that the Immaculate Conception. It's a beautiful way to celebrate God's design, God's plan. He always wants to bring us closer to Himself, free us from our sins, and return us to the Garden of Eden. From the first moment of her life in her own mother's womb, she—by a privilege given her by God the Father, anticipating the redemption of His and her Son, Jesus—was preserved from sin.

At the center of history, when B.C. became A.D., is that woman and her baby, Jesus. At His first miracle, under His cross, at the first Pentecost, is found that same woman. The poet Wordsworth called her "our tainted nature's solitary boast."

In a few weeks, much of the world will come to a stop to celebrate a mother and the birth of her baby. It's a great Advent feast because it celebrates God's providential plan.

DECEMBER 9

For here we have no lasting city,
but we seek the one that is to come.
—HEBREWS 13:14

It was a damp winter day in 1973. I was a seminarian walking through Saint Peter's Square and saw a small but excited crowd near the obelisk. Over I went only to see in the middle of the dozens of people Archbishop Fulton J. Sheen. Among the handshakes, flashbulbs, and autographs, someone shouted, "What are you doing in Rome, Archbishop Sheen?"

"I just came from an audience with Pope Paul VI," he replied. "What did the Holy Father say to you?" inquired another in the crowd. Archbishop Sheen blushed a bit and replied, "The Holy Father looked at me, took my hand, and said, 'Fulton Sheen, you will have a high place in heaven.'"

"What did you say back?" pestered another.

"Well," responded our man with that familiar sparkle and grin, "I replied, 'Your Holiness, would you mind making that an infallible statement?'"

Which I propose to you is the key message of Fulton J. Sheen: He wanted to get to heaven; he wanted to bring the world with him.

All of his philosophy and theology, all of his radio and TV, his avalanche of books and articles, his tapes, retreats, and conferences . . . all for one purpose: to help us discover the purpose of life—eternal union with God.

Fulton J. Sheen wanted to get to heaven. He wanted to bring all of us with him.

He wanted to be a saint. He wanted us to be saints, too. His pivotal insight, central to revelation, was that Jesus Christ was the way to heaven, the truth about how to get there, the life we hope to share for all eternity. This is the anniversary of his death.

DECEMBER 10

But if we hope for what we do not see,
we wait with endurance.
—ROMANS 8:25

We Christians take Advent seriously, which means that we are in a time of preparation for Christmas—a grand feast we really do not begin to celebrate until Christmas Eve.

That is certainly the case in our liturgy, as is evident in our churches, where we don't begin to celebrate Christmas until the actual day.

Biblical wisdom and the wise mother we tenderly call the Church advise us that "good things come to those who wait."

That's a tough sell today, I'm afraid. We want our fun, our pleasure, and we want it now. No waiting, no preparing, no putting it off. I'm guilty of this immediate gratification myself. That is all the more reason to push ourselves to truly live out this Advent season.

We may feel unconventional by society's standards for focusing more on Advent and delaying the celebration of Christmas until afterward, but we may really feel like outsiders when we continue to celebrate Christmas for twelve days after Advent. The tree stays up, the carols are still sung, the holidays go on—at least until Epiphany.

"We're tired of Christmas," people sigh. No wonder. The decorations have been up since the day after Halloween!

So let's try to keep Advent as much as we do Christmas.

Good things come to those who wait.

Whoever follows me will not walk in darkness,
but will have the light of life.
—JOHN 8:12

When I think about the world today, two words come somberly to mind.

The first word is *darkness.* There's a lot of dreariness out there to make the world a bleak, shadowy place: war, violence, persecution, hunger, terrorism, immorality, family breakdown, poverty.

There's no denying it: Our world can seem dark because we often feel that evil, sin, and suffering are winning.

The second word is *fear.* Forces are out there that frighten us. That fear can paralyze us, depress us, or make us irrational.

Then we hear God's Holy Word through Isaiah: "The people who walked in darkness have seen a great light." That great light is Jesus, the Savior of the world.

When He was born, "The angel said to them, 'Do not be afraid.'"

An antidote to this fear is the birth of a baby, for every newborn baby is a sign from God that He wants life to go on. He is not afraid of the future.

The infant born in Bethlehem that first Christmas was God's proclamation that "fear is useless; what is needed is trust," as that baby would teach when He grew up.

We need Christ! He turns the darkness around and evaporates fear, for as He said, "I am the Light of the World."

DECEMBER 12

Feast of
Our Lady of Guadalupe

When I consider the image of Our Lady of Guadalupe, a number of thoughts come to mind. First, the site of Guadalupe is near the center of the two American continents. Mary appeared there to tell us about her special care for the Americas, both North and South.

Second, she appears as a pregnant woman. The cord tied around her waist was a sign to the Native peoples that a woman was expecting. Thus, as we gaze upon Our Lady of Guadalupe, we venerate her and worship the baby in her womb. No wonder she has become a special patroness for the pro-life movement.

Third, researchers who have studied the image of Mary on the *tílma* (cloak) of Juan Diego, the peasant Native to whom she appeared, have discovered the image of a man in the pupils of Mary's eyes. The image is not obvious without the aid of magnifying devices, but we know that the man is Juan Diego. Not only is this evidence of the supernatural character of the cloak, it is a consoling message that Mary loves us as a mother loves a child, that she looks at us, and that she has us in her eyes. We remember with gratitude her words to Saint Juan Diego: "Am I not here, who is your Mother? Are you not under my protection?"

Saint John Paul II designated Mary, under her title of Our Lady of Guadalupe, as "patroness of America." That includes us!

But when the kindness and generous love of God our savior appeared,
not because of any righteous deeds we had done but because of his mercy,
he saved us through the bath of rebirth and renewal by the holy Spirit,
which he richly poured out on us through Jesus Christ.

—TITUS 3:4-6

From the moment our first parents, Adam and Eve, sinned, God our Father knew that He would redeem us with His Son. After Adam and Eve, every creature was born at odds with God, lacking His grace.

But our Father, who wants only to love and save us, already had a plan of redemption in mind: He would send His Son, born of a woman, to restore us to friendship with Him and to erase Original Sin. Part of His eternal plan of mercy was to choose a woman to bear the Messiah, and this woman had to be free from the sin her offspring would cancel.

Thus, we praise God the Father, who planned our salvation from the beginning and would not allow Original Sin to frustrate His design. As Our Lady would remind us, she did nothing to merit such grace; it came to her, as all spiritual gifts do, only because of the "fruit of her womb," as she shared early in the redemption achieved by her son's dying and rising.

God the Father had Christmas, Good Friday, and Easter in mind from all eternity. Thus, we are moved to praise the wonder and majesty of God's promises and God's ways, and we are prompted to glorify Jesus for the redemption He won for us by His Death and Resurrection.

As our Blessed Mother would tell us, "It's not about me, it's about the Lord. I am but a servant."

DECEMBER 14

The Lord's acts of mercy are not exhausted, his compassion is not spent;
They are renewed each morning.
—LAMENTATIONS 3:22-23

We are a Church of new beginnings, and Advent powerfully reminds us of that. We have a God who loves fresh starts, who always wants us to have a future full of hope, and who forever gives us another chance. We have a God who, no matter how long the darkness of night might seem, always causes the sun to rise the next morning.

That's the hope Advent brings as we prepare for the arrival of the Light of the World, the brightness of whose birth shattered the midnight darkness of a cold night in the fields of Bethlehem.

Do you find yourself in the dark? Are you suffering from sickness or despair? Are you searching for something you can't quite find? Are you overwhelmed with loneliness? Are money problems causing you anxiety? Have you experienced the death of someone dear? Do you feel discouraged? Is your family hurt by addiction?

Does it seem to you at times that it is all over and you can't go on?

It's not! Christ is your beginning.

The celebration of the birth of the only one who can definitively answer the question every human being poses is nigh. Hope is the message that the tiny baby in the stable brings.

It's morning in the Church. The darkness has passed.

The cycle of God's love and salvation is starting all over again!

And stretching out his hand toward his disciples, he said, "Here are my mother
and my brothers. For whoever does the will of my heavenly Father
is my brother, and sister, and mother."
—MATTHEW 12:49-50

Have you noticed how, around Christmastime, joy seems to be everywhere? It's safe to say that we all want joy. Joy certainly sells. If a quick look around shops and at advertisements is any indication, it sells doughnuts. And home improvement. It emblazons a sparkly money holder for the child who doesn't need Santa to bother with toys but will just take the money, thank you.

Yet you and I both know that joy is not something money can buy. Now, I grant you, I'm not likely to pass up a jelly doughnut if one is offered, but we know that a momentary delight is not joy.

If the local mall is unreliable on this front, just where do you go for joy?

You were created in love by Love Himself. He made you for Himself, destined for life with Him for eternity. He wants us to know we are loved by the Creator of the Universe. This is the source of joy.

It may be hard to hear God's voice in your life or understand how He might want to meet you with that quiet joy of His love.

Yet amid life's struggles and hardships, I encourage you to allow Jesus to be the source of your joy!

DECEMBER 16

A voice of one crying out in the desert: "Prepare the way of the Lord, make straight his paths."

—MARK 1:3

I was on a flight from St. Louis to New York and sat next to this wonderful young Jewish man who was flying back to the city for college.

"Oh, my gosh," he kindly pointed out, "you Catholics are in the season for Advent. That's important for you, right?" I said yes, it is, with a bit of hope and yearning. I hope we take Advent seriously.

Advent is our four weeks of spiritual preparation for the coming of Christ. *Adventus* is the Latin word for "coming" or "arrival." Thus, Advent is the time when you and I prepare inside, in our hearts and souls, for the coming of Christ.

In our Catholic understanding, the Lord arrives in three different ways. In other words, there are three different comings of Christ: History. Mystery. Majesty.

The Lord has come to us in history. He arrived in history that first Christmas, born in a crib in Bethlehem.

He comes to us in mystery. He is here with us, every day of our lives, in the mysteries of the sacramental life of the Church and in the ordinariness of our days.

He comes to us in majesty. At the end of time, with his Second Coming, He will judge the living and the dead.

These are the three Advents. They are the three arrivals of Our Lord that I invite you to contemplate with me during this season.

DECEMBER 17

God is light, and in him there is
no darkness at all.
—1 JOHN 1:5

Christmas is about light—the Light of the World. Our goal this season is to stay focused on Him.

On Christmas Eve 1979, I was on pilgrimage in the Holy Land and looked forward to concelebrating Midnight Mass in Bethlehem. Christmas Eve came cold and drizzly as we pilgrims assembled in a parking lot for the five-mile bus ride. After waiting two hours, we were searched and packed onto buses. But before long we were halted, taken off the bus, made to wait an hour outside, searched again, and allowed back on. The bus continued for a mile or so, only to be stopped and searched again. We started up once more, but by then we were all cold, tired, crabby, wet, and impatient. And guess what happened. We were stopped again.

This time a young couple boarded the bus. The mother carried a baby, who looked out at us frustrated people with big black radiant eyes, plump red cheeks, and a spontaneous smile that attracted every person on that chilly bus. Before long, we were all smiling. The whole tenor of the bus had been transformed, and we began to laugh and sing Christmas carols. That baby changed everyone and united us in joy and friendship.

I thought to myself: I just witnessed what God did that first Christmas and what He continues to do—transform tired, crabby people into warm, friendly pilgrims.

That's the power of the Divine Infant. Let Him on your bus this Christmas!

DECEMBER 18

But to those who did accept him he gave power to become
children of God, to those who believe in his name.
—JOHN 1:12

In Advent, we wait for Jesus.

We wait for His grace and mercy, which are sure to come.

We wait for Him to answer our prayers. We are sure that He will, but we don't know when, where, or how.

We wait for reasons to explain the suffering, struggle, and worries in our lives.

We wait for Him to call us to be with Him for all eternity.

And lest we forget, the Lord waits for us!

Jesus waits for us to open up to His grace and mercy.

He waits for us to admit that we do in fact need a Savior.

He waits for us to admit that He is the answer to the questions that our lives of searching pose each and every day.

He waits for our ultimate return to Him, for He has gone to prepare a place for us, and He longs for us to spend eternity with Him.

Christ will come! In the waiting is the very arrival. And deep down inside, cradled in the soul, where no one but the One who counts can detect it, is again an empty manger where the Son of God wants to be reborn.

Because you are precious in my eyes and honored, and I love you,
I give people in return for you and nations in exchange for your life.
—ISAIAH 43:4

I was about ten years old when my dad asked me to go with him to deliver Christmas gifts to a needy family.

As we carried the boxes of food, clothing, and wrapped gifts into the shack, four young kids hurried around us, excited at the delivery. The mom, obviously pregnant, seemed delighted. Only the dad seemed somewhat confused, embarrassed, and nervous.

My dad immediately sensed the father's restlessness and remarked, "I was just down at the store, and the owner asked if I'd drop off the groceries and presents you ordered last week."

I could sense the relief in the other dad's face, and he thanked us.

My dad had helped the other father save face. That other dad's wife and family were beaming at their husband and dad, grateful that he had taken care of them.

For the two dads, this was personal. For mine, this was not just a drop-off. For the other father, his personal reputation had been not only preserved but enhanced.

Christmas shows us that God is personal. He is hardly just a distant, aloof observer, delivering blessings in a businesslike way.

We sometimes use the phrase "It's not personal" to assure someone that the transaction at hand is just business. God would never use that phrase. For Him, it is very personal.

He personally and passionately loves us. The Bible tells us that He loves us as a father loves his wife and children. That's about as personal as you can get!

She wrapped him in swaddling clothes and laid him in a manger,
because there was no room for them in the inn.
—LUKE 2:7

One of the biggest errors we make in our faith is to think that Jesus comes to us only with thunder and lightning, with drama and flair.

Not so. He still arrives as softly, unexpectedly, and meekly as He did in the crib at Bethlehem.

Here's an example: Christmas Eve 2002 was a rough one for me. I had served lunch to the homeless that Christmas Eve before heading to a jam-packed Christmas Eve vigil Mass.

Then I headed home—to an empty house. I had six hours to kill until Midnight Mass.

I made a sandwich and began to feel sorry for myself, wondering when the joy of Jesus would arrive.

I went into the chapel to pray my Divine Office, go over my homily for Midnight Mass, and wish I were with family and friends.

I turned on the lights on the little tree, put on a Christmas CD, and began my prayers.

The cadence of the psalms and the beauty of the biblical readings calmed me down. The sanctuary light reminded me of the Real Presence of Jesus in the tabernacle. The long list of names of family members and friends to whom I had promised prayers sat on the kneeler in front of me, reminding me of all the wonderful people in my life.

The Lord came to me then, right there, reminding me that I was not alone. His presence was gentle and unassuming, just as it was in Bethlehem.

DECEMBER 21

In God I trust, I do not fear.
What can man do to me?
—PSALM 56:12

God's Holy Word is supposed to be good news.

Never is the hope of the good news of God's promise and fulfillment erased for a believer, and the more it is tested, the stronger it gets.

Today, December 21, is the darkest day of the year—the day of least light as the sun is at its lowest point.

Anthropologists tell us that our ancestors millennia ago were gripped with fear and anxiety on this day, wondering if the sun would reverse its descent and start back up into the sky, if the days gradually would get longer and the light more obvious.

Year after year they would hold their breath with fear, only to discover that yes, tomorrow the sun would be reborn and start upward. No wonder every ancient civilization celebrated the "rebirth of the sun" in the days after things looked scariest.

Fear eventually became trust as life and community went on, showing that nature and her god would always guarantee that light would conquer darkness.

At the darkest time of the night, near the darkest day of the year, Jesus, the Light of the World, was born in Bethlehem.

He teaches us in His own birth, life, death, and Resurrection that light conquers darkness, hope conquers despair, and love defeats hate.

Fear, doubt, and confusion all flooded Mary's heart, yet she trusted, and she conceived the Light of the World! When we're tempted to fear, He whispers, "Fear is useless. What is needed is trust."

DECEMBER 22

*He should ask in faith, not doubting, for the one who doubts is like
a wave of the sea that is driven and tossed about by the wind.*

—JAMES 1:6

Several years ago, I went to a spectacular Catholic Charities Christmas luncheon at which I had the honor of reading the story of the first Christmas from the Gospel of Luke. While I was reading, children—dressed as angels, shepherds, wise men, and Joseph and Mary—slowly and reverently formed a silent "Christmas Tableau" of the Nativity on the stage.

When I finished reading, all simply gazed upon the scene with wonder. From my place on the stage, I could see every person in the vast hall, eyes riveted upon the scene. It was simply awesome.

All 800 of us were uplifted in prayer, conscious of God's presence, grateful for the mystery of Christmas, and filled with faith, hope, and love.

My wish for you is that these final days of Advent and the grand holy days of Christmas may find you, like those at the luncheon, in prayer before the crib.

It doesn't matter if it's the Nativity scene in your church, the one beneath your tree, or the image of the first Christmas in your imagination. Let wonder and awe guide you. Enjoy the silence. Let your heart acknowledge Jesus as our Savior and let God know we sure need one. Tell Jesus that you love Him, you believe in Him, you need Him, you thank Him.

The Nativity happened. Christmas is true. It's not just a myth or a story. God did become one of us. His name is Jesus. And He is Our Lord and Savior.

*Glory to God in the highest and on earth
peace to those on whom his favor rests.*
—LUKE 2:14

"Where will you have your Christmas?"

A common question this time of the year.

Usually, the person asking is wondering where you'll have Christmas dinner or where you'll be when the presents under the tree are opened.

But for us as believers, the essence of Christmas is not the festive meal or even where we'll gather with family and friends to exchange presents.

No. For us as Catholics, the heart of Christmas is the Mass. Even the name of the holiday—Christ-Mass—implies the centrality of the Holy Sacrifice of the Mass on this radiant feast of the Nativity of the Lord.

Jesus was born in Bethlehem, Hebrew for "House of Bread."

Thus, on His birthday, we approach the Eucharist to receive this bread of life in Holy Communion.

In the baby Jesus, the divine was hidden within the tender, innocent, humble human nature of an infant.

So in the Holy Eucharist, the divine is hidden under the simple, routine, natural elements of bread and wine.

That first Christmas, God the Son assumed flesh and blood. At every Mass, Jesus Christ—body, blood, soul, and divinity—comes into our midst on the altar, into our souls.

In a way, every celebration of the Eucharist is Christmas again as Jesus comes to us in the Blessed Sacrament.

The tree, lights, carols, gifts, family, friends, cookies, and dinner are all cherished Christmas traditions. But the greatest custom of all is Mass on the feast of Christmas!

DECEMBER 24

And the Word became flesh and made his dwelling among us, and we saw
his glory, the glory as of the Father's only Son, full of grace and truth.
—JOHN 1:14

To conquer the darkness in the world, He whose birth was announced by the dazzle of a star came to be the Light of the World.

As we will hear Isaiah bellow out at the Eucharist on Christmas, at midnight, when the earth is in darkness, "The people who walked in darkness have seen a great light. Upon those who lived in a land of gloom a light has shone."

Our Jewish neighbors recognized this invitation from nature long before we did as they begin their annual Festival of Lights—Hanukkah—as we anticipate Christmas.

Just as nature tells us annually that the sun trumps darkness, so does "supernature" teach us that the only begotten Son of God is victorious over the darkness of sin, selfishness, Satan, and death itself.

For this baby will go from the wood of the manger to the lumber of the cross. On that Good Friday afternoon, midday became as bleak as midnight as "darkness covered the earth" and even the sun covered its face in shame.

But the following Sunday morning, as the sun came up to announce that the night was over, the Son rose!

The darkest day of the year does not have the last word. December 25 does! Light the candles! Illuminate the trees! Belt out "Alleluia" with Handel! Gaze upon the menorah! Acclaim the Son as the Light of the World!

DECEMBER 25

*Today in the city of David a savior has been born
for you who is Messiah and Lord.*
—LUKE 2:11

Today is born a Savior, Christ the Lord!

The joyful message of the angels to the shepherds that first Christmas in Bethlehem announced the birth of our Savior. If that is not "good news," I don't know what is!

I invite you to meditate with me for a moment on one word in that good news message from the angels: *today*.

Christmas is indeed the celebration of a real event that occurred over 2,000 years ago, but Christmas is also the celebration of something sacred and joyful happening right now—today—because Jesus was born to be reborn every day in the hearts of believers.

The birth of Christ happens today!

Today, millions will receive Christ in the Eucharist. Christ is reborn in our hearts. Today, families will bow their heads in prayer, gaze upon the crib, and come together in love. Christ is reborn. Today, friends will embrace, the poor will be fed, anger and bitterness will fade, and people will be filled with joy. Christ is reborn.

Today, peace will reign and love will win. Christ is reborn.

Yes, what happened that first Christmas is the central event of all history, but Christ was born so that He could be reborn now in our hearts as we believe, trust, and love Him.

The angels are right: Today is born a Savior; He is Christ the Lord.

Merry Christmas!

DECEMBER 26

Each must do as already determined, without sadness or compulsion,
for God loves a cheerful giver.
—2 CORINTHIANS 9:7

Christmas festivities end sooner or later, don't they? That's why we're forever asking the question, "How can we make the joy, light, and love of Christmas last all year?"

Well, here are some ideas. One is to concentrate on the Eucharist. Jesus told us from the beginning that He is the "living bread" and He came to be "food" for our souls. We see that promise kept in the Holy Eucharist. When you think about it, every Mass is Bethlehem revisited, where Jesus becomes our living bread.

Christ takes flesh and blood again at every Mass. The Incarnation goes on! Christmas continues.

God became man so that we men and women could become divine! That happens every time we receive Him at Mass, as we share His divine life!

As we pray before Him in the tabernacle or adore Him in the exposed Eucharist, we behold Christmas again: He is Emmanuel, "God is with us," really and truly present in the Blessed Sacrament.

A second way to prolong Christmas? Charity.

Our food pantries, soup kitchens, and clothing depots report that in the days right before and after Christmas, they're brimming over with supplies. But then, as the trees come down and the carols halt, the pantries are strapped, soup kitchens are adding more water to the stew, and clothing and monetary donations dwindle.

Christmas sparks love, sharing, and giving. If you want to keep Christmas going all year, keep on loving, sharing, and giving.

DECEMBER 27

Feast of Saint John the Apostle

Because we celebrate Saint John's feast day just two days after Christmas, December 27 is almost forgotten. It's a "down day," unfortunately, after the intensity of Advent and Christmas.

We priests love to look back often on the joy and fervor of our ordination and first Mass. That's probably not true of those first priests, the Apostles. Within hours after their ordination at the Last Supper, some had fallen asleep on the Master, one betrayed Him for thirty pieces of silver, one denied three times even knowing Him, and all ran off and abandoned Him just when He needed them most. Not a good track record for that first ordination class!

Only one of the first twelve remained faithful—Saint John.

I've often wondered if we can discover any hints as to why Saint John was able to remain faithful to Our Lord, and I propose two reasons for his fidelity.

The first is that he was closest to the Lord at the Last Supper. He was so close, in fact, that he had his head on His shoulder. There's the first explanation of Saint John's fidelity: He was close to Jesus at the Eucharist.

The second comes the next day on Calvary, at the foot of the cross, as Saint John stands next to Mary, our Sorrowful Mother.

I believe that John's fidelity is a direct result of his closeness to the Eucharist and to Mary and that this closeness is a critically important lesson for us today. When we stay close to Christ and His mother, fidelity comes easily.

DECEMBER 28

Feast of the Holy Innocents

After Christ was born, King Herod was terrified of the threat posed by this baby king. In an attempt to save his crown, he had all the male infants in Bethlehem killed. Through a dream, God told Joseph to take Mary and Baby Jesus and flee to safety in Egypt. Joseph obediently and immediately took his Holy Family out of harm's way. Sadly, an untold number of innocent babies lost their lives at Herod's command.

Today, we still worry about the safety of babies—both boys and girls.

Although all tragedy moves us, when a baby is involved or hurt, we shake our heads in disbelief a bit more vigorously in worry and sadness.

We worry when preborn babies are killed before ever having a chance to live outside the womb.

We worry when children don't have enough to eat.

We worry when children are abused, hurt, and neglected.

Babies are vitally important to us as families and as a society. Our country is greater when our national drive is to see that our children have even more opportunities than we did and when we protect each and every one.

Feast of the
Holy Family

One of the feasts of the Christmas season that I very much enjoy is the Sunday after Christmas, the Feast of the Holy Family.

That baby born a few days ago is true God for sure but also true man. As a true man, he has a mother, Mary, and an earthly foster father, Saint Joseph. Together, they are the Holy Family.

During the Christmas holy days, we seem most grateful for our families. To be a member of a warm, loving, united family is such a savored part of the human project that God did not want His only begotten Son to miss out on it!

When God our Father looks upon us, He beholds a family of people all created in His own image and likeness.

Then of course He smiles as He gives us our natural family. Our Christian tradition so honors the family that we consider it a reflection of God Himself.

God also gives us our Church family. Like any family, we look out for and take care of our members who are sick, poor, or suffering.

Today we praise God for our natural family and our spiritual one. Our identity as a member of this one, holy, catholic, and apostolic Church cannot be erased.

I have the strength for everything through him
who empowers me.
—PHILIPPIANS 4:13

The new year is almost upon us, and I want to suggest a couple of resolutions. There are a few promises we can make about the first things in life.

Number one: First thing, every day, is a morning offering. Our first thought daily is of the Lord. We wake up because of Him; we got through the night because of Him; we'll make it through this new day only because of His grace and mercy. As soon as we awake, we think of Him in prayer. We tell Him we love Him, we need Him, we thank Him, we trust Him, and we offer the new day to Him.

Number two: First day, every week, is Sunday Mass. We catch our breath from the just-concluded week and place the coming week in His providential hands. There's no better way to do that than by joining our spiritual family, the Church, in the most sacred Sunday meal of all—the Holy Sacrifice of the Mass.

Number three: First Friday, every month, we approach the Sacrament of Penance. Remember the beautiful custom of First Friday? Jesus died on the cross to save us on a Friday. The first Friday of every month we tell Him we're sorry for our sins and ask for His mercy with a good confession.

Rejoice in the new year! We have a God of newness. We have a God always eager to give us a fresh start.

As for me, to be near God is my good,
to make the Lord GOD my refuge.
—PSALM 73:28

In many churches, you will find a statue of our Blessed Mother called Our Lady of Guadalupe, and she is pregnant.

At this time of year, you will find another image in a different part of the church: a mother next to her newborn baby.

Your church also may have an image of the Pietà. Mary's baby is now thirty-three, and once again she is holding Him. This time, though, her Son is dead, taken down from the cross, bloody and beaten, and put into her arms.

Same woman, same Son. Mary and Jesus.

From the pregnant Virgin of Guadalupe to the joyful mother that first Christmas at Bethlehem to the sorrowful mother at the foot of the cross that first Good Friday on Calvary, she is there with Jesus.

What was this past year like for you? Was it one of loss? Sadness? Sickness? Death? Struggles? Happiness? New birth? Prosperity? Peace?

Probably some or all of these things, if you're like the rest of us.

What will next year be like? Once again, probably a balance of good and evil, light and darkness, life and death.

No wonder we turn to her as we conclude one year and commence another.

Mary had supreme joy at Bethlehem and deep sorrow on Calvary. In both, she simply stayed close to Jesus.

Not a bad New Year's resolution.

After all is said and done, always stay close to Christ.

ACKNOWLEDGMENTS

Thanks to Joe Zwilling, Lino Rulli, Susan Ciancio, and Gary Jansen for their inspiration, support, and encouragement.

ABOUT THE AUTHOR

CARDINAL TIMOTHY DOLAN was named Archbishop of New York by Pope Benedict XVI in 2009. He was ordained to the priesthood on June 19, 1976, in his hometown of St. Louis, Missouri. On the twenty-fifth anniversary of his ordination, Cardinal (then Father) Dolan was named the Auxiliary Bishop of St. Louis and in 2002 was named Archbishop of Milwaukee by Pope Saint John Paul II. Cardinal Dolan's Episcopal motto is the profession of faith of Saint Peter: *Ad quem íbimus,* "Lord, to whom shall we go?" (John 6:68). Cardinal Dolan is the author of numerous books, including *Called to Be Holy* and *Doers of the Word.*

ABOUT THE TYPE

This book was set in Requiem, a typeface designed by the Hoefler Type Foundry. It is a modern typeface inspired by inscriptional capitals in Ludovico Vicentino degli Arrighi's 1523 writing manual, *Il modo de temperare le penne*. An original lowercase, a set of figures, and an italic in the chancery style that Arrighi (fl. 1522) helped popularize were created to make this adaptation of a classical design into a complete font family.